For Rebuilding
OF SAN FRANCISCO
See Page 3

The San Francisco Examiner

WITHDRAWN

SAN FRANCISCO, SUNDAY, APRIL 22, 1906

STREET CARS START IN SAN FRANCISCO TO-DAY

Junction of Post and Montgomery Streets as It Is To-Day and a Panorama of the Ruins From the Site of the Hopkins Institute of Art.

Street cars will be in operation to-day from the Ferry Building, and construction of the entire transportation system will be begun.

An offer of $400,000, for a strip of Market-street property was emphatically refused yesterday.

Mayor Schmitz has issued a proclamation stating that after to-day no further seizures of automobiles or carts will be made.

The condition of the homeless and shelterless who are camped in various points of the city is remarkably fine.

Offers of substantial financial assistance are being rapidly received from many cities in all sections of the United States.

FUTURE IS BRIGHT FOR SAN FRANCISCO

Considering the catastrophe that descended upon San Francisco without a moment's warning, conditions here are simply marvelous. Though from the water front to Van Ness avenue the city is laid waste, westward lie well-paved streets and solid houses, while the parks and squares are as green and inviting as ever.

There is absolutely no panic of any kind. Instead every one is cheerful, nay, enthusiastic over the prospects of the future. So far from being prostrated by misfortune, the citizens have banded together in a determination not only to reconstruct, but to establish a San Francisco that will be known as the most beautiful and attractive city in the wonderland of California.

Of course there are pessimists in every community. So it is no wonder that for the past three days ugly rumors have been spread. It was reported yesterday, for instance, that pestilence had broken out, that the whole of Golden Gate Park was under quarantine and that in a day or two the entire city would be cut off from the world by the authorities.

There is no epidemic of any kind, nor will there be if the Board of Health makes the proper sanitary arrangements without delay.

NO CLASH BETWEEN AUTHORITIES.

Then there were rumors of a clash between the civil and military authorities. No such thing has occurred. The city is under martial law just now, which is the very best thing for it until the conditions are relieved.

So San Francisco is to spring up again, and quickly. This very day street cars will be running from the ferries out Market street and by Turk and Eddy streets to Fillmore, where the great power-house stands almost uninjured. Mayor Schmitz has given the United Railroads a special permit to operate an overhead trolley system, and by it people will be carried free of charge.

Gangs of men will be at once set to work to remove the debris from the street.

Yesterday the good news was sent forth that there was no need to remove the postoffice to Oakland. The handsome structure on Seventh and Mission streets received a twisting from the earthquake,

(Continued on Page Two.)

MARKET STREET CARS WILL BE RUN TO-DAY

Manager Mullaly of the United Railroads announces that cars will be operated to-day from the Ferry through the city to Turk, Eddy and Fillmore streets, and that within a few days the temporary service to be established would cover the greater part of the city. Transportation for all passengers and supplies will be free until conditions are relieved. Mayor Schmitz, in this connection, announces that he had guaranteed a temporary franchise for a trolley system down Market street, to remain in force until revoked.

Rufus P. Jennings, secretary of the Citizens' Committee, yesterday morning requested General Funston to furnish fifty men to aid in starting transportation on the Fillmore system. A few cars may be run with horses.

METCALF CHECKS STREAM OF IMMIGRANTS TO CITY

NEW YORK, April 21.—Orders not to sell tickets to immigrants who may desire to go to San Francisco were received to-day by the New York immigration officials from Secretary Metcalf of te Department of Commerce and Labor.

SALT LAKE, April 21.—"People should not go to San Francisco," is the warning the press is requested to give the public, by General Manager W. H. Bancroft of the Harriman Western lines to give the public. At every place along the line hundreds are clamoring for tickets and transportation. "Please point out the folly of this," said Mr. Bancroft. "Every arrival at San Francisco increases the trouble of the authorities and enhances the danger. The authorities are doing everything that can possibly be done. Instead of helping the sufferers an influx of outsiders at this time will add to the confusion and impede the work of relief."

RELIEF FUND $4,154,000

The following is a tabulated statement of the amount of money raised yesterday for relief purposes. The grand total takes in all the moneys subscribed to date:

State of Massachusetts and the citizens of the city of Boston	$500,000
Portland	100,000
Government of Dominion of Canada	100,000
City of Philadelphia	100,000
State of Colorado	100,000
Waldorf-Astoria Hotel, New York	100,000
International Banking Association	100,000
Modern Woodmen of the World	100,000
John D. Rockefeller	100,000
Standard Oil Company	100,000
Pacific Coast Lumber Association	50,000
Guggenheims, bankers, New York	50,000
Salt Lake	30,000
Kansas City	25,000
Americans in London, Eng.	12,500
Provincial Government of British Columbia	10,000
Pacific States Telephone Co.	10,000
Lewiston, Idaho	7,500
S. Kockland, San Francisco	7,500
Business Men's Association of Helena, Mont.	6,000
Walla Walla, Wash.	5,000
American Bankers' Association	5,000
Napa	5,000
Silverton, Wash.	3,500
Aberdeen, Wash.	3,000
Woodburn, Wash.	2,500
McMinnville, Ore.	2,500
W. F. Herrin, San Francisco	1,000
Williams, Dimond & Co., San Francisco	500
H. Ducon, San Francisco	500
Pacific Portland Cement Co.	500
Hensey-Greene Company	500
C. E. Wilson, Clinton, Ia.	500
Total subscribed during day	$1,678,500
Amount subscribed Friday	2,475,500
Grand total to date	**$4,154,000**

INSURANCE COMPANIES PREPARE FOR WORK

Several of the companies have already leased offices for a year in Oakland, and they will be down to business in no time. There is no limit to the liability of stockholders in the California companies.

"There is no disposition here to raise any question as to the liability for earthquake damage," said T. C. Coogan, attorney for the Board of Underwriters, yesterday. "The question is being looked into for the information of Eastern and European owners, but here nobody so much as hints that any quibble will be made over paying earthquake losses."

RECORDS BELIEVED TO BE UNHARMED.

Insurance Commissioner E. Myron Wolf says that he carried all the records of his office to the basement of the Trust Company on California street, just east of the Kohl Building. The flames got into the structure, but it is thought the basement and the records were not harmed.

At the meeting of the Board of Underwriters yesterday President G. W. Spencer presided.

The board will meet again this morning at Reed Hall, its regular headquarters from now on till San Francisco is rebuilt.

ESTIMATE OF INSURANCE LOSS.

Now as to the amount of that loss. The actual loss can be placed at almost any figure, but the fixing is mere guesswork. It runs into figures beyond human comprehension. But the insurance loss can be estimated even when the books are in the fire-smitten vaults. An insurance man who is quick at figures estimated the loss for "The Examiner" yesterday.

He said the actual insurance loss is $225,000,000.

That makes Chicago's $120,000,000 seem cheap and Baltimore's $35,000,000 a mere trifle. This is how he figures it:

The 105 insurance companies doing business in California last year took in $2,600,000 in premiums. They probably wrote their business at an average rate of 90 cents. That would represent policies amounting to a total of $234,000,000.

The board will meet again to-morrow morning at Reed Hall, its regular headquarters from now on till San Francisco is rebuilt.

BURNED POLICIES TO BE HONORED.

In cases where insurance policies have been lost or burned the

(Continued on Page Two.)

GOVERNOR DECLARES TODAY A LEGAL HOLIDAY

EXTRA

Berkeley Reporter

EXTRA

VOL. IV.   BERKELEY, CALIFORNIA, THURSDAY, APRIL 19, 1906.   No. 133

BERKELEY A PLACE OF REFUGE

MILLIONS IN FLAMES

FIRE STILL RAGES IN SAN FRANCISCO

MEETING OF BANKERS

LIST OF BUILDINGS DESTROYED BY THE FIRE

At present it is impossible to correctly estimate the loss of life in San Francisco, but it is thought that it will pass the half-thousand mark. Every available building has been pressed into service as a hospital, and the dead and wounded are laid out on the floors of these buildings, side by side, and the wounded given such attention as the crude appliances at the disposal of the surgeons in attendance will permit, while the dead are held waiting identification and burial. Many of the bodies of the victims have not been received as yet, and no attempt will be made to recover them until the flames subdue and the living have been properly cared for.

While it is known that the property loss will run into the hundreds of millions, it would be useless to attempt to make an estimate of the loss at this time, as there are no figures at our disposal, and furthermore, it does not look as tho' the fire has anywhere near reached the end. To give an idea of the damage done we will give a partial list of some of the big buildings ruined:

St. Mary's Hospital.
The St. Francis Hotel.
The Alcazar Theatre.
The San Francisco Call Building.
The Lick House.
The Emporium Building.
Blake, Moffitt & Towne
A. Zellerbach & Co.
The Examiner Building.
The Masonic Temple.
The Occidental Hotel.
The Chronicle Building.

(Continued on Page 8)

COUNTY FINANCIERS TO CO-OPERATE WITH PARDEE

The bankers of Alameda county held a meeting last night to consider the great catastrophe and to undertake such measures of relief as suggested by its effect upon financial affairs.

Governor Pardee sent a telegram to the effect that he would arrive in Oakland at 11 p. m. to confer and act with the bankers. But the train bearing the governor was stalled by sinking and shifting of the railway track along the Suisun marshes.

Later a second dispatch was received, to the effect that the governor would arrive at 2 a. m., which message, having left calls for the hour when the governor was expected.

On his arrival, one of the things they suggested to him was a proclamation declaring the next three days legal holidays, so that collections might not be enforced or notes protested while many of the bank vaults across the bay, in which so many of our Alameda county banks carry their surplus, are buried under mountains of glowing coals.

There were many other things to be considered, and the governor's presence was deemed absolutely necessary to the purpose of the meeting.

Upon his arrival he acquiesced in the suggestions of the committee, and the desired proclamation will follow.

IN SAN FRANCISCO pandemonium reigns. The fierce fire which followed immediately in the wake of the violent temblor continues to spread and at four o'clock this morning it seemed very problematical as to when or where the fire demon would call a halt. On all sides havoc has been wrought by the action of the flames and the holdings of the rich and the poor alike have paid tribute to this foul monster which has come upon San Francisco unannounced and so unceremoniously. But few of the landmarks have been left on the south side of Market street between the water-front and Twelfth street and on the north side the devastation has been equally severe and the entire commercial and wholesale district east of Kearny street has been completely wiped out. So great has the damage been that one might easily be forgiven for failing to locate Market street when emerging from the Ferry building at the foot of the famous thoroughfare.

When our last message was received from the scene of horrors the flames were still spreading and sweeping everything in their path, and there seemed no likelihood of getting them under control for some time.

The firemen are putting up a brave fight under such adverse circumstances, but owing to the scarcity of water it seems at times that the only thing to do is to retire and let the flames take their course undisputed; but such action would not be in keeping with the proud record of the San Francisco fire department, and they are contesting every foot of the way; but it seems that the fight is against too great odds, and that the entire city is doomed to destruction.

EX-SUPERVISOR BAILEY SERIOUSLY INJURED IN SAN JOSE DISASTER

SUPERVISOR MITCHELL IS ALSO HURT

Many Fires and Much Damage in the Wake of the Temblor —Many Buildings are Shaken up and Some Fatalities Reported — Damages Will Exceed $200,000

San Jose, April 18.—Among the notables in San Jose last night were representatives from every county in the State attending the annual conventions of the sheriffs and supervisors of the State, and they were scattered throughout the city in the various hotels. Many of these buildings were unable to resist the violent wrenchings of the earthquake and soon crash after crash gave warning tha the worst was happening and that many of San Jose's supposedly substantial buildings were being wrecked and that in many instances lives were being sacrificed. When it became known that such buildings as the St. Francis and the Menlo were wrecked rescuing parties were organized and the work of getting out the bodies commenced. Many were kill ed and likewise many injured and the work of rescue was pushed with all possible speed, but in several instances many hours were required to get bodies of the dead and to liberate those who were still alive but pinioned under some of the heavy timbers. The work of rescue was push-

FRESNO ESCAPES WITH SLIGHT CASUALTIES

Fresno, April 19.—This city felt the earthquake this morning, but beyond the breaking of windows, the toppling of chimneys and cracking of plates, it destroyed no property. There was no loss of life, and no person sustained physical injury worth reckoning.

The same story applies to all the San Joaquin valley. But little damage was done in any of the counties adjoining ᵍthis.

Help for San Francisco will be forthcoming from Fresno within a few hours after daylight of Thursday.

MANY PERISH AT THE STATE HOSPITAL OF INSANE AT AGNEWS

BUILDINGS WRECKED AND INMATES ESCAPE

Sheriffs of the State in Convention in San Jose are Asked to Assist in Rounding up the Seven Hundred Unfortunates —All Now Confined in one Large Pen

San Jose, April 18.—Great consternation raged among the inmates of the State Hospital for the Insane at Agnews when the temblor in all its fury broke forth. Crouched in the corners of the cells with a feeling that something terrible was happening, but not realizing their true danger, the poor unfortunates awaited the outcome of the visitation. In a moment all was over. The walls of almost every building, of which there were many, soon succumbed to the violent wrenching and bricks and timbers were hurled upon the heads of the defenseless inmates of this institution and when it was possible to take an inventory of the damage it was found that about 225 of the insane patients had been killed. Some bore marks and bruises which denoted the manner in which the end overtook them while others were free from any sign of injury and were apparently scared to death. Those who escaped death were not slow to realize that they were at liberty to leave their places of confinement and soon

(Continued on Page 8)

A Legal Holiday

Governor Pardee arrived in Oakland at two o'clock this morning, and after a consultation with W. G. Palmanteer of the Central Bank, who is a vice president of the Alameda Bankers' association, decided to declare today a legal holiday in compliance with the request of the association. It is likely that Friday and Saturday will also be made holidays. This action is taken that no trouble may be brought on as a result of so many of the San Francisco banks being destroyed.

LOS ANGELES DOES NOT NEED HELP

Los Angeles, April 18.—The earthquake shock was a severe one here, but its consequences were far less serious than those reported from the north. No loss of life has been reported. Several fires, caused by overturning of lamps and stoves, followed the earthquake, but all were quenched before they could spread. Interruption of telegraphic service by the earthquake caused much uneasiness and apprehension concerning the sit- uation in the north, but the apprehension was not sufficient to prepare the population here for the frightful news from San Francisco.

Los Angeles is in no need of outside help. On the contrary, organization has already been effected, under direction of the Chamber of Commerce, to extend aid to San Francisco. A trainload of supplies will be sent to the stricken city tomorrow, and with it will go men and women trained to the work of rescue and of nursing.

GOOD WORK OF THE RELIEF COMMITTEE

By 1:40 o'clock this morning the relief committee had received 238 refugees from San Francisco and had found lodgings for them.

Most of them were sufficiently clothed, but a few had not had time to completely dress themselves. A small portion had brought small luggage with them, and there were some who had carried bedding. It was a heavy task to care for them all. The workers were too few. Messrs. Kilbourn, Preston, Galla- ger, Spencer and Aguirre remained until the last Southern Pacific train had come in. Each train brought its quota of the fire-evicted refugees. A few of these had suffered minor wounds, but there was not seriously injured among the night's arrivals. Some were hungry, and these were fed. The members of the Provisions Committee, Messrs. S. J. Sill and E. L. Coryell, had made hasty arrangements to that effect. These arrangements will be perfected and extended today.

Denial of Disaster

San Francisco Chronicle.

VOL. LXXXIII. SAN FRANCISCO, CAL., WEDNESDAY, APRIL 18, 1906—SIXTEEN PAGES. NO 93.

GOVERNMENT TO USE HUGHES' TALENTS

To Prosecute Coal Cases

YOUNG LAWYER ONE OF MAIN COUNSEL

Retained by the Department of Justice in Connection With the Commerce Inquiry.

Special Dispatch to the "Chronicle."

WASHINGTON, April 17.—Attorney-General Moody to-day gave out the following statement: Charles E. Hughes of New York, who gained fame in the insurance inquiry, has Alexander Simpson Jr. of Philadelphia have been retained by the Department of Justice to take under consideration all the facts now known, or which can be ascertained, relating to the transportation and sale of coal in interstate commerce, to advise what, if any, legal proceedings should be taken and to conduct, under the direction of the Attorney-General, such suits or prosecutions, if any may be warranted by the evidence in hand and forthcoming.

The Attorney-General adds that he believes that sufficient evidence has been developed in the investigation of the Interstate Commerce Commission and otherwise to warrant the employment of counsel under the provision of the appropriation act of February 25, 1903, authorizing the employment of counsel in proceedings of this nature.

THREE KILLED ON A BRITISH BATTLE-SHIP

Boiler Explodes on the Prince of Wales During Speed Trials.

MALTA, April 17.—Three members of the crew of the British battle-ship Prince of Wales were killed to-day and four others injured by a boiler explosion while she was undergoing her speed trials.

M'VICKER WILL CONTEST ENDS

Under Compromise to Protect Name of Horace McVicker, Mrs. Effey Gets $17,500.

Special Dispatch to the "Chronicle."

CHICAGO, April 17.—To protect the good name of McVicker, as it was admitted in court to-day, the legal battle over the estate of Mrs. Harriet G. McVicker was compromised. By the terms of the agreement Mrs. Minnie M. Effey, who attacked the will, is to receive $17,500 of the $275,000 estate.

The decree was signed after Attorney L. D. Conde, who took the witness stand, had explained to the Court that in the event of a trial before a jury, which was the course originally planned, the name of McVicker might suffer. It is possible that a charge would be made reflecting on Horace McVicker, who was Harriet G. McVicker's stepson, the lawyer.

The proceedings in court came as a surprise to persons interested in the suit. The case had been set for trial on Judge McEwen's May calendar and the work of taking the depositions of witnesses in many States from Maine to California was about to be undertaken.

Ever since the death of Mrs. McVicker, which took place in Pasadena, Cal., in August, 1904, relatives and others have been squabbling over the estate. Dr. L. C. H. Zeigler claimed $100,000 for medical services, but was allowed only $10,000. Mrs. Minnie M. Effey, who receives $17,500 under the compromise, is the wife of Robert Effey of 957 Hayes street, San Francisco, and was a niece of Mrs. McVicker. Mrs. Effey expected to share the estate with Mrs. Clara Belle Game, another niece, also of this city, but Mrs. Effey was not mentioned in any of the several wills found. One will left Horace McVicker, the stepson, three-fourths of the income of the estate, and Mrs. Game one-fourth; three-fourths of the estate went to Horace McVicker and one-fourth to Dr. Zeigler.

DEATH LIST OF THE KEARSARGE GROWING

Two More Added, Including Frederick Thomas Fisher of This City.

WASHINGTON, April 17.—The Navy Department was advised to-day that two more deaths had occurred as the result of the explosion on the battle-ship Kearsarge last Friday. They were Frederick Thomas Fisher, chief gunner's mate, and James B. McCardle, electrician, first class. Fisher was a resident of San Francisco.

GUANTANAMO

GUANTANAMO (Cuba), April 17.—Another officer, according to reports here, has died as a result of the explosion on board the battle-ship Kearsarge. Ten of the sailors who were injured at the time of the explosion were believed to be in a serious condition.

KING EDWARD AT ATHENS

ATHENS, April 17.—King Edward, Queen Alexandra and the Prince and Princess of Wales arrived here to-day.

DOWIE REJECTS OVERTURES OF ZION

Negotiations for a Peaceful Settlement Broken Off by the Deposed First Apostle.

SAYS VOLIVA IS NO LONGER IN THE CHURCH

Fight Must Be Made in Courts—Ousted Leader Plans to Return to City He Founded and Excommunicate Rival.

Special Dispatch to the "Chronicle."

CHICAGO, April 17.—All negotiations looking toward a peaceful settlement of the question as to who shall control Zion City and its vast resources were broken off to-day. John Alexander Dowie, through his attorneys, rejected the proposition advanced by General Overseer W. G. Voliva yesterday to the effect that the $21,000,000 estate be turned over to a board of control to consist of nine members, four of them to be selected by Dowie and five by Voliva, the ninth man to be selected by the board as created.

It was stipulated that the action of the members thereof be final in determining whether or not the deposed "first apostle" or Voliva be the recognized head of the Christian Catholic church. Dowie rejected the proposal on the ground that not only would he not acquiesce in the appointment of Voliva on the board, but that he no longer recognized the new leader as a member of the church.

In speaking of the ultimatum, Attorney P. C. Haley, representing Dowie, said: "As soon as we can obtain the necessary information we will file a bill in chancery. This instrument will be a petition that the transfer of the property of Zion City executed by General Overseer Voliva, giving to Deacon Alexander Granger full title thereof, be declared void. We are handicapped to the extent that Voliva and his forces have in their possession all of the books and papers concerning Zion City and its property. It may be necessary for us to go into court to get possession of these. As soon as we obtain the desired information the bill will be filed.

Dowie, it is said, will go to Zion City.

Voliva, they say, will be excommunicated.

STRIKERS' WIVES FIGHT SOLDIERS

Rioting Renewed in the French Coal Mines and Authorities Call for More Assistance.

LENS (France), April 17.—There was a renewal to-day of the disturbances consequent on the strike of the miners in the Pas de Calais district. The wife of a miner who had refused to strike was attacked in her home by 150 women, the wives of strikers, her clothing torn off and her furniture wrecked. Gendarmes who interfered to stop the riot were stoned by the women, and cavalry ordered to assist the gendarmes were similarly resisted.

A cavalry officer and two soldiers were severely injured and fifteen others received minor wounds. Several women were arrested, but they subsequently were released. The General Prefect here received with shouts of "Long live the revolution!" Rioting was resumed to-night. The local authorities are calling urgently for reinforcements.

FORTUNE LEFT TO FRIEND'S WIDOW

Portland Millionaire Rewards Family of Doctor Who Assisted Him When in Want.

Special Dispatch to the "Chronicle."

NEW YORK, April 17.—Mrs. Clara Goldsmith, widow of Dr. M. K. Goldsmith, and her three children are the sole beneficiaries under the will of L. K. G. Smith of Portland, Or., who died recently. The estate is said to be worth $1,500,000. It consists of securities and Oregon land.

Before Dr. Goldsmith's death Smith had made a will leaving everything to him, and when Goldsmith died he drew the present will, writing in it that his reason for so disposing of his estate was "because Dr. Goldsmith assisted me with the last means at his command while I was in need and want; for and in consideration of his long friendship for and in consideration of the fact that I always have been single and unmarried, and in consideration of the fact that nobody else has or can have any claim upon me and my possessions, either direct or indirect."

COMEDIAN LEECH DYING

LANCASTER (Pa.), April 17.—Al Leech, the well-known comedian, is dying at the Lancaster Hotel. Though very ill, he played last night, but collapsed this morning. His physician says there is no hope for his recovery.

CANARY VOLCANO REVIVING

MADRID, April 17.—The newspapers here report that the dormant volcano at Palma, Canary Islands, is showing signs of resumption. Columns of smoke are issuing from the crater.

DIVORCE RULING WILL CAUSE TROUBLE

Lawyers Say Property Titles in Later Generations Will Be Unsettled by the Decision.

STATUS OF CHILDREN ONE OF PROBLEMS

Attorneys Not in Accord as to Effect of Decision by United States Supreme Court—The Dakota Industry Continues.

Special Dispatch to the "Chronicle."

NEW YORK, April 17.—While the decision of the United States Supreme Court in the Haddock divorce case was generally discussed to-day in the County Courthouse, lawyers who have made divorce a special study expressed the opinion that there was nothing either radical, new or unexpected in it and that it merely reiterated the decision of the same court. As the same time there was much discussion of that phase of the decision that evidently brands as illegitimate thousands of children born to previously divorced parents.

It is pointed out that the decision may cause legal complications several generations hence in families not immediately affected. Therefore it would appear that some step should be taken to determine at once the status of the persons to whom the principle applies. So far as the children of persons not properly divorced are concerned, it is pointed out that there are two methods of offsetting the evil results. First, a new suit for divorce might be brought by consent of both parties to the former marriage in a court of competent jurisdiction, the children of the later marriage becoming legitimate. Secondly, parties to the second marriage could appeal to the Legislature of the state in which the child was born to have the offspring legitimatized by special enactment.

CHICAGO, April 17.—It is estimated by Chicago lawyers that the decision of the Supreme Court of the United States holding illegal all divorces except where both parties to the suit reside within the same jurisdiction will make illegal 100 divorces now pending in this city alone.

NEARLY EIGHTY AND YET ABOUT TO WED.

Los Angeles Man and Wisconsin Woman Will Marry at Ripe Old Age.

WAUKESHA (Wis.), April 17.—Mrs. Mary E. Billings of this city and Captain Enos B. Baily of Los Angeles, Cal., will be married here Saturday. Mrs. Billings is 79 years of age and Captain Baily is 75. They have been friends for over fifty years. Mrs. Billings has been married twice before. Her first husband was Captain Baily's brother.

CO-EDS ROBBED BY CHEERFUL THIEF

Burglar at Depauw Chats With His Frightened Victims as He Takes Their Money.

GREEN CASTLE (Ind.), April 17.—"Now, ladies, I want your money. I'm not after stuff," said a burglar, who early this morning, entered the Kappa sorority house, the home of many co-eds at DePauw University in the startled girls, who were awakened by a dark lantern flashing in their faces. "If you make any sound I will kill you," added the burglar as he displaced their watches, pins, rings and other jewelry, collected before awakening them to discover where their money was laid. After the frightened girls had surrendered their purses the burglar chatted affably with them, telling them he knew most of their beaux, asked kindly after their parents and desired to know what progress they were making on account of the endowment trying to force a local company to join with them to contribute into his pockets. He saw a young man and did not wear a mask. He explained that he was sorry in disturbing them, but he really needed the money. His victims netted him about $200 in money and jewelry.

FATHER WEALTHY BUT CHECK IS NO GOOD

Young Man From New York Said to Have Spent $30,000 Since the First of January.

PUT IN JAIL FOR GIVING A BAD CHECK

When His Money Ran Out Max Jaegerhuber Raised Funds to Play the Races by Forging His Father's Name.

"I'm a good fellow. I often give two bits or four bits to poor devils like these that they are putting into cells here now. Every one will tell you that I'm a good fellow and I always stop at the best hotels, of course, for I've been reared in luxury and always have had everything I wanted. Why father is worth $30,000,000."

After Max Jaegerhuber Jr's fund of personal anecdote ran out, however, he was escorted back to a cell like the "poor devils" because he is charged with feloniously obtaining money by false pretenses from the management of the Hotel St. Francis, where he has had apartments for the past six days. It was last Friday when he had the hotel people cash a check for $50, purporting to be drawn by his father in his favor on the Jackson Trust and Savings Bank of Chicago, but when a telegram was received yesterday stating that the check was refused on account of "no funds" complaint was lodged at police headquarters and Detective Sergeants Taylor and Braig, aided by Special Policeman Hirsch, took Jaegerhuber into custody at the hotel and locked him up.

He is a young man of 20, full of autobiography and according to his own admission so loaded down with erratic notions regarding the running of the ponies that car fare is not safe in his pockets. He does not deny that he did wrong in taking liberties with his father's name on a check, but ingeniously explains that he expected to make a killing on a "good thing" at the track when he would have taken up the incriminating bit of paper. The "good thing" is still running and he says that he will take his medicine and won't think of such a foolish course any more.

LODGE ASKS POLICE AID

Sons of Hermann Stirred Up Over Disappearance of Effects of Deceased Member.

Special Dispatch to the "Chronicle."

LOS ANGELES, April 17.—Police aid was sought to-day by the Sons of Hermann, a German fraternal and benevolent society, to solve the mystery of the disappearance of a trunk supposed to contain a large amount of money, a pawn ticket and trunk receipt held by a member who died in Los Angeles three months ago. The dead man, Librecht Martin, was a member of Mission Lodge, No. 9, of San Francisco.

BULLETS END A RUSSIAN MUTINY

Seven Rebellious Soldiers Killed by Volley Fired by Loyal Troops—Trouble Stopped.

ST. PETERSBURG, April 17.—The news published in the United States that there was a part of the garrison at St. Petersburg has been mutilated and that in a fight between the mutineers and loyal troops 215 soldiers had been killed and 85 wounded, probably originated with a report published in the Russkoe Slovo on April 15th of a meeting of soldiers at Tiflis on present certain grievances of which they complained.

ELLIS ISLAND SWAMPED.

NEW YORK, April 17.—Sixteen thousand immigrants, that could not be subjected to restraint on board the vessels on which they came to this country, went to sleep to-night in the steerage of transatlantic liners. This was because a record-breaking rush of immigration has swamped the bureau on Ellis Island, which has facilities for examining only 5000 newcomers a day.

BLANCHE WALSH PLAYS LIFE SAVER

GORKY WEARY OF AMERICA

Russian Finds Personal Liberty Hampered Here as Much as It Is in the Czar's Realm.

Special Dispatch to the "Chronicle."

NEW YORK, April 17.—A cable to the Sun from Paris says: Maxim Gorky has sent a telegram to the director of a French publication for which he is writing his impressions of the United States. The director appraises Gorky's bitterest comments, but leaves enough to show that the Russian has formed had impressions of America and American ways.

Rescues Kathérine Bell

Actress Tumbles Out of Launch at

Special Dispatch to the "Chronicle."

SEATTLE (Wash.), April 17.—Blanche Walsh, appearing at a local theater in "The Woman in the Case," jumped from a launch this afternoon to rescue Katherine Bell, a member of her company. The accident occurred on Lake Washington on which Miss Walsh was entertaining some friends with a launch party. Miss Bell was leaning over the side of the boat trailing her hand in the water, when she lost her balance and with a scream fell into the lake.

San Francisco Chronicle *edition for April 18, 1906. This edition was on the street when the earthquake struck.*

Denial of Disaster

by
Gladys Hansen
and
Emmet Condon

David Fowler, Editor
Richard Hansen, Photo Researcher

*This book is dedicated to the known and unknown victims
who suffered and died in the last Great Earthquake,
and to those who will suffer and die in the next.*

A special mention of appreciation must be made to
Robert E. Burger
for his contribution of organizational expertise
and for his editorial and literary skills.

Published by
Cameron and Company, San Francisco

Such a book as this does not reach publication without more than the usual amount of cooperation from many people. So, for their encouragement and expertise, we thank the following:

Vetelmo V. Bertero, Merijane Block, Willie Brown, LaCienne Bryant, Jeffrey M. Burns, Todd Cameron, Andrew C. Casper, Donald Cheu, Arnold Chung, Raymond Clary, Barbara Cox, Octavia Coffey Cox, Henry Degenkolb, Ron Eguchi, Tim Findley, Richard Frick, Kathleen Griffin, Michael Griffith, Michael Housh, Thomas Johnston, George Kovatch, Frank McClure, Phil McDonald, John B. McGloin, John Masek, William Murray, Michael E. Myers, Robert D. Nason, Patricia O'Grady, Rena Phillips, Bernadette Quineri, Frank R. Quinn, Ray Siemers, Carol Ruth Silver, Charmaine Wong, Staff of the Military History Room, National Archives, Washington, D.C., Staff of the San Francisco Archives, Public Library.

Helicopter pilots:
James E. Larsen and James M. Larsen.

Credits for Historical Photographs:
Blue Lake Museum Society
California Earthquake History Program
San Francisco Archives, Public Library
Mrs. Rita Little.

CAMERON and COMPANY
543 Howard Street   San Francisco, California 94105   (415) 777-5582

Library of Congress Catalog Number: 88-070156
Denial of Disaster ISBN 0-918684-33-1
©1989 Robert W. Cameron and Company, Inc. All rights reserved.

First Edition 1989

Book design by
JANE OLAUG KRISTIANSEN

Color Photographs on pages 137 through 151 by Robert Cameron, San Francisco
Typography by Parker-Smith Typography, San Francisco
Photo Retouching by Alice Marie Mutrux and Jerome Vloeberghs, San Francisco
Camera work by Color Comp Graphics, San Francisco
Cover photo and page 62 by Modern Effects, San Francisco (Courtesy of Maxwell Galleries, Ltd., San Francisco)
Color Separations and Printing by Dai Nippon Printing Co., Tokyo, Japan

TABLE OF CONTENTS

Commerce and Labor Secretary Victor Metcalf was struck by the devastation he saw upon his arrival in San Francisco, and sent this telegram to President Roosevelt one week after the earthquake and fire. "As regards industrial and commercial losses, the conditions are appalling; figures and distances convey slight conceptions of realities.

"Not only have the business and industrial houses and establishments of one-half million people disappeared, leaving them destitute financially and their means of livelihood temporarily gone, but the complicated system of transportation indispensable to the daily comfort and interest of one-half millions of people, has been almost totally destroyed."

This panoramic photograph of the ruins was taken from Bush and Jones Streets looking toward Market Street.

The San Andreas Fault cuts across the history of California as it cuts across its geography. That recorded history is short; little more than 200 years. Thus, the frequent and violent earthquakes in that short time must be considered ominous.

San Francisco lies between two major faults, the San Andreas and the Hayward.

Records of the California Missions and those of the Spanish Army told of an earthquake on June 10, 1836, that opened fissures from San Pablo to Mission San Jose. Then, in June 1838, an earthquake damaged Mission Dolores and cracked walls at the Presidio of San Francisco.

Both the *Alta California* and *San Francisco Herald* newspapers, in 1852, began to comment on this strange earthquake phenomenon, a danger second only to the persistent fires that had burned large parts of San Francisco to the ground six times between Christmas Eve, 1849 and June 22, 1851.

To reduce the fire danger, brick buildings were constructed on the warm ashes of the wooden structures that burned – then came the earthquake of 1857.

This earthquake on the then-unnamed San Andreas Fault caused grave concern and alarm in San Francisco which, in turn, sparked a steep but temporary drop of real estate prices.

It was not clear to San Francisco's inhabitants whether the instability of brick in earthquakes or the fire hazard from wooden structures was the greater financial or life-safety threat to the city.

An 1860 state history book categorically, and erroneously, reported "no sizeable earthquake has ever been recorded north of the 35th parallel" which is, in the West, just north of San Luis Obispo, California. In the minds of early white settlers major earthquakes were a Southern California phenomenon.

But the earthquake of October 8, 1865 prompted Mark Twain to write an "Earthquake Almanac," in the *San Francisco Dramatic Chronicle*. His acidic and humorous entries for October 24, 25 and 26th were: "Shaky." "Occasional shakes, followed by light showers of bricks and plastering. About this time expect more earthquakes, but do not look out for them, on account of the bricks."

Twain's journalistic contemporary Bret Harte took a different and more serious view of the earthquake threat. He wrote, in 1866, "In spite of the fears of alarmists, I do not think that the prosperity and future of California is disturbed by these shocks, and I believe that there is more danger to be apprehended from the concealment of facts, or the tacit silence of the public press on this topic, than in free and open discussion of the subject and speculation for the future."

The Great Hayward Earthquake of October 21, 1868 damaged enough property and killed enough people in San Francisco to convince major property owners and builders of the pressing need for solid foundations and structural reinforcement. This was an economic move, as some property values tended to fall for a few months after each large earthquake. So-called "made ground" or "filled land" was composed of garbage, rotting wood, debris from past fires and even old sailing ships abandoned during the Gold Rush. Buildings on "made ground" suffered badly in this earthquake, and five people were killed.

Two severe earthquakes within three years were of great concern to the editor of the

(Continued on page 11)

The domes of the California Hotel on Bush Street near Kearny Street dominate this 1905 photograph. A chimney from the hotel fell upon the neighboring fire station and fatally injured Fire Chief Engineer Dennis Sullivan. Goldberg, Bowen & Company's warehouse is seen on the left. The Hopkins Institute of Art and the new Fairmont Hotel are seen in the distance.

This photograph taken from Rincon Hill shows the city as it was in 1905. The Selby Shot Tower is at First and Howard Streets.

Smokestack of the San Francisco Brick Company dominates this picture that looks from Twentieth and Castro Streets toward Corona Heights. The brick company's smokestack fell during the earthquake.

View of Montgomery Street before the earthquake as photographed from the second floor of the Palace Hotel. Crocker-Woolworth Bank is at left.

City Hall Avenue in front of City Hall before the earthquake and fire. McAllister Street is at the right. City Hall Avenue ran diagonally southwest from about Leavenworth and McAllister Streets to Grove and Larkin Streets.

The 18-story Call Building, also known as the Claus Spreckels Building, is shown at Third and Market Streets. The building survives today, although the exterior was savagely altered during remodeling in the 1930s. This photograph taken from Third and Mission Streets also shows the Mutual Bank Building in the center, and the clock of the San Francisco Chronicle Building can just be seen over the structural steel of the Monadnock Building.

Kearny Street as it was in August 1905. The Chronicle Building at Market and Kearny Streets is in the distance.

(Continued from page 8)

San Francisco Real Estate Circular who suggested in the October 1868 edition: "The late shock will undoubtedly have the effect of keeping the prices of lots upon 'made ground' stationary, if it does not actually make them retrograde. Only the best built and anchored houses are safe on 'made ground.' Just three years elapsed between the heavy shock of 1865 and the late one. If we neglect the precautions which have been so strongly urged upon us, we may feel reasonably certain that the day of reckoning for such neglect is not more than a very few years distant, and, what

adds to its terror, it always comes upon us like a thief in the night."

Regardless of these dangers, the need for usable land for expansion in the economic boom which followed the Gold Rush, and extended into the Civil War era, gave real estate speculators the economic incentive to continue to fill Yerba Buena Cove – with anything that could be hauled to the water's edge and dumped.

The shoreline of 1849 at Montgomery and Jackson Streets, curving around to the present Fremont and Howard Streets, was steadily extended into the Bay. Soil samples taken

in the 1970s showed the same landfill composition in the former swamps along the shoreline of Mission Bay south of Howard Street. Mission Bay swamps came inland to what is now the James Rolph Jr. Civic Center, where a grand City Hall was built. Upon its completion in 1896, the gigantic San Francisco City Hall was not only the largest structure west of Chicago, but one of the largest municipal buildings in the world.

By 1906, one-sixth of the city's 410,000 population lived on some form of "made or filled ground."

An 1880s view of the Palace Hotel as seen from Second and Howard Streets. The steeple of St. Patrick's Church is seen slightly to the left of the center of the photograph.

Mechanics' Pavilion as it was in the early 1900s. This site at Grove and Larkin Streets is today occupied by Exposition Hall, which serves as San Francisco's Civic Auditorium.

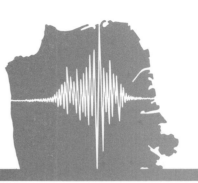

The Great Earthquake

This extraordinary panoramic view of the disaster South of Market was taken from the rear of the Grand Hotel. Fires along Fremont Street and blazes from cheap rooming houses are about to descend upon the intersection of Second and Mission Streets.

At 5:12:05 a.m., Wednesday, April 18, 1906, two of the world's greatest tectonic plates, the Pacific and the North American – unable to further bear the geologic tension – lurched past each other a distance of nine to 21 feet along the California Coast. The break stretched some 290 miles, from Mendocino to Monterey counties.

This was the full fury of the longest fault line in the world, mapped and named 11 years earlier by a young geologist from the University of California at Berkeley. Professor Andrew Lawson called it "San Andreas" after a reservoir of that name a few miles south of San Francisco which exhibited ancient earth movements. This 1906 slippage of the recently-named fault sent shock waves speeding at 7,000 miles per hour through the then-largest population center of the Western United States.

By 1906, Alexander G. McAdie had been in charge of the San Francisco office of the U.S. Weather Bureau for 12 years. It was among his responsibilities to record all earthquake shocks for the bureau's records. Professor McAdie, who had developed a personal interest in earthquakes after Charleston, South Carolina, was wrecked in 1886, left a detailed record of the major earthquake and the aftershocks as recorded in San Francisco.

The first shock wave from the San Andreas Fault lasted, he said, "approximately 45 seconds." Seismic stations in Tokyo, Washington, D.C. and elsewhere confirmed the observations made in San Francisco that the earthquake came in two parts with a 10-12 sec-

13

The San Francisco Gas and Electric fire attacked earthquake-damaged buildings on Market Street. The earthquake also ripped the facade from the Shiels Apartment

Building at 32 O'Farrell Street. Fire Engine No. 2 was quartered directly under the Curtaz Piano sign at 22 O'Farrell.

ond pause between them, followed by the heaviest jolt.

Scientists at the turn of the century used the Rossi-Forel scale of intensity that ran from one to ten, with ten denoting complete destruction.

Professor McAdie classified the 1906 earthquake as a Rossi-Forel No. 9. He said, "Earthquake No. 9 of the scale being used, is an earthquake which throws down badly built buildings and will give in the streets of the city a large amount of debris. It is about as severe an earthquake as can be experienced without total destruction, without great yawning chasms and complete destruction of life and property. The effect is more pronounced upon filled-in ground, loose soil, made land and alluvial soil, than upon rock formation."

The professor recorded all the subsequent earthquake shocks felt in San Francisco. "On April 18th, 1906, we had 27 earthquakes. The earthquake of next severest intensity after the first earthquake occurred at 8:14:28, and would be classified as a No. 5 . . . [that] would displace loose masonry, and buildings not

securely built . . . might be wrecked," he said. Professor McAdie described the other 25 shocks as in the number two and three range, slightly stronger than a gentle rocking.

Seventeen of the most significant aftershocks recorded by the professor were at 5:18 a.m, which lasted a few seconds, then another at 5:25 a.m.; another at 5:42 a.m. There were no more aftershocks that morning until the five-second tremor at 8:14 a.m., then smaller shocks followed at 9:13, 9:25, 10:49 and 11:05. The afternoon brought shocks at 12:03, 12:10, 2:23, 2:27, 4:50, 6:49 and 7 o'clock.

In later years people spoke of "before The Fire" or "after The Fire" as historical bench marks, as future generations would reference the attack on Pearl Harbor or the assassination of President John F. Kennedy. Yet, the earthquake alone, without the fire, would have significantly changed the history of San Francisco, just as it altered the lives of all who went through it.

The Great Fire and dynamiting done to stop the conflagration also obliterated much

of the physical evidence scientists and structural engineers would later need to study the quality of construction relative to the widely-varying geologic conditions throughout the city. This loss of solid, scientific data would lead to accusations of shoddy construction and stories of miraculous survivability of certain buildings. It would mask an unrecorded death toll that reached into the thousands.

The earthquake story began for *San Francisco Examiner* reporter Fred J. Hewitt at 5 a.m. as he walked north on Larkin Street past City Hall. He had just spoken with two policemen headed for the City Hall Police Station quartered on the first floor of that structure. Central Emergency Hospital, one of several such small municipal hospitals in the City, was in the basement of the huge building. After a brief chat with the officers he continued north on Larkin Street to the intersection of Golden Gate Avenue. Then came the first shock wave.

Later, Mr. Hewitt would write from one of the refugee camps, "It is impossible to judge

RICHTER SCALE	
Richter Scale Magnitude	Equivalent Energy
1.0	6 ounces TNT
1.5	2 pounds TNT
2.0	13 pounds TNT
2.5	63 pounds TNT
3.0	397 pounds TNT
3.5	1,990 pounds TNT
4.0	6 tons TNT
4.5	32 tons TNT
5.0	199 tons TNT
5.5	1,000 tons TNT
6.0	6,270 tons TNT
6.5	31,550 tons TNT
7.0	199,000 tons TNT
7.5	1,000,000 tons TNT
8.0	6,270,000 tons TNT
8.5	31,550,000 tons TNT
9.0	199,000,000 tons TNT

(Based on California Division of Mines and Geology data)

Richter scale increases are measured logarithmically by a factor of 10.

Earthquake-caused subsidence at Market and Spear Streets.

Ruins of City Hall seen from Fulton Street near Larkin Street before the building caught fire. The damaged Fulton House is on the right, the Strathmore Apartment Building is on the left.

the length of that shock. To me it seemed an eternity. I was thrown . . . on my back and the pavement pulsated like a living thing. Around me the huge buildings, looming up were terrible because of the queer dance they were performing, wobbled and veered. Crash following crash resounded on all sides. Screeches rent the air as terrified humanity streamed out into the open in agony of despair. Frightened horses dashed headlong into ruins as they raced away in their abject fear.

"The first portion of that shock was just a mild forerunning of what was to follow. The pause in the action of the earth's surface couldn't have been more than a fraction of a second . . . then came the second and most terrific crash.

"The street beds heaved in frightful fashion. The earth rocked and then came the blow that wrecked San Francisco from the bay shore to the Ocean Beach and from the Golden Gate to the end of the peninsula. . . ."

Collapse of buildings in the area raised a dust cloud around City Hall, and Mr. Hewitt

was unable to see the gigantic building. As the dust cloud dispersed he said, "The dome appeared like a huge birdcage against the morning dawn. The upper works of the entire building lay . . . in the street below."

Worse than the destruction, it was the "condition of an excitement-crazed populace" that made a lasting impression on the *Examiner* reporter. "Herds of huddled creatures . . . each and every person I saw was temporarily insane. Laughing idiots commented on the fun they were having. Terror marked other faces. Strong men bellowed like babies in their furor. No one knew which way to turn, when on all sides destruction stared them in the very eye. A number of slight tremors followed the first series of shocks. As each came in turn fearful agony spread . . . on every brow."

Reporter Hewitt's somewhat dramatic eyewitness account is similar to those written by people in other areas of "made ground." In general, though, eyewitness accounts from people on more stable ground are less vivid.

This grand City Hall Mr. Hewitt described

was constructed between 1872 and 1896 on part of the Mission Bay swamplands, and portions of the massive structure had already begun to settle into the "made ground." The earthquake as Mr. Hewitt described caused the skin of the dome to peel and fall into the surrounding streets. Portions of the exterior walls also fell away.

Perhaps the clearest description of what happened inside City Hall, as part of the building collapsed, came from San Francisco Police Officer Edward J. Plume, who wrote this account a few weeks after the disaster. "I was seated at a desk in the office [of the City Hall Police Station] when I felt a slight trembling of the great building. This had lasted a few seconds when Officer Jeremiah M. Dwyer said, 'that's an earthquake.'

"Then the seemingly light temblor began to increase in violence and all of a sudden I was thrown clear out of the chair. As I was then being tossed from one side to the other by the shocks, I tried to find something to hold onto and prevent myself from falling.

"Meanwhile the noise from the outside

became deafening. I could hear the massive pillars that upheld the cornices and cupola of the City Hall go cracking, with reports like cannon, then falling with crashes like thunder. Huge stones and lumps of masonry came crashing down outside our doors; the large chandelier swung to and fro, then fell from the ceiling with a bang.

"In an instant the room was full of dust as well as soot and smoke from the fireplace. It seemed to be reeling like the cabin of a ship in a gale. Feeling sure that the building could never survive such shocks, and expecting every moment to be buried under a mass of ruins, I shouted to Officer Dwyer to get out.

"The lights were then out, and though the dawn had come outside, the station, owing to the dust and smoke inside, and the ruins and dust outside, was all in darkness.

"Dwyer and I made a rush for the nearest door, stumbling over chairs and desks and other litter as we scrambled out to Larkin Street.

"It was dark in the street, and choking with dust. We ran across to a small alley. The dust from the buildings that were still falling made it impossible to see anything.

"As I reached the alley, the front walls of the Strathmore [apartment building at 207 Larkin Street] began to fall. There was a vacant lot about fifty feet away, and I ran there and stood along a high fence waiting for the ruin to become complete. Dwyer had tripped when crossing Larkin Street and had not joined me.

"Then the quaking stopped, and we could hear screams in all directions."

Officer Plume was about one block south of where Mr. Hewitt was thrown down by the earthquake at Larkin Street and Golden Gate Avenue and Plume's account of the human condition is strikingly similar to the *Examiner* reporter's.

Officer Plume wrote, "Presently, as the smother [dust] cleared away, we could see the people that were screaming. Men and women from the Strathmore and other [apartment] houses were running about in all directions, some clad only in their underwear, some in their night clothes.

"Then I remembered the prisoners we had locked up in the Station – two women and a man – and also we had left Lieutenant Bernard McManus there.

"I called to Officer Dwyer and started back to the station. But this time I tripped several times over wires that had fallen, but I did not seem to mind hurting myself.

"Dwyer had hurt himself and was limping. But we had not time to notice these things. I was wondering if the prisoners had been caught in the mess and killed, so I hurried to get the keys of the cells and find out what I could about their fate. The cells were then in perfect darkness.

"When we got to the prison door, the man inside was shaking his cell door and howling to be let out. There was not a sound from

Smoke from the burning Mechanics' Pavilion obscured parts of the ruined City Hall. This view from Larkin Street and Golden Gate Avenue shows the high fence against which Officer Plume of the San Francisco Police Department stood to wait for the earthquake to stop.

Fire attacked earthquake-damaged buildings in the 500 block of Sansome Street on the afternoon of April 18.

Officer Max Fenner was said to have been the strongest man on the police department. He was killed when a wall fell upon him on Mason Street near Eddy Street.

Below, Officer Fenner's children mourn their father, the only on-duty policeman killed during the earthquake.

the women.

"The cells appeared to be unharmed, as far as we could judge. We opened the women's cell and found them both lying on the floor senseless. The unfortunate girls had fainted from terror.

"We let the man out of his cell and, by Lieutenant McManus' orders, we released him. He was held only on some misdemeanor charge. The girls we had to carry out between us, and then, with a wet towel, I tried to revive them. One was hysterical when she came to, and it was some time before she could control herself.

"They had been arrested during the night, on Mason Street, by Officer Max Fenner. We guessed he would not mind our letting them free after the terrible fright and punishment they had been through. But we then had no idea that poor Max Fenner had been killed by the quake a few minutes earlier, near the very spot where he had arrested these girls."

Officer Fenner was the only police officer killed during the earthquake. His friend, Officer Maurice S. Behan was working on another beat when a man ran up to him and said a police officer was buried under rubble at the Oriental Bar and Cafe at 138 Mason Street near Eddy. Max Fenner had been speaking to the man in charge of the cafe-bar when the shock came. The cafe man ran out of the building, and hugging the wall, went south on Mason Street. The officer began to run across the street when the cornice and part of the upper wall of the cafe fell on him.

When Officer Behan got there he could see nothing of Max Fenner. Wrote Officer Behan, "He was buried under the pile of debris, and on top of the pile lay the body of a very lovely girl, stone dead. She had jumped out of a window five stories above, and was killed instantly.

"They lifted off her body and dug down to Max Fenner. When they got out Max, he was utterly crushed, but his eyes were open and he was still breathing."

He was carried by his fellow police officers in the direction of Central Emergency Hospital at City Hall.

At the time the earthquake struck, Police Officer Edmund F. Parquet was in the basement Emergency Hospital talking with hospital matron Mrs. Rose Kane. Collapse of the exterior walls described by Officer Plume covered the outer entrance and windows of the hospital with rubble and effectively trapped Dr. Arthur McGinty, Matron Kane, Officer Parquet, and several insane patients held in locked cells. No one knew they were alive until about 6 a.m., when Dr. Charles B. Pinkham arrived and found the hospital entrance choked with debris, and injured earthquake victims milling about. Doctor Pinkham ran to the Underwriters' Fire Patrol station nearby on City Hall Avenue, and got the men to dig away at the rubble and tear the iron bars from the Larkin Street windows to allow the trapped to escape.

The wreckage of the massive City Hall was bad enough, but the worst destruction by earthquake in any city in the continental United States occurred just a few blocks south of City Hall. The area is not large; just 12 by 6 blocks. But within this South of Market zone lay the largest concentration of dead and injured in the San Francisco Earthquake. Until the 1980s, these casualties were also the least recorded.

If there were a "ground zero" for destruction in the South of Market zone, it would be Sixth and Howard Streets, once part of the old Mission Bay Swamp. Small streets in the area – Natoma, Minna, Jessie, Tehama, Clementina, Shipley, Clara – were and are precariously paved over "made ground."

The 1900 census statistics and the *Great Voter Register* record a population density in the South of Market area second only to that of Chinatown. Structures along Sixth Street, from Howard to Folsom, were predominantly two- and three-story wood-frame buildings with rooming houses on the upper floors. The first floors generally contained small stores or restaurants. Larger five-story wood-frame buildings, some with as many as 300 small rooms, dominated corner lots at most major intersections, and most were hotels and rooming houses for transients.

To the south – a little more than one block from this "ground zero" – was San Francisco Fire Engine Station No. 6 at 311 Sixth Street, between Folsom and Shipley Streets. A little background about the way the San Francisco Fire Department functioned is important before telling the story of Fire Engine Station No. 6.

In 1906, firefighters were on duty 24 hours per day in 10 day cycles with three days off per month. Firefighters could eat at home if it were near their assigned station, but they were required to sleep in the firehouse. Most, however, were not married and took up permanent residence in the firehouses.

Uniformed strength of the San Francisco Fire Department on April 10, 1906 – the most accurate figure that can be found – was 575 men, roughly twice as many as are on duty in the department today. And, there was actually far more manpower available should a major fire strike. In addition to 38 engines and 12 ladder companies, there were eight chemical companies, two monitor batteries and one water tower. Steam engines had a rated pumping capacity of about 500 gallons-per-minute, and the department possessed only 30,000 feet of hose for day-to-day use. Nine men and one officer were assigned to

Refugees' camp near Fort Mason as the fire swept into North Beach.

each fire engine, about twice as many as assigned to a modern fire engine in San Francisco. An additional five relief companies were manned by fire department support personnel and "substitutes," hired to take the place of regular firefighters who could afford to pay them to allow for extra days off. These substitute and relief firefighters, however, were not counted in the department's annual manpower report.

The total number of able-bodied firefighters available at the time of the earthquake was probably closer to 700, if the substitute and relief manpower is taken into account.

Spring Valley Water Company's system of mains for fire hydrants was considered barely adequate, and the 57 underground cisterns, relics of the Gold Rush days, were no longer considered by fire insurance companies to be a factor in fire protection. Many cisterns had been filled with trash and garbage, or utility companies had run pipes or conduits through them, although most still contained water. Knowledge of where the cisterns were located resided in the memories of the older San Francisco firefighters.

The amount of fire department manpower on duty on April 18, or the adequacy or inadequacy of the water system, is somewhat academic because the department simply never had a chance. Too many disasters happened at the same time – thousands of people caught in wreckage – damage to the fire stations which trapped the engines and caused the horses to run away – destruction of the telephone and fire alarm system – all would have exhausted, disorganized or fragmented the resources of the San Francisco Fire Department, even if there had been no fires.

Captain Charles J. Cullen of Engine No. 6, like many other fire department officers in the disaster, was forced to make crucial life and death decisions as how to best utilize his limited resources.

For many years, Captain Cullen's account of the fire and earthquake rested in the Bancroft Library at the University of California at Berkeley. This heavily-edited transcript of his fire station journal and those of other fire department officers had been used as stipulated testimony in the many insurance court cases which followed the Great Fire.

Fire Engine Station No. 6 was a 25 by 75-foot two-story wood-frame building. When the earthquake struck, the rear of the station settled over three feet into the made ground and the floor parted in the center. Captain Cullen wrote, "Immediately after the first shake ... the doors of our engine house shook open and our horses ran into the

Fire Captain Charles J. Cullen (front row, third from left) surrounded by members of Engine Cos. No. 4 and No. 6. This photograph was taken inside Fire Engine Station No. 6 shortly before the earthquake.

streets and escaped. It was with great difficulty that we got our apparatus out of the station.

"Our first rescue was on both sides of the engine house. At 313 Sixth Street the place was completely wrecked and the bare foot of a child could be seen in a pile of debris. We cut our way into the premises with axes and shortly afterwards rescued three little children and five adults."

The crew of the fire engine company was able to rescue three men and two women from the home of fireman John T. Titus at 309 Sixth Street also next to the fire station. "The house was still standing," wrote Captain Cullen, "but seemed to be in a dangerous condition, having partly caved in."

According to Lieutenant Edward H. Daunet of Engine No. 6, most of the wood-frame buildings on the west side of Sixth Street between Folsom and Harrison Streets had partially collapsed. Most, he said, had second-floor collapses, leaving the first stories intact. Wholesale destruction like that described by the lieutenant inevitably foreshadowed what firefighters had long feared for San Francisco.

The first fire in Captain Cullen's district broke out just a block from the firehouse, in Nicholas Prost's Bakery which had collapsed at 234 Sixth Street, on the west side between Howard and Folsom.

The crew of Engine No. 6 worked its way through fallen electric and telephone wires and Captain Cullen split his company into two squads, one to fight the fire and the other to continue rescue efforts.

Corona House, a three-story wood-frame hotel on the northwest corner of Sixth and Folsom Streets, about 150 feet from the firehouse, sank two stories into the made ground and the top story collapsed into the street.

After the initial rescues on either side of the fire station, his men tried to work their way through the roof of the Corona House, now at street level, chopping frantically to rescue trapped victims they could hear desperately screaming for help.

"At this time," Captain Cullen wrote, "my crew helped rescue a man and woman from the Corona House, [and] approximately forty people were killed by the collapsing of this hotel. The two survivors rescued were pinned on the top floor near a sky-light."

Without horses, Captain Cullen's men pulled the heavy Clapp and Jones steam fire engine by hand along Folsom Street. There was no water, either, in the hydrants at Sixth and Folsom or Sixth and Shipley Streets, on either side of the firehouse.

Captain Cullen did find some water in sewer lines, the source of which came from a broken water main at Seventh and Howard Streets. For a time, this helped keep the blaze from crossing from the bakery on the west side of Sixth Street to the east side. However, by 6:15 a.m., about one hour after the earthquake, the bakery fire began to rapidly

Fire attacked the lower floors of the Call Building at Third and Market Streets. Buildings to the right were severely damaged by the earthquake.

spread, and the men of Engine No. 6 were forced to pull the heavy steam engine out of the intersection and away from the fire.

"Our water supply gave out," wrote Captain Cullen, "and the fire was then raging around our engine. It would have proved fatal for us then to stay there any longer, and with wet sacks around our heads we assisted our engineer to . . . pull the engine by hand along Folsom Street. . . ."

Altogether, a minimum of fifty people died from the direct effects of fire or earthquake within 100 feet of the intersection of Sixth and Folsom Streets by the time Engine No. 6 was forced to evacuate. "Stopping occasionally we tried to obtain water from the sewers, only to find them dry or filled with mud; finally on Fifth Street we succeeded in drafting a small amount of water from the sewer and tried once again to the fight the fire."

Captain Cullen then made the decision to abandon fire fighting and concentrate his few resources on rescue operations. Finally, he wrote, "The heat became so intense it proved

impossible to save our engine and we had to move westward, and abandon our hose in the middle of Fifth Street, between Folsom and Clementina."

Had the captain and his firefighters dragged the engine north on Sixth Street another block, they would have become involved in the worst single disaster so far recorded in the 1906 earthquake – a disaster that no firefighter saw.

Brunswick House was the largest of four wood-frame hotels and rooming houses in one short block and occupied the northwest corner of Sixth and Howard Streets. Next to the Brunswick House, from south to north along the west side of Sixth Street, were the Ohio House, the Lormor and, on the southwest corner of Natoma and Sixth Streets, the Nevada House.

These hotels for transients occupied a portion of Mission Swamp once known as Pioche's Lake, a depression created by the

(Continued on page 23)

Fire from the Chinese Laundry across from Fire Engine Station No. 4 burned along Howard Street near Hawthorne Street.

Post-disaster view of Chinatown and Telegraph Hill. The Hall of Justice is at the right.

Smoke from fires on both sides of Market Street obscured the Ferry Building in the distance.

(Continued from page 20)
Great Hayward Earthquake of 1868, and later filled. The earthquake created a domino-like effect that began with the collapse of the Nevada House at 132 Sixth Street. The falling Nevada House slammed into the Lormor at 136 Sixth Street which, in turn, fell upon the Ohio House at 142 Sixth. Ohio House then rammed most of the Brunswick House into Howard Street as far as the car tracks in the middle of the intersection. All four hotels, combined, contained about one-thousand rooms.

Druggist Frederick Rockstroh made his way toward Sixth Street shortly after he was routed from his room at Seventh and Howard Streets by the earthquake. Girard House on the northwest corner of Seventh and Howard Streets and the Kingsbury next to it had "caved in" and both buildings were partially "lying on the sidewalk," he said. He could also see the huge Brunswick House start to burn.

Alfred F. Giddings, another of the business-men who typically lived near his work place, approached the Brunswick House from the south – Folsom Street. He saw that fully half the buildings in his view on Sixth Street – all wood-frame – "were down."

Messrs. Rockstroh and Giddings were two of more than 120 witnesses called by the Commercial Union Fire Insurance Company of New York in defense of a lawsuit by the California Wine Association argued before the California Supreme Court three years after the earthquake. Dozens of insurers either refused to pay fire losses or insisted on compromises, alleging the earthquake had wrecked the buildings.

Transcripts of these trials record remarkable first-hand eyewitness accounts of the disaster South of Market that were not available to reporters and writers of the time.

Joseph Balcera was a saloon keeper whose bar was on the first floor of the Corona House at Sixth and Folsom Streets. "When I saw my building a half hour after the earthquake," he testified, "the fire was next door to it. The building itself had sunk, and although it was a three-story building only one story was above the ground." Mr. Balcera's account corroborates Captain Cullen's report of the swift spread of the fire.

In the grotesque wreckage of the Brunswick House and others on the block the greatest horror was the pitiful moaning and pleading of the trapped and dying victims. Survivors of the top floors of these structures either crawled from the wreckage or were quickly rescued by bystanders. Two police officers who came across the disaster worked frantically to dig down through the roofs of the flattened hotels.

The fire that started in the wreckage of the Brunswick House grew bigger, and people held blankets between the two officers and the flames to allow just a few more minutes to rescue trapped victims they heard screaming for help.

Doctors Margaret Mahoney and Louisa Linscott were staying with one another at 929-1/2 Howard Street and were at the Brunswick House wreckage within a few minutes. "There was a terrible, low, heart-rending cry of utter resignation" from the trapped occupants, Dr. Mahoney later wrote. Eyewitnesses put the death toll at the Brunswick House, alone, at anywhere from 150 to 300.

James Madison Jacobs was one of a handful of survivors from the Brunswick House disaster. He lived in room 56 on the third floor, near the Sixth and Howard Street corner of the building. "I jumped out of bed and made a grab for my clothes; but before I could get into them the second quake came. It was much more severe than the first and its effects were immediate and indescribable. There were noises of cracking, and rending, and shrieks and everything; and while these noises were terrorizing everybody, the building itself broke asunder into three parts."

Mr. Jacobs' reference to "the second quake" is quite common to many eyewitness accounts. Those in some large structures or in buildings on made ground felt a distinctive second jolt during the main shock. Some described the second part of the earthquake as having a rotary or twisting motion to it. In the Palace Hotel, as an example, nearly every eyewitness reported the "rotary motion" of the earthquake.

James Madison Jacobs' account continued. "One part pitched into Sixth Street, another into Howard Street, and the third section, which comprised what would be the northwest corner of the building, diagonally back from the street corner, remained standing."

His room was partly telescoped by the collapse of the floors and roof above him. He had just enough space to pull on his clothes, and he then started to dig upward toward the light. "I had not gone far when I came on to another roomer who was held fast between some timbers and was crying for help. He was not badly gripped and between us we got him loose and he was able to come

The four-story Valencia Street Hotel shortly after dawn on the morning of April 18. The broken Spring Valley Water Company main has flooded part of the street and drowned most of the occupants of the lower three floors which had sunk into the old marsh.

A coroner's wagon stood by to remove the dead as rescuers worked to tear apart the Valencia Street Hotel. Note the excessive damage to the wood-frame structures on both sides of Valencia Street between Eighteenth and Nineteenth Streets.

Rescuers abandoned the Valencia Street Hotel late Thursday, after demolishing most of the roof during the rescue attempt.

along with me. We then started climbing upward to a big opening in front of us, and by climbing about ten feet we found ourselves on part of the roof that had pitched over into Sixth Street. We had been buried behind and to the west of it as the part of the building we were in slid forward in that direction.

"We could hear wailings and cries for help in every direction, but we were too shaken and nerveless to think of anything but escape from the ruins, and the man I had helped to get out was so badly crushed that he had to be assisted over the debris.

"From the debris where we escaped, flames were already licking at us, and I was hard pressed taking the other roomer away from this danger onto the ground on Sixth Street."

Destruction of the Brunswick House overshadowed the disasters at other large rooming houses and cheap hotels. The scene at the Girard and Kingsbury buildings was just as horrible, but apparently fewer people survived the simultaneous collapse of the structures.

Here again, fire followed the collapse of these buildings. In the wood-frame Girard House, Levi D. Peacock had just made a fire in the stove of his restaurant. He said the earthquake shock caused the brick Kingsbury House to fall onto the Girard House.

Mr. Peacock and a patron, John McKeever, managed to escape by kicking out the front door glass. Mr. McKeever said, "I saw the Kingsbury building on Seventh Street collapse. That occurred at the last vibration of the earthquake." A few minutes later, before survivors could be rescued, the fire broke out.

Eyewitness accounts conflict as to how fast these collapsed rooming houses burned, but, by mid-morning, it was clear that victims trapped in the wreckage of more than 30 structures in the South of Market area had to be abandoned to the rapidly moving fires which approached from three sides.

There are no known photographs of the this extensive South of Market destruction, only the hundreds of graphic eyewitness accounts. But one horrifying hotel collapse happened in the Mission District of which there is ample photographic evidence.

The Valencia Street Hotel at 718 Valencia, between Eighteenth and Nineteenth Streets, was a four-story frame structure with a brick foundation built on the site of a stagnant swamp known at various times as Laguna de Manantial, Laguna de los Dolores and Lake McCoppin.

In the mid-1870s, that area extending irregularly from Dolores to Harrison, between Seventeenth and Nineteenth Streets, was filled in and a large wooden sewer installed to carry away the runoff from the hills behind Mission Dolores.

The Valencia Street Hotel sank three stories and then collapsed upon itself, leaving one story above ground level. The settling swamp also snapped cable car conduits and broke the major Spring Valley Water Company main that supplied water to downtown San Francisco. Subsidence of the swamp was also responsible for the sinking and collapse of other wood-frame homes and businesses along Valencia between Eighteenth and Nineteenth Streets.

Most of victims trapped in the lower three floors of the Valencia Street Hotel probably drowned within a few minutes of the earthquake. People in the neighborhood broke into hardware and mercantile stores to get ropes, axes and pry-bars to begin a rescue effort that continued for two days and nights. Rescuers progressively tore apart the top of the building and saved about a dozen people.

Fire Engine No. 7 briefly stopped at the Valencia Street Hotel early on the first day and cut eight bodies out of the wreckage, but was soon called away to the spreading Hayes Valley fire. Exactly how many were killed in the collapse is not known, but survivors say about 20 victims were left in the building when the Great Fire finally swept into this part of the Mission District on the third day.

The Valencia Street Hotel was on the western tip of this mass of made ground that extended down to Harrison Street. The State Earthquake Investigation Commission report of 1908 made only passing reference to this densely populated zone of mostly wood-frame buildings. "From Folsom Street between Seventeenth and Eighteenth to the vicinity of Valencia at Eighteenth, great destruction was conspicuously prevalent. Less than a third of the frame dwellings in this tract remained in their vertical positions, and a few collapsed completely. Others remained standing only by leaning against each other."

The worst of the collapses seemed to follow the contour of the filled-in lands, or that of the original shoreline of Yerba Buena Cove and Mission Bay.

Most of the brick structures in the 200 and 300 block of lower Washington Street, in the wholesale district, collapsed and killed several produce dealers. Destruction by earthquake was just as savage in the Fish Market District on Merchant Street, a few blocks below Chinatown. Alex Paladini of the firm A. Paladini and Company at 520 Merchant Street was unloading the morning catch from a wagon when the buildings around him began to shake.

"Merchant Street," Mr. Paladini wrote, "began waving in billows, houses began to waggle and topple, horses screamed as the masonry crashed down on them and the wagons, men hollered, everything seemed to go smash. I just dropped the fish, quit business and ran for shelter.

"Up near Montgomery Street, opposite but to the west of us, another big building fell out in the same fashion, burying and killing some men and horses. But the worst crash was the one nearer Sansome Street, at Enea's

Fire Underwriters' Patrol fire engine burned near Second and Harrison Streets during the Rincon Hill firestorm. The engine had been removed from its station at Second and Natoma Streets and brought to Rincon Hill to save it from the fire.

Earthquake wreckage of the Martel Power Company generating station at 149-153 Fremont Street. Every brick structure in the block bounded by Fremont, Mission, Beale and Howard Streets, on filled land, collapsed during the tremor.

Earthquake damage was also excessive in the Fish Market area near Clay and Merchant Streets. Here, rubble from fallen buildings trapped fishermen and horses on Merchant Street near Alex Paladini's fish dealership.

where ten or twelve men were killed, and I think fifteen horses."

A. Enea and Company, fish dealers, occupied the building at 513 Merchant Street, just across from Mr. Paladini's. Police officers came down from the nearby Hall of Justice to dig trapped fish dealers and workers out of the wreckage. Other officers went through Clay, Sansome and Montgomery Streets and shot injured horses trapped in the rubble.

Police Officer Edward J. Wiskotchill's account is one of the few eyewitness reports of the destruction in Chinatown. The damage was horrendous, and the number of dead apparently quite high. No organized, systematic building-by-building search was made because of the extraordinary damage. Further, the complexity of searching buildings with barricaded iron doors and false walls, built to hide gambling halls, opium dens and houses of prostitution, so prevalent in preearthquake Chinatown, was too great.

Officer Wiskotchill was on Commercial, between Grant and Kearny Streets, with fellow officer Edwin E. Lloyd when the earthquake rolled through Chinatown.

"The walls of the buildings seemed to be grinding, and this seemed to be filling the air with dust," Officer Wiskotchill wrote in his eyewitness report. "It was really the falling walls and cornices and things that were raising the dust; but the idea in my head just then was that the grinding of the masonry was doing it. That idea seemed to be increased as the dust made it grow dark.

"As soon as the quake stopped Lloyd and I started up Commercial Street again to see what we could do to rescue the people we believed must be crushed, and otherwise help as far as lay in our power.

"The front walls had fallen out of most of the houses, and the men and women – mostly women – were running out, scrambling over the debris, to the safety of the middle of the street. Some of these poor women were very scantily clad. Some had snatched up kimonos or other garments to cover themselves. Most were in their bare feet."

The two officers went to the whorehouses on Commercial Street and found prostitutes and their male customers running around nude.

"Therefore all we could do was to calm those that threatened to become hysterical, and coax those that had too few garments over them to go back into their houses and get more clothes. Some of them were too scared to return to their ruins; so Lloyd and I went in and fossicked [rummaged] among the debris for whatever skirts and petticoats and things we could find.

"Most of the men bolted like rabbits as soon as they felt the coast was clear, and seemed to be wholly indifferent to what they were wearing and what they were not. A few seemed willing to face the music and stay around and help the girls away from the scene of the disaster."

Other police officers in Chinatown found injured Chinese wandering the streets but left them to Chinese doctors who moved through the rubble treating the injured. There is no record of any Chinese person taken to any Emergency Hospital immediately after the earthquake.

James C. Kelly, the Fire Alarm Operator on duty at the alarm office at 15 Brenham Place, was startled to see "... the suddenness with which Portsmouth Square, in front of the office, filled with Chinese from the adjacent Chinatown Blocks. It seemed not more than several minutes after the shock before the Square was literally packed with hundreds of Chinese, of all ages, sexes, and conditions of apparel, jabbering and gesticulating in excited terror."

The Reverend Ralph Hunt was asleep in the rectory of St. Patrick's Church on the north side of Mission between Third and Fourth Streets. Directly behind St. Patrick's, on Jessie Street, was one of the electrical plants of the San Francisco Gas and Electric Company. This plant not only generated electricity but was also served as the downtown distribution point for SFG&E power from a major plant in the Potrero District.

Father Hunt wrote, "I awoke with the first shake and was waiting for the thing to stop so that I could finish my sleep. But it continued in dead earnest and my bed began to jump around the room. In a moment I heard the immense spire of the Church topple down beside my window and the big chimney of the electric plant come down behind the house. I then realized the extreme peril of the situation – I was in a brick house and it swayed and groaned so terribly that I thought every moment was the last.

"I peeped through the door but could see nothing distinctly because of the cloud of dust raised by the falling buildings. Steam also was escaping from a nearby boiler and was quickly filling the house, nearly stifling us. I met some of my brother priests at the door who had hastened to make their escape. One in particular has impressed himself on my mind. He had received a scratch upon his cheek which was bleeding freely and I suppose he rubbed it with his hand and in doing so he smeared the blood all over his face. I thought he was badly hurt and my fears were confirmed when he dropped to his knees for absolution. I gave it to him and he in turn gave it to me. This scene was repeated upstairs by two others, and it will give you some idea of our state of mind. We were certain it was all over with us – in fact, as I heard afterwards, some priests were waiting for the archangel to sound his trumpet."

St. Vincent's School at 669 Mission Street was a block west of St. Patrick's; Father Hunt walked there to check the condition of the Sisters and the students. "It was only on my way there that the real horror of the situation dawned upon me. On the east corner of Third and Mission Streets was a saloon. It had collapsed upon the occupants and I saw men being dragged out of the ruins, some of them horribly bruised and mangled.

"Harrowing scenes met the eye on every side. The streets were crowded with people who feared to stay indoors. The men seemed

Earthquake damage to buildings on the south side of Market Street at Beale Street.

dazed; the women were, some of them, so terrified that they did not know where they were or what they did. I saw women that morning rushing like frightened geese against the walls of the houses, seeking escape from the earthquake which they thought every moment was pursuing them."

Father Hunt worked his way through his parish along Third and Fourth Streets and into the smaller Natoma, Minna and Tehama Streets, ministering to the dead and consoling the injured. "The fire spread with amazing rapidity. It was not a fire starting in one place and then gradually gaining ground. Dozens of fires broke out at the same time, sometimes two or three or more in the same block. On that account the fire spread so rapidly that many were burned alive who might otherwise have been rescued, for the rescuing parties were driven back by the flames before they could reach the unfortunate victims."

It would be years before hundreds of the smaller tragedies could be reconstructed: drunks who refused to be pulled from waterfront dives, complete families suffocated in ramshackle flats, infants who were never found or were killed in baby buggies by flying cinders.

If anyone had a right to suffer a heart attack it was William J. Dutton. His attack came as he was leaving the badly shaken Palace Hotel, and fires breaking out all over the city may have been the reason, or perhaps it was the result of the violent shaking of the huge structure. Mr. Dutton was, however, president of Fireman's Fund Insurance Company, and the prophecy of a great conflagration in San Fran-

cisco was coming true.

There is little scientific data about the condition of the hotel after the earthquake. Charles Gilman Hyde, of the University of California, did make minor reference to the hotel. "It appears no serious damage was caused by the earthquake, although some plaster was shaken down in some portions of the building. It is stated that book cases on the the north and south walls of the building were undisturbed, but those on the east and west walls were thrown westward."

The Palace and Grand Hotels were owned by the Sharon Estate Company, whose president, William F. Herrin, was also chief counsel of the Southern Pacific Company's law department, and was thought of as the political boss of California. Another partner in the Sharon Estate Company was U. S. Senator Francis Griffith Newlands of Nevada, one of railroad's chief apologists in Congress.

Conditions in the Palace Hotel must have been frightful. Nearly all eyewitness accounts from the hotel contain descriptions of some of the most violent shaking reported in the earthquake.

Cora Older, wife of the *Builetin's* Fremont Older, described the sensation of the earthquake as resembling the roaring of a monstrous train. She later wrote, "The Palace Hotel turned on its axis; the building twisted and moaned. The sound of the earth grew more ominous, then in the living room of our suite a crash as if the walls had collapsed. I found myself out of bed kneeling in the passageway between the bedroom and the living room. A bust of our friend . . . Gertrude Atherton had been thrown from its pedestal

and crashed to the floor."

John H. Hollister's description of the earthquake is another of many that told of the twisting sensation common to many eyewitness accounts in the Palace Hotel. "We were awakened instantly from a sound sleep and at once recognized that an earthquake was convulsing everything around us. The rotary motion of the immense building, and when one vertical thud was succeeded by a second, it seemed as though a third would bring walls crashing down upon us. The heavy ornamentation had fallen, and broken glass was all around us, but the walls of our room were intact and we were unhurt. The doors were no longer perpendicular and ours could not be opened."

Ernest Goerlitz, manager of the Conreid Opera Company, which had staged *Carmen* at the Mission Opera House a few hours earlier, wrote, "I was awakened by a noise and a trembling of the building which I first mistook for an explosion in the cellar of the hotel or a nearby building. However, during the next few seconds the shaking of the building became furious and I realized it was due to an earthquake. Furniture, bric-a-brac from the mantlepiece, especially around the bay window, fell topsy-turvy around us. The noise from the rumbling of the earth, and as I afterwards saw, from the falling of buildings was deafening. It is impossible for me, and perhaps for anyone else to accurately describe our experience. I looked out the window and saw the Grand Hotel, situated opposite our room being shaken as by a terrific explosion. I cannot better describe the motion of the Palace . . . it seemed to dance a jig.

"All I hoped for was that we would be killed outright and not be suffering from broken limbs under the debris . . . what will remain incomprehensible to me at the end of my life is the fact that the building, after being torn out of its angles during an entire minute, can return to its original position and stand instead of burying its inmates."

Those windows Mr. Goerlitz spoke of were of great concern to the National Board of Fire Underwriters, which, in its 1904 report on the structure, contended that, "The earthquake-proof Palace hotel is declared to be made structurally weak by numerous frame bay windows."

Enrico Caruso, the most famous operatic tenor in the world, was thrown from his bed in the hotel. "Everything in the room was going round and round. The chandelier was trying to touch the ceiling, and the chairs were all chasing each other. Crash – crash – crash! It was a terrible scene. Everywhere the walls were falling and clouds of yellow dust were rising. The earth was still quaking. My God! I thought it would never stop."

Henry Hahn, Manager of Waldhams and Co., Portland, said, "On being awaked by the first tremor, I noted that the building shook perceptibly. Plaster fell from walls and ceiling, followed by chandeliers in the hall and

Dazed crowd at Third and Market Streets near the Palace Hotel (right) Thousands of people ran to the streets during the earthquake, and eyewitnesses described their aimless, dazed wanderings after the tremor.

The 400-room Grand Hotel at Market and New Montgomery Streets was completed in 1870, five years before the Palace Hotel opened.

corridors and continued crashing, mingling with the noise of breaking glass. The electric wires were rent by the blow and the hotel was in darkness."

L. B. Brunswig described the pandemonium following the earthquake "as though bedlam had broken loose. Of the hundred guests who rushed from their rooms, not one was entirely clothed. All were crying and shrieking, and they had cause to. Great roars and crashes went up from the city. . . . It was rumored that thieves had entered vacated rooms and were looting them of valuables."

Cora and Fremont Older cleared away the rubble in their suite and "we put on our dressing gowns and went into the hall. People in night attire were standing in their doorways in a state of shock, and a wrinkled woman with peroxided hair was dashing from one [person] to another, crying 'Save me! Save me!' All were as terrified as she, but her panic was so grotesque . . . when we came into the hall again, the elevators were not running and people in various states of undress were scrambling down the stairs. As we walked down we met sculptor Waldo Story panting and puffing to the gallant rescue of Bessie Abbott, who had sung the role

of 'Micaela' at the Opera House a few hours before."

Egbert H. Gould was asleep on the sixth floor of the hotel and said, "I was thrown out of my bed and half way across the room. Fearing that the building was about to collapse, I made my way down the 6 flights of stairs and into the main corridor. I was the first guest to appear. The clerks and hotel employees were running about as if they were mad."

A. D. Evans also ran from his room, downstairs to the grand lobby, and, "within two minutes after I had appeared, other guests began to flock into the corridors, not many of them wore other than their night clothing. Women and children with blanched faces stood as if dazed. The children and women cried, the men were hardly less affected."

Ernest Goerlitz of the opera company began to look for members of his troupe and, "on arriving in the beautiful courtyard of the hotel, I found a number of our artists, most of them greatly excited. I was told that Caruso had already left on a hired truck with his belongings and that Miss Allen [of the opera company] had also hurried out of the building after trying in vain to communicate

with the Lord over the telephone."

L. B. Brunswig said of the opera stars, "And a more frenzied lot of people I never saw. They cried their fear in Italian and French and questioned every one near to what it meant. I was unable to speak the only language they could speak. I came into contact with them, but no amount of assurance on my part sufficed to allay their fright."

E. C. Kendall and John H. Hollister both had the same idea; to check out of the Palace Hotel as soon as possible. Mr. Kendall said, "I went into the office of the Palace Hotel, and there men, women and children were rushing about, crazed and frantic in their night clothes." Mr. Hollister brought his wife down from their damaged room and found, "by the glimmer of a tallow candle, that the office had opened for business. I went thither, found an old gentleman, utterly confused, but trying to do his best to run the finance, and settled my bill. . . ."

Many of the people didn't bother to check out. According to J. F. Baker of the Wells Fargo Express Co., "Men screamed and rushed about. Women called for help, alternately adding prayers to their entreaties and conducting themselves as though they had not

"I don't like earthquakes. I'm getting out of here." That's what Selim Woolworth said after the earthquake of 1868. Mr. Woolworth sold his Market Street property to William Ralston who began construction of the Palace Hotel on the site.

the slightest realization of destruction. From both the Palace and Grand Hotels, the frightened occupants poured in throngs and soon the sidewalks were jammed with crowds that stood like so many sheep, unable to determine in which direction to seek flight." Zebedee R. Winslow also observed the post-earthquake fright and said, ". . . we went outside and found that almost the whole city had been shattered. The crowds in the streets were dazed, they rambled about as if stunned speechless, contemplating the ruin without apparent fright, like herds of sheep."

Mr. Baker then saw something else that startled him. Two longhorned steers "made their way into Market Street and rushed madly down the thorofare. I saw a commercial [sales] man heading in their direction carrying 2 grips. He seemed to be under a spell and made no effort to evade the frenzied animals. One of them struck him under the shoulder and he was tossed as though he was a baby. He was not injured."

Terrence Owens, chief of the Denver Fire Department, and certainly a credible witness, had been with Fire Chief Engineer Sullivan the previous evening and had gone with him to a Mission District fire. Chief Owens and

his family were at the Grand Hotel and, "when the first shock came, my wife sprang up from bed and a moment after she had, quite a heavy dresser was thrown on it. It would surely have killed her had she remained there. I quickly got my wife and child to the street. Going back I got our things together and took them down where my wife was when I saw a fire burst out a few blocks away.

"Market street, when we got out of the hotel," he said, "was in a frightful state. Wires were down, naked and half naked men and women were running along the streets, cattle and horses were mixed up with the nude and the scene was one of indescribable confusion. Some we met were cut about the face and hands by falling glass or windows, and others had been hit by stones. The air seemed to be sort of a bluish yellow. To make matters worse there was the most peculiar smell in the air."

This strange smell in the air was also noted by A. D. Evans, who said, "In the vicinity of the Palace Hotel . . . the air was impregnated with an odor that resembled creosote, and the reason for the odor I cannot imagine for I recognized not the least trace of sewer gas

or sulphuretted hydrogen which would have seemed to be most natural odors in such an event. . . ." The precise nature of this unusual odor can't be explained, but it may have been related to the destruction of the gas pipeline system.

A remarkable eyewitness account of the initial effects of the Great Earthquake came from Clarence E. Judson of 1396 Forty-seventh Avenue, near what is now Judah Street. Mr. Judson was a mechanic for United Railroads and lived in what was really a small village out at the Ocean Beach. He was swimming in the Pacific Ocean when the earthquake rolled along the coast. He may have been the person closest to the San Andreas Fault in the city, and the only one so far known to experience the so-called luminous phenomena of earthquakes in the San Francisco disaster.

"I got up to take my usual dip in the surf —my daily custom for two years past. The breakers were not so very large, but they came in crosswise and in broken lines, with a vicious, snappy sort of rip-and-tear fashion. However I got in up to my armpits almost, and a breaker larger than usual came in and shot away up the beach, probably seventy-five feet, not a very unusual thing, however. It almost took me off my feet, and I started to go out, and instantly there came such a shock. I was thrown to my knees. I got up and was down again. I was dazed and stunned, and being tossed about by the breakers, my ears full of salt water and about a gallon in my stomach. I was thrown down three times, and only by desperate fighting did I get out at all. It was a close call.

"The motion of the quake was like the waves of the ocean – about twenty feet between crests – but they came swift and choppy, with a kind of grinding noise – enough for anyone.

"I tried to run to where my shoes, hat and bath robe lay, but I guess I must have described all kinds of figures in the sand. I thought I was paralyzed. Then I thought of lightning, as the beach was full of phosphorus. Every step I took left a brilliant, incandescent streak. I jumped on my bath robe to save me. I began to think the world was coming to an end. I reached for my shoes and landed with both feet onto my hat, twice. I finally got dressed after being thrown to the ground a few more times. I reeled and staggered like a drunken man. I thought of my wife and babies; I had left them asleep. I realized we had just had a terrible earthquake. When I got to the new road up on the sand dunes [the Great Highway] I saw the road was badly cracked, houses were out of plumb, men, women and children were coming out in the streets, dogs were barking and chickens cackling. I ran and ran at top speed and finally arrived at home, to find the wife frantic with fright, trying to manage the babies – a boy of 2 and twin baby girls.

"Someone started a tidal wave scare and the result was that the night of the 18th and 19th nearly all the population of the district and hundreds of refugees gathered up blankets and wended their way back to the sand hills a half dozen blocks from the beach where they camped in safety."

Adobe structures at the nearby Presidio were badly damaged by the earthquake, as was the submarine cable connecting the post with Angel and Alcatraz Islands. The earthquake pulled the undersea cable apart, and communications were lost.

Major James Stephenson, in charge of the Fort Mason post hospital, was shocked at the strength of the earthquake, but was more shocked when he arrived there to find injured people streaming in. Earthquake damage to the U. S. Army General Hospital left his small facility, and the Presidio post hospital, the only two military facilities fully capable of immediate operation after the tremor.

The major's staff was already busy before the first civilian refugees arrived, treating 30 soldiers who jumped from second story barrack windows during the earthquake and were brought to the post hospital for emergency treatment.

Lieutenant-Colonel George H. Torney, Chief Surgeon of the Army's Department of California and commanding officer of the Army General Hospital at the Presidio, said his facility "... was badly wrecked by the earthquake. The power plant was disabled and water shut off by a break in the pipes of the city water mains. The ward ventilators, heavy brick structures, were thrown upon the roofs of the wards, crushing through the roofs; sheets of plaster fell from the ceilings and walls of all buildings, and all telegraphic and telephonic communications were broken. This, of course, does not fully describe the extent of the damage, but is merely a statement made that the condition of the hospital may be understood." He asked the War Department for a $75,000 appropriation to repair the structure.

The hospital was built in 1899 of wood-frame construction on a concrete and brick foundation, at a cost of $113,329.50. If Lieutenant-Colonel Torney's loss figure were correct, earthquake damage to the hospital was roughly two-thirds of the structure's value.

Two days after the earthquake, General Funston issued *General Orders No. 37* that gave the lieutenant colonel full and unrestricted control of health services in San Francisco. The order read: "Lt. Col. George H. Torney, Medical Department U. S. Army, is hereby placed in charge of the sanitary arrangements of the city of San Francisco. All his orders must be strictly obeyed by all parties whomsoever. By command of Brigadier-General Funston."

It was years before a candid discussion of the condition of San Francisco gas mains was fully addressed. Edward C. Jones, Chief Engineer of the San Francisco Gas and Electric Company, opened his speech to the Pacific Coast Gas Association with the most unusual

The charismatic Mayor Eugene Schmitz.

The Ocean Beach, where Clarence Judson was thrown to the ground during the earthquake.

The earthquake caused this part of Ninth Street, between Bryant and Brannan Streets, to sink.

admission. "The brave builders of the new city have long ago ceased to speak of the natural calamity, the earthquake, and in speaking of the sad days following April 18th, they are referred to as after the 'fire.' It is therefore with some hesitation and regret that the writer is compelled to describe the physical effect on gas property due to earthquake."

Two of the gas generating plants suffered little earthquake damage, according to Mr. Jones. They were the Independent plant in the Potrero District and Martin Station just south of San Francisco, in what is now Daly City. But, the big North Beach facility, in the block bounded by Bay, Fillmore, Buchanan and Pierce Streets, was destroyed by the earthquake, and one of the large gas holders collapsed. Mr. Jones closed the valves of the surviving tanks and went to the Independent plant in the Potrero District to shut down the entire gas supply to the city.

"At this time the fire was raging South of Market street, and had not made great headway, so that the early shutting off of the gas supply," in his words, "prevented the addition of fuel to the flames." Mr. Jones closed the valves at the Potrero District station just before 7:30 a.m. and claimed to have reported the gas shut-off to Mayor Schmitz.

"Beginning at seven o'clock Wednesday morning there were successive explosions in the feeding mains connecting the Potrero and North Beach stations," he said.

"On the thirty-inch main, running from the Potrero works on Kentucky [now Third Street], Mariposa, Potrero Avenue, Tenth, Market, and Fell to Van Ness Avenue, and thence along Van Ness to Broadway, there were twenty-one explosions. In nearly every case the explosion took place at a line drip or cross, where the main was weakest, and the earth around the main was thrown up, leaving openings of various sizes up to twelve feet wide and thirty feet long, and on the line of the [parallel] twenty-four inch feeding main connecting the two stations there were as many as forty breaks due to explosions. . . . Nearly all of the explosions occurred after the gas had been shut off to the city mains, and fortunately these explosions did no damage to life or property."

Mr. Jones' assertion of "no damage to life or property" from the explosions is not correct. These large gas mains were along those major streets used by refugees to flee San Francisco. Substantial numbers of eyewitnesses claim to have seen people injured, and others killed, as the result of exploding gas mains along the streets as described by Mr. Jones, and in other parts of the city; not just those along the route of the major gas lines.

Thirteen-year-old James J. O'Brien was one such witness. "Down Tenth street, we went and after crossing [the] Tenth and Howard intersection the street blew up. The gas mains on Tenth exploded, the cobblestones on the street blew very high, and many people were hurt."

Mr. Jones also neglected to say that an employee at the North Beach station, 37-year-old James Benjamin McIntyre, was killed when the gas works collapsed.

He continued his description of the damage. "Gas mains in the streets running east and west were broken and drawn apart, while the street mains in streets running north and south were crushed together and telescoped, or else raised out of the ground in inverted Vs. This rule applied generally with but few exceptions."

Louis E. Reynolds, Mr. Jones' counterpart in the electrical department of San Francisco Gas and Electric Company, described to the Gas Association audience the wreckage of the Central electrical station on Jessie Street known as Station C, behind St. Patrick's Church. A six-story brick wall, which may have been part of the Opera House or the Call Building powerhouse, as well as steel from the adjoining building and a crane used for the installation of electrical generators, fell on top of the power station. He did not mention how the station's large smoke stack collapsed and apparently ruptured the boiler of the station's 2000 horsepower steam engine, or that an employee, Gerald Stanley Kirkpatrick, was killed in the structure. This was the explosion that terrorized Reverend Hunt and other priests in the rectory of St. Patrick's and filled the building with steam.

Mr. Reynolds was, however, candid about severe earthquake damage to underground utilities in the South of Market area and described how four underground cables were so badly wrecked by the earthquake and gas explosions as to be out of commission for some 10 or 12 days. "Along Seventh Street," he said, "the underground extension of these lines was so badly damaged that the conduit and manholes had to be reconstructed in

A leaflet from the Committee on History. The committee gathered thousands of pages of documents and eyewitness accounts from survivors, but apparently never issued or published a final report. Only a few of the committee's original documents have been found.

General Frederick Funston.

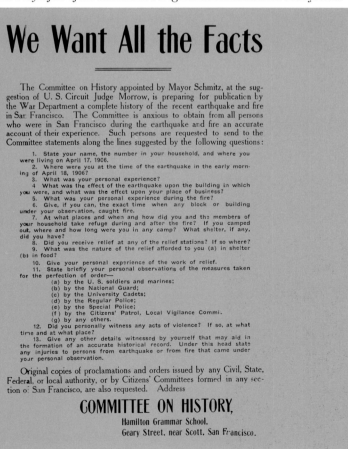

We Want All the Facts

The Committee on History appointed by Mayor Schmitz, at the suggestion of U. S. Circuit Judge Morrow, is preparing for publication by the War Department a complete history of the recent earthquake and fire in San Francisco. The Committee is anxious to obtain from all persons who were in San Francisco during the earthquake and fire an accurate account of their experience. Such persons are requested to send to the Committee statements along the lines suggested by the following questions:

1. State your name, the number in your household, and where you were living on April 17, 1906.
2. Where were you at the time of the earthquake in the early morning of April 18, 1906?
3. What was your personal experience?
4. What was the effect of the earthquake upon the building in which you were, and what was the effect upon your place of business?
5. What was your personal experience during the fire?
6. Give, if you can, the exact time when any block or building under your observation, caught fire.
7. At what places and when and how did you and the members of your household take refuge during and after the fire? If you camped out, where and how long were you in any camp? What shelter, if any, did you have?
8. Did you receive relief at any of the relief stations? If so where?
9. What was the nature of the relief afforded to you (a) in shelter (b) in food?
10. Give your personal experience of the work of relief.
11. State briefly your personal observations of the measures taken for the perfection of order—
   (a) by the U. S. soldiers and marines;
   (b) by the National Guard;
   (c) by the University Cadets;
   (d) by the Regular Police;
   (e) by the Special Police;
   (f) by the Citizens' Patrol, Local Vigilance Commi.
   (g) by any others.
12. Did you personally witness any acts of violence? If so, at what time and at what place?
13. Give any other details witnessed by yourself that may aid in the formation of an accurate historical record. Under this head state any injuries to persons from earthquake or from fire that came under your personal observation.

Original copies of proclamations and orders issued by any Civil, State, Federal, or local authority, or by Citizens' Committees formed in any section of San Francisco, are also requested. Address

COMMITTEE ON HISTORY,
Hamilton Grammar School.
Geary Street, near Scott, San Francisco.

East side of Eighteenth Street between Capp and Howard (now South Van Ness Avenue) Streets showing earthquake damage to sidewalks.

Rubble at Montgomery and Sacramento Streets.

many places. Along Seventh Street, from Mission to Howard, the earth was displaced from five to eight feet in a direction lengthwise to the conduit. This caused some of the manholes to crush like eggshells, although they were twelve-inch-thick concrete walls. The conduit was pulled apart at other places, and cables were wrenched and torn from their boxes and in some places pulled apart between manholes, so that these breaks were not discovered until after we tested with full voltage."

Massive destruction of the underground conduiting system also wrecked telephone and telegraph cables, as well as a good part of the water system. Distribution mains from two major Spring Valley Water Company reservoirs inside the City of San Francisco were severed by the earthquake, and those from the Lake Honda reservoir in the foothills of Twin Peaks were badly damaged.

A panel with the unwieldy title "Sub-committee on Water Supply and Fire Protection to the Committee on the Reconstruction of San Francisco" suggested all serious breaks in the water system within the city occurred in "made ground." "These breaks rapidly wasted the water stored in the city reservoirs and cut off entirely the direct supply to the districts where the main fires originated. The failure to control the fire was not due to the breaking of out-of-town conduits, but primarily to the fact that the eighty million gallons of water stored in the distributing reservoirs within the city, a quantity sufficient to check even such a conflagration, was rendered unavailable by reason of breaks in important distributing mains. The failures in the pipes of the distributing system occurred only in filled or soft ground and were not due in any case to the use of poor material."

Later inspection of the water supply system showed distribution main breaks in so-called good ground, including earthquake breaks in the 22-inch main along Market Street.

San Francisco Call reporter James Hopper was to make his reputation with vivid accounts of how the earthquake sounded, looked and felt. For the benefit of national magazine readers, his writing style was somewhat florid, yet he seemed to have been everywhere.

With barely an hour's sleep from his stint at the paper, he was awakened in his apartment at 631 Post Street by the roar of bricks falling from his building. The mass of bricks struck a series of little wooden houses in the alley below (on Cottage Place). "I saw them crash in like emptied eggs, the bricks passing through the roofs as through tissue paper." From his window he could see the back of the St. Francis Hotel, "waving to and fro with a swing as violent and exaggerated as a tree in a tempest."

The 12-story St. Francis Hotel was the tallest occupied structure in San Francisco. Eyewitnesses in the hotel were also badly shaken but did not speak or write of the "twisting" or "rotary" motion reported by those in the Palace Hotel. August Busch of the St. Louis brewing family, on the 10th floor when the shock came, said the building swayed so violently that several members of his party were thrown from their beds and onto the floor.

J. C. Gill, on the second floor, said, "We were awakened by the rocking of our beds. They seemed to be lifted from their legs, suspended in the air and as suddenly dropped, while the plaster began cracking and falling. We arose and left our room after putting on a few clothes. We felt that with every step we were treading on glass and that the ten stories above us would fall, not allowing us to escape alive."

Dr. W. Edward Hibbard described a phenomenon often reported by eyewitnesses who watched the tall structures in the downtown area during the earthquake. He said "The St. Francis felt like it would tip over . . . I ran to the window and saw the big buildings waving like stalks in the wind."

Mr. and Mrs. W. R. Harriman were on the 12th, or top, floor. Mr. Harriman said, "The room seemed to twist out of shape and the door stuck and it required all my strength to open it. Men were shouting and women screaming hysterically, and everybody was endeavoring to get to the elevators and stairways . . . it was soon discovered that the elevators were not running, and the people literally fell and rolled down the narrow stairway. My wife and I descended and on the first floor we found a mass of people whom the hotel employees were imploring to remain, as it was the safest place, but all seemed determined to get outside."

Ella Ransom wrote, "The lobby of the great hotel was filled with an excited throng! People were dazed and did not know which way to turn."

"One of the first men we saw," said Mrs. John Ryan, "was Captain Porter of the [Pacific Mail Steamship] Mongolia scurrying down the hall. We hurried downstairs to the office, clad, like everybody else, in our night clothing. While the women were directed into one of the parlors, there came another shock, and it wasn't any wonder that most of the women screamed frantically.

"At 8:30 they had us all go into the grillroom and the waiters served buns and coffee . . . one man ordered a breakfast steak and the waiter turned to him and said, 'Well, sah, if you wait long enough you can have the whole hotel.' The coffee and buns were all we had until evening."

Famed photographer Arnold Genthe walked to the St. Francis from his Sacramento Street apartment to survey the damage. He wrote, "Near the entrance we saw Enrico Caruso with a fur coat over his pajamas smoking a cigarette and muttering 'ell of a place!, 'ell of a place!, 'ell of a place! I never come

(Continued on page 36)

St. Francis Hotel after the fire The dome of City Hall can be seen to the left of the Dewey Monument.

Photographer Arnold Genthe who heard Enrico Caruso say "I never come back here" to San Francisco.

Rescuers pulled rubble away board by board at the Wilcox House as they tried to saved trapped victims. According to the New York Times, Fathers Hogan, Rogers and Huber of St. Patrick's Church gave the trapped and dying victims last rites "while a mass of coping overhead threatened to crush the priests to death. At least three of the victims died."

Refugees streamed along Second Street at Jessie Street as rescuers worked to save the trapped victims from the collapsed Wilcox House. These rescuers continued their rescue efforts until driven away by the fire. The San Francisco Gas and Electric fire can be seen spreading along Third Street.

An unusual photograph of a San Francisco firefighter pulling a victim from the rubble of the Wilcox House.

Terrible earthquake damage to wood-frame buildings was reported throughout the South of Market area. These buildings at Ninth and Brannan Streets were torn apart when the filled ground under them liquified during the earthquake.

The earthquake shifted the tracks of the Presidio and Ferries cable line on Union Street near Steiner Street.

Refugees from the fire rushed past a wrecked saloon on the southwest corner of Golden Gate Avenue and Hyde Street.

*Houses built on the filled-in bed of Mission Creek col-
lapsed during the earthquake. These buildings were
on the south side of Howard Street near Eighteenth
Street.*

Damaged houses on Howard Street near Seventeenth Street.

*Typical earthquake damage to wood-frame structures
in the Mission District.*

Fire engine at Broadway and Leavenworth drew water from a cistern on Union as the fire engine in the center of the picture retreated along with the refugees.

Reporter James Hopper.

A crowd gathered around the Seventh and Stevenson Street entrance to the U. S. Post Office to mail letters. The burned-out chambers of Judge John De Haven are above the entrance.

(Continued from page 33)
back here.'" The tenor had gone to the St. Francis to find other members of the Conreid Opera Company who were staying there.

Walter V. Marsh of Albany, New York, was at the Hotel Savoy, diagonally across Post Street from the St. Francis. The Savoy handled overflow bookings from the larger, more famous hotel. Mr. Marsh said, "We went over to the St. Francis, where, although the [exterior] upper portion showed little effects . . . the lower floors were badly demoralized. The windows were all smashed and the solid marble floor of the lobby was pulverized into gravel and powder."

One of few references to the St. Francis Hotel in scientific literature of the era states, "The exterior walls fronting on streets are faced with sandstone blocks. The main front of this building was cracked by the earthquake, especially at the left of the entrance on Powell Street, southeast corner, showing heavy earthquake cracks in the first story of the sandstone front."

Everyone searched for a simile to describe the shaking. Mr. Hopper said, "It pounced on the earth like a bulldog." Others felt the city was in the grip of a giant fist or like a rat shaken by a terrier. A musician sensed the violence of the sound more than anything else "like a thousand violins playing off key." The Metropolitan Opera's Alfred Hertz contemplated professionally on the way the disaster was scored. "Something comparable to the mezzo forte roll on a cymbal or gong."

It was left to Mr. Hopper's imagination to describe how human silence was the true measure of the terror. "Throughout the long quaking, I had not heard a cry, not a sound, not a sob, not a whisper. And now, when the roar of crumbling buildings was over, and only a brick fell here and there, this silence continued, and it was an awful thing." Fifteen minutes later, when he reached the street, he saw that the streets "were full of people, half-clad, dishevelled, but silent, absolutely silent, as if suddenly they had become speechless idiots . . . All of them had a singular hurt expression – not of physical pain, but rather one of injured sensibilities, as if some trusted friend had wronged them. . . ."

Mr. Hopper was thrown immediately into the thick of things when he saw a man trying to escape from The Geary, a three-story wooden rooming house at 239 Geary Street across from Union Square. The building had been smashed by the collapse of a brick wall of what is now the I. Magnin department store and a small fire had begun in the wreckage. He and members of Engine No. 2 climbed through fallen lath and plaster, rescued several trapped women, unearthed bodies and finally had to abandon the mass of rubble that would have taken days to untangle.

Mr. Hopper then went down to Mission Street after a brief stop at the Call Building at Third and Market. He moved along Mission to the U. S. Mint at Fifth and the U. S. Post Office on the northwest corner of Seventh and Mission Streets. He noted that the exteriors of both structures were relatively intact, but the ground in front of the Post Office, completed in 1905, had sunk six feet. This structure had been built on piles driven into Mission Bay Swamp, and some engineers and geologists felt the piling had not been driven deep enough to support such a monumental building. The State Earthquake Investigation Commission said: "At the southwest corner, the streets are deformed in great waves, some with an amplitude of 3 feet, causing fissures and sharp compressional arches in the pavement and sidewalks . . . [the Post Office] building appears damaged to the casual

The U. S. Post Office at Seventh and Mission Streets was saved because ten employees ignored orders of the U. S. Army to leave. The fire penetrated the third story of the building on the west side of the structure near Stevenson Street. Mail sacks dipped in water from the tank which ran the elevator system were used to stop the fire.

However, the earthquake thoroughly ruined the interior of the building. According to William F. Burke, Assistant to the Postmaster, "... walls had been thrown into the middle of various rooms, destroying furniture and covering everything with dust. In the registry division the handle was broken from the vault by falling bricks, furniture was thrown in all directions and valuable mail lay scattered on the floor. In the main corridors the marble was split and cracked, while mosaics were shattered and had come rattling down upon the floor. Chandeliers were rent and twisted by falling arches and ceilings."

observer. It is terribly shaken and greatly damaged – such injuries as the destruction of mosiacs in the arches of the corridor helped to increase the loss – but not in peril of collapse, tho one of the low walls had to be supported by timbers."

Charles Derleth Jr., of the University of California School of Engineering, was a bit more skeptical when he wrote, "The site of the general Post Office was very unhappily chosen. That structure, while it stood and was saved from the fire, was severely racked and its beautiful granite fronts were badly cracked on all sides. The hollow tile partitions of the general Post Office have been dreadfully shattered by the earthquake . . . . The structure represents an example of a building with heavy masonry walls with a partial and too light a steel frame. Considering the material upon which it rests, the building withstood the earthquake surprisingly well."

Other Federal buildings, such as the Appraisers' Building on Sansome, between Washington and Jackson Streets, had fared better than most of the other large structures in the city. More important, workers remained behind in these structures to fight

the coming conflagration. They had the authority and the manpower – at the Appraisers' Building an infantry regiment was garrisoned in the basement. In contrast, city structures burned after they were ordered abandoned by the army.

Forty-one city schools which the fire never reached sustained moderate damage – anywhere from $100 to more than $6,000 at Mission High School at Eighteenth and Dolores Streets. All-brick Girls' High School at Scott and Geary Streets was a total loss, valued at $150,000 in 1906 dollars. Wood-frame Sutro Grammar School on Twelfth Avenue between Clement and California Streets collapsed as did the wood-frame Ocean House Grammar School building near what is now Nineteenth and Ocean Avenues.

If the large Lincoln Grammar School on Fifth near Market Street was indicative of earthquake damage, then many of the 28 others in the burned area would also have been damaged beyond restoration – had they escaped the fire.

The San Francisco Chronicle reported "every institution for care of children" was damaged or wrecked by the earthquake. "Roofs tumbled in, furniture was shattered,

window glass flew in all directions, and panic among the children resulted. . . ." The Ladies' Protective and Relief Society Building at Geary and Franklin Streets, one of the few adobe buildings left in San Francisco, "was a wreck within ten seconds of the giant shock."

Children's Hospital at California and Maple Streets, the Chronicle reported, was severely damaged. "Every chimney was down, the two upper floors were completely wrecked, and the roof of the nurses' quarters was perforated by the tumbling of the tall chimney on the laundry. Falling brick also wrecked the room of the maternity cottage. . . ."

The Catholic Youth's Directory at Nineteenth and Guerrero Streets, on the very edge of Lake McCoppin, partially collapsed in the earthquake.

The entire front of the Maria Kip Episcopal Orphanage on Lake Street near Seventh Avenue collapsed as did the front of the San Francisco Nursery for Homeless Children at Lake Street and Thirteenth Avenue.

Pacific Hebrew Orphan Asylum at 600 Divisadero was also badly damaged. Edna Laurel Calhan lived directly across the street. "Their laundry was next to Hayes and it had a very high brick chimney. That brick chimney crashed down and made a terrible noise. Our brick chimney had also fallen in. That added to all the confusion. It was all quite frightening."

Rabbi Rudolph I. Coffee wrote, "Not a single child of the 190 wards suffered the slightest from the catastrophe. The building of the asylum was badly damaged. The work of repair has not yet been completed. For two nights the children slept in the open air, and for the succeeding 5 weeks stayed in the gymnasium that was improvised as a dormitory. The record is all the more remarkable when we consider that every other orphan asylum building in San Francisco, Catholic, Protestant or non-sectarian – was either totally demolished or so badly damaged that the children had to be removed to some neighboring town."

San Francisco's old City Jail on Broadway, a relic of the Gold Rush days, fell into rubble. For the inmates at the Hall of Justice, the shaking was excruciating; all around them came sounds of crashing walls and general pandemonium. Prisoners thrown back and forth by the earthquake beat their heads against the bars, pleading to be released. Some prayed, others fainted or vomited. In this pandemonium, jailers tried, with great difficulty, to open damaged cell doors. It took some time to get the hysterical prisoners out of the building.

The drama of trapped victims and a helpless fire department was repeated at many South of Market fire stations. Fire Engine Station No. 4 at 676 Howard Street was partially wrecked by the falling wall of the American Hotel next door. Firefighter James O'Neill was killed by the brickfall. At the same time, a Chinese laundry directly across the street collapsed, and fire broke out in the rubble. Trapped Chinese cried for help in the wreckage. Firefighters had to try to rescue O'Neill, salvage their fire apparatus from the damaged station, and deal with the collapsed and burning Chinese laundry at the same time.

A general assessment of the extent of physical earthquake damage appeared in the respected San Francisco insurance journal *Coast Review.* "The cheaper kinds of frame buildings in the earthquake districts – especially those put up by contractors to sell – were damaged more or less by the quake. Plastering fell in sheets, exposing the lathing. Fairly good homes were moved slightly at one end often, on their foundations. Houses with slender or rotten under-pinning took a tumble or at least sent 'out of plumb.'

"Even on good ground there was not infrequently some damage. The cheaper grade of new brick family hotels were sufferers, the back brick walls falling out one or two stories from the top. Poorly constructed brick buildings were rammed by un-anchored roof timbers and lost cornices, gable-points, fire walls, etc.

Earthquake damage to the Youth's Directory on the southeast corner of Nineteenth and Guerrero Streets.

Looters caught by the U. S. Army. Many looters were shot by police and soldiers under what Police Captain Thomas S. Duke called "the Law of Necessity." Captain Duke had been in command of Central Police Station in the Hall of Justice at the time of the earthquake, and later wrote, "Reports reached headquarters that thieves were burglarizing wrecked stores and deserted homes, and it was also learned that in the Mission District the body of a woman was found, the finger upon which she wore several valuable rings having been amputated, evidentally by some thief."

These five looters were luckier than most.

The Graft-Hunters.

Left to right: Prosecutor Francis J. Heney, William J. Burns of the Secret Service, Fremont Older, Publisher of the San Francisco Bulletin, *and millionaire Rudolph Spreckels, who along with James D. Phelan, bankrolled the graft investigation.*

San Francisco's political boss Abraham Ruef entered the temporary courtroom at Congregation Beth Israel to be sentenced to San Quentin prison for his part in the graft scandal.

"On poor ground the damages were frequent and excessive, the fallen debris obstructing the streets here and there. The ground-filling subsided in some degree, irregularly, and tilted or twisted frame buildings.

"As a rule, churches, halls, theaters, breweries and all large area buildings were extensively damaged, by falling towers, domes and roofs, it requiring but little departure from vertical lines at the roofs to create a wreck."

The War Department report on the earthquake commented that 95 percent of all chimneys in San Francisco fell in the tremor.

Mayor Eugene Schmitz' home at 2849 Fillmore Street was ten minutes away from the Hall of Justice by car. Elected in 1905 for a third two-year term, this tall, handsome man – with carefully trimmed beard and mustache – was a compromise politician. From humble beginnings he had threaded a narrow course to the top: musician, conductor of the Columbia Theater orchestra, president of the Musician's Union. He had been picked by a manipulative lawyer and Republican party regular, Abraham Ruef, to fill a void in the leadership of the newly-formed Union Labor Party.

The mayor was a Roman Catholic, a teetotaler, a family man with two daughters and an extremely convincing and charismatic speaker. As appealing as Eugene Schmitz was as a politician, however, he was patently on the take. No city contract was awarded during his administration without the expected cut for Mr. Ruef, for the mayor and for the Board of Supervisors.

Eugene Schmitz was well aware of a political disaster on the horizon. His predecessor in office, the respected James Duval Phelan, had joined with fellow millionaire Rudolph Spreckels to launch an investigation of the massive graft scandal.

This scandal had national political impact. Southern Pacific Company controlled both California and San Francisco politics. Abraham Ruef was employed by the railroad as a "fixer," and was considered the political boss of San Francisco.

President Theodore Roosevelt wanted Southern Pacific's grip on California politics broken and was willing to send William J. Burns from the Secret Service to San Francisco to be chief investigator. Francis J. Heney, a special prosecutor famous for handling corruption cases in Oregon, was recruited and paid from a $100,000 fund supplied by Rudolph Spreckels.

A big break in the corruption investigation came just before the Great Earthquake. William H. Langdon, Mr. Ruef's hand-picked District Attorney, turned on the Southern Pacific machine and began to cooperate with Messrs. Heney and Burns, much to the consternation of Mr. Ruef and Mayor Schmitz. To put additional pressure on Mr. Ruef, on the mayor and on the Southern Pacific political machine, the crusading Fremont Older, editor of the vigilant *San Francisco Bulletin,* was about to publish an exposé of the graft investigation.

The earthquake and the following fires, more than 60, took Mayor Schmitz's mind off the graft investigations. At the Hall of Justice, after six a.m., he met with Chief of Police Jeremiah Dinan and learned the stunning news that Fire Chief Engineer Dennis Sullivan had been taken to the Southern Pacific Company Hospital with possibly fatal injuries.

Brick chimneys and the east wall of the California Hotel had crashed 60 feet through the adjoining fire station, Chemical Company No. 3, at 410-412 Bush Street where Chief Engineer Sullivan lived with his wife Margaret.

Firefighters who survived the destruction of the station frantically dug through rubble to rescue the chief and his wife. They were aided by three police officers and a few employees of Fremont Older's *San Francisco Bulletin,* which had its offices directly across the street.

Chief Engineer Sullivan's head and shoulders were soon uncovered and he raised himself to a half sitting position. Fire Lieutenant Jeremiah Collins and Hoseman Peter T.

Gallagher pulled him out and, with his arms around their shoulders, they assisted him to St. George's Stables next door, at 408 Bush Street.

He had a slight fracture of the skull, several broken ribs, one of them punctured a lung; his right hip was badly lacerated and his body was covered with bruises and abrasions. The most dreadful injuries were caused by steam and scalding water from the radiator that was in the spot where he was carried by the avalanche of rubble and was spurting on him while the rescuers were at work.

Chief Engineer Sullivan lingered near death for four days and finally died at the Presidio's U. S. Army General Hospital, where he was taken when the Southern Pacific Company Hospital was evacuated.

The mayor replaced him on the morning of the 18th with First Assistant Chief Engineer John Dougherty. He, Chief Dinan, and the mayor went to the basement of the severely-damaged Hall of Justice to assess the situation. The scope and magnitude of the disaster overwhelmed them.

The Ferry Building tower was standing but near collapse and was mobbed by thousands of people trying to flee the burning city. Mar-

ket Street, the pride of a great commercial city, was littered with the debris of fallen buildings. The worst had always been feared for South of Market and it had happened.

Police and fire department forces were scattered, and at the Hall of Justice no one knew clearly where they were, because destruction of the Municipal Police Telephone System and the fire department's Street Telegraph System had cut all communication with police and fire stations. Commercial telephone and telegraph service had stopped and the entire electrical and water supply failed.

Mayor Schmitz saw a city panicked by aftershocks and threatened with extinction by fire. Over the next few days there would be chaos, hunger, desperation and mob violence.

There was another major concern. A report came from Harbor Police Station, by messenger, that 150 men had looted thousands of boxes of cigars from Tillman and Bendel's wholesale tobacco store at 313 Battery Street. It was one of just several reports streaming into the mayor's Hall of Justice headquarters with the fearsome word: looting.

Plaque commemorating the death of Dennis T. Sullivan on the wall of the San Francisco Fire Chief's residence at 870 Bush Street.

The assembly hall of St. Ignatius College on Van Ness Avenue at Grove Street before the Hayes Valley fire swept the area. The spire of St. Ignatius Church can be

seen in the background. Davies Symphony Hall currently occupies this site.

Burnt and dynamited shell of the Southern Pacific Company Hospital on the southwest corner of Fourteenth and Mission Streets. Reporter James Hopper went to the hospital shortly after the earthquake, and wrote, "Carts, trucks, express wagons, vehicles of all kinds

laden with wounded, were blocking the gates. Upon the porch stood two interns, and their white aprons were red-spotted as those of butchers. There were 125 wounded inside and eight dead. Among the wounded was Chief Sullivan of the Fire Department. . . ."

First Assistant Fire Chief Engineer John Dougherty, with white mustache at left, during a test of Water Tower No. 1 before the earthquake. He was appointed to the rank of Acting Fire Chief Engineer when Dennis Sullivan was seriously injured. Chief Dougherty retired two months after the fire.

San Francisco Chief of Police Jeremiah F. Dinan.

Map of fault lines and water works structures drawn for the American Society of Civil Engineers' report on the earthquake.

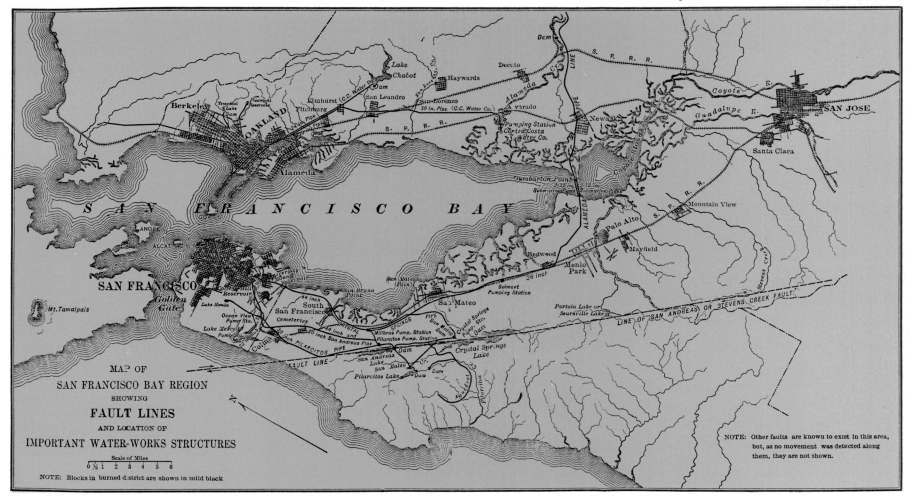

View of the Hayes Valley fire as it swept the rubble of
the wrecked City Hall. This photograph was taken from
McAllister and Larkin Streets. Fulton Street intersects
Larkin Street at right.

Fires spread through the Wholesale and Financial
Districts on the first day of the fire. Note the damage
to the spire of St. Mary's Church at Dupont (Grant
Avenue) and California Streets. The small area in the
lower left hand corner of the picture is actually a collapsed building.

Stragglers escaping from the South of Market District crossed Mission Street at Third Street as the Chinese Laundry fire merged with the San Francisco Gas and Electric fire. Several hours earlier, Father Ralph Hunt passed through this intersection on his way to St. Vincent's School. Father Hunt watched as rescuers pulled victims from the rubble of the collapsed building on the left. Captain Thomas Duke of the San Francisco Police Department wrote that one of the men trapped in the rubble begged bystanders to kill him because of the advancing fire. "After some hesitation," he wrote, "a large, middle-aged man stepped forward, and after a few words with the unfortunate prisoner, he whipped out a revolver and shot him through the head, killing him instantly. He then requested the witnesses to accompany him to the Hall of Justice, where the Mayor, who after hearing the circumstances and seeing the man's distressed appearance, commended him for his humane act."

Buildings at this intersection also collapsed in the earthquakes of 1865 and 1868.

The earthquake snapped the top of the smokestack at the cable car powerhouse at Washington and Mason Streets. The falling smokestack tore through the roof of the structure.

The Great Fire

Panoramic view of the burning city taken from the roof of the St. Francis Hotel.

Gold Rush San Francisco was destroyed by fire six times between 1849 and 1851. But as the frontier town became a city, the volunteer fire companies, in 1866, became a paid, professional, fire department.

Yet, San Francisco from its founding was built to burn, and the Fire Department's chief engineer, Dennis Sullivan, entertained no illusions about so-called "fireproof" buildings, a poor water supply with low pressure in the fire hydrants, an abandoned and deteriorated underground cistern system – a relic of the volunteer fire department days – or wide streets that were supposed to act as firebreaks.

Chief Sullivan should have been concerned with the 1905 Fire Underwriters' report that questioned the condition of the fire engines and the preparedness of the firefighters. "There are 38 steam fire engines in service, and 12 in reserve. In the tests the average discharge was less than 70 percent of their rated capacity, a low figure. The ability of the men handling the engines was in general below a proper standard," said the report.

As the major city on the West Coast, San Francisco was the headquarters of the U. S. Army's Pacific Division, as well as the Department of California. Brigadier-General Frederick W. Funston was commander of the Department, as well as acting commander of the Pacific Division in the absence of Major-General Adolphus W. Greely who was on leave the week of the earthquake, and did not return to the city until April 22.

General Funston left his home at Washington and Jones Streets a few minutes after the earthquake to survey the damage. He walked to the crest of Nob Hill near the Mark Hopkins mansion, site of the present Mark Hopkins Hotel, and watched the fires burn South of Market. He walked down Nob Hill to the Phelan Building, headquarters of the U. S. Army's Department of California, and found the interior of the structure in shambles.

Fire had already broken out in the area of California and Sansome Streets and spewed acrid fumes into the dust from fallen parapets and shattered walls. Idle fire engines stood in the middle of streets amid lengths of flat hose as firefighters checked hydrant after

Rare photograph shows the fire as it burned through the rear of the Cosmopolitan House on the southwest corner of Fifth and Mission Streets. The U. S. Mint is to the left.

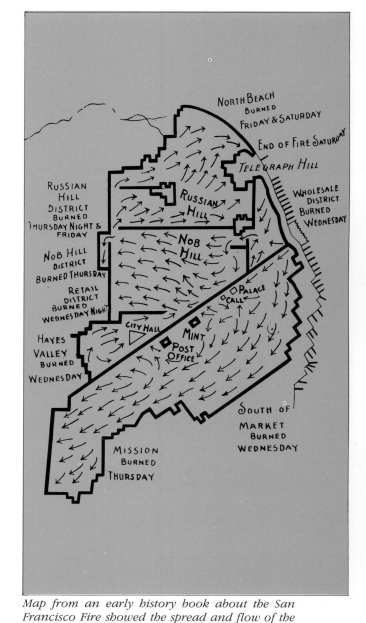

Map from an early history book about the San Francisco Fire showed the spread and flow of the conflagration.

hydrant for water.

General Funston ran back up Nob Hill to his stables at Pine and Hyde Streets. There, he gave his carriage driver a note to commanding officers at Fort Mason and the Presidio to bring all available troops into San Francisco and report to the Hall of Justice.

His driver arrived at Fort Mason at about 6:45 a.m. and reported to Captain Meriweather L. Walker of the Corps of Engineers and Fort Mason's commanding officer.

Captain Walker later wrote in his official report that he opened the door of his quarters and "found a civilian who said General Funston, Department Commander, ordered that I bring all available men to the Hall of Justice at once, and report to the mayor for duty, as the city was all in flames. Assuming that the message was all straight, I dressed hurriedly and sent orders for all officers and men to turn out in field equipment and twenty rounds of ball ammunition. The command, 5 officers and 150 men, moved out at 7:15 a.m., about, leaving 1 officer and necessary guard and working force to keep kitchen, quartermaster, commissary and stables running.

"At about 7:45 a.m., April 18, 1906 I reported to Mayor Schmitz at the Hall of Justice.

He directed me to protect public and private property, and that I should go to the extent of taking life if necessary."

Mayor Schmitz' order to Captain Walker came as an absolute surprise to Colonel Charles Morris of the Coast Artillery, who had also reported to the Hall of Justice from the Presidio on General Funston's orders.

"Anticipating that looting would take place," wrote Mayor Schmitz, "I had already seen some of it on my trip downtown – and realizing that we would have no place in which to keep prisoners if we arrested any, and that it was time for firm and decisive action, I told Colonel Morris and also the captain who reported to me from General Funston, to let the news be widely spread that anyone caught looting should not be arrested but should be shot. Colonel Morris asked me if I would be responsible for that order and I told him Yes; that I would be responsible for that order; we could not take prisoners; we must stop looting, and therefore to shoot anyone caught looting. The same order was also issued to the Police Department."

Seventy five of Captain Walker's troops from Companies C and D, Engineer Corps, were assigned to the financial district along

Montgomery Street. Another 75 were assigned along Market from Third Street to the City Hall, where $7,000,000 cash was held in the city treasury.

At 8 a.m., troops from the Presidio – the 10th, 29th, 38th, 66th, 67th, 70th and 105th Companies of Coast Artillery, Troops I and K of the 14th Cavalry and the First, Ninth, and 24th Batteries of Field Artillery – began arriving in the downtown area.

Major Carroll A. Devol, Pacific Division Quartermaster, wrote in the *Journal of the United States Infantry Association*, "Most fortunately for San Francisco they had a live mayor, a man ready, tactful and resourceful. He at once ordered all saloons closed and kept them closed. The benefits of this order were far-reaching and assisted the army very greatly in keeping order.

"The Headquarters and First Battalion 22nd Infantry, were brought from Fort McDowell by boat, arriving at 10:00 a.m., and were held for a time in reserve at O'Farrell Street. They were later utilized as patrols and as an assistance to the fire department. The Fort Miley troops, the 25th and 64th Companies Coast Artillery, had a longer march and did not arrive until 11:30 a.m."

General Funston had 1500 troops in the

The Girard House fire as it attacked the U. S. Post Office at Seventh and Mission Streets. Note the large amount of debris that fell from the Odd Fellows' building on the southwest corner of Seventh and Market Streets. The Grant Building is to the immediate left.

city by noon; an armed force that more than equalled the combined strength of the police and fire departments.

"I have no doubt," General Funston wrote, "and have heard the same opinion expressed by scores of citizens, that had it not been for the prompt arrival of the large force of Regular Troops, who were acting under orders to shoot all looters, the saloons would have been broken into, and then the crowd, becoming turbulent, would have begun sacking the banks and jewelry stores. The city police, however brave and efficient, would have been totally unable from mere lack of numbers to have dealt with such a situation."

Panicked people who milled in the streets seemed to accept the troops as an expected precaution. There was a general assumption that martial law was in force, even though it was not. At best, San Francisco was an occupied city under military rule because the U. S. Army was the only disciplined, cohesive force operating within the city.

In this case, the erroneous assumption on the part of the people that some form of military rule was in force, or "Martial Law Proper," was as effective as any declaration.

In these early hours of the disaster, the mayor's and the general's perception of the

danger quickly changed. The mayor's order to Chief Dinan to close the city's saloons was a stiff one for the overworked, uncoordinated and disorganized 700-man force. General Funston telegraphed the War Department for enough tents and rations for 20,000 people, and within an hour raised that figure to 100,000. He also tried to reach the Presidio of Monterey by telegraph for more troops, but the lines had been wrecked by the earthquake.

In these first hours, San Francisco's only connection with the outside world was one military telephone circuit, two insecure commercial telegraph lines to Oakland and the trans-Pacific cable to Manila. The entire commercial telephone system stopped when frightened operators abandoned switchboards and ran from phone offices. The earthquake also threw down overhead lines and wrecked parts of the underground telephone and telegraph networks.

What little communication the city would have with the outside was patched together by Captain Leonard D. Wildman of the U. S. Army Signal Corps, who wrote of this immense effort, "The earthquake had scarcely ceased when General Funston, realizing that the services of the Army would be necessary,

attempted to communicate with the troops in the immediate vicinity for the purpose of assisting the police and the firefighters. The lines were all down. His first official order was sent by his coachman, mounted upon a carriage horse. His second order was transmitted to troops across the bay by a boat. His third order to troops was transmitted from the Presidio to Fort Miley by the single telephone wire which remained intact. The fact that the operators at the telephone switch-boards at the military post were attending to their duties immediately after the earthquake, in the midst of confusion, is an illustration of the value of the discipline of the military organization."

Captain Wildman's report continued. "At 10 o'clock on the morning of the 18th, the first flying [portable] telegraph office was established by the Signal Corps, connecting the Presidio Central [telegraph exchange] by a line which was ordered constructed after 8 o'clock that morning. This telegraph office was at the very western outskirts of the fire at all times during the day, and was utilized for the transmission of orders concerning explosives, troops and transportation. On the other side of the fire, the Commanding General had a clear right of way over the Postal Telegraph wire to Washington until 3 o'clock, while at the same hour all arrangements had been made to keep communication with Washington by means of cables from Oakland to the Ferry Building, which was unburned. All of this work was done by seven men of the Signal Corps of the Army, stationed in San Francisco and the Presidio."

Though in a state of shock and panic, people who crowded the downtown streets had little concept of the general conflagration forming from the numerous isolated fires. No one could guess where the safest part of the city might be – though it was clear that South of Market and the wholesale districts were the most dangerous areas.

Custodians of the famous Adolph Sutro Library felt that fires approaching the Montgomery Block were a threat to the late mayor's magnificent collection of some 200,000 volumes, and they had it loaded aboard wagons early in the morning and taken to the Mechanics' Pavilion across from City Hall. This collection, which included rare Renaissance and Elizabethan volumes, would go up in smoke by noon. The Montgomery Block, though in the middle of the fire zone, would survive.

Without direction or much assistance from the overwhelmed fire and police departments, the people in the South of Market district fought desperately to rescue those trapped and to fight fires. Some helped beleaguered firefighters pull fire engines through the streets by hand, carry hose or haul the injured to the Harbor Emergency Hospital and Mechanics' Pavilion. Others began to pack a few meager belongings and prepared to flee.

Refugees from around City Hall and Hayes Valley tried to reach the Southern Pacific Company yards at Third and Townsend Streets, or the Ferry Building by detouring through the South of Market area. Sixth Street was in shambles, and in Seventh Street past the U. S. Post Office and Court House, fires had begun in the collapsed rooming houses, so the pitiful line of refugees went down Tenth and then around to Townsend Street.

Others from the South of Market district fled east to the Ferry Building or north into Union Square. Author Charles Caldwell Dobie was horrified by what he saw. "The square was swarming with refugees from 'South of Market' districts. This was the cheap, poor quarter of the town and many of the wretches who had fled from the flames looked as if they had not faced the morning sunlight for years. They were like rats startled out of their holes, this beer-sodden, frowsy crew of dreadful men and still more dreadful women. A breed that has passed out of American life completely – red-faced, bloated, blowsy." This type of pronounced sense of class prejudice, prevalent among middle or upper-class San Franciscans of the time, was a contributing factor in the Army's zealous

The big exit doors along the Polk Street side of Mechanics' Pavilion were thrown open to begin the mass evacuation of the wounded. Injured patients were taken on an agonizing ride to Golden Gate Park or the U. S. Marine Hospital on Lake Street.

Abandoned hospital beds along the Hayes Street side of the Mechanics' Pavilion after the evacuation.

Victims removed from the Mechanics' Pavilion are unloaded at a temporary hospital in the Golden Gate Park Panhandle.

The fearsome scene of San Francisco burning, as viewed from a ferryboat on the morning of April 18 was unlike anything seen before. The overall effect was unnerving. Novelist Mary Austin described it as "a surly, lurid glow like the unearthly flush on the face of a dying man." *Fire conditions like these were not seen again until the firebombings of World War II.*

The "U.S.S. Chicago," flagship of the Pacific Squadron, berthed at the earthquake-damaged Pier 9.

Oakland's Board of Public Works sent sprinkler wagons to San Francisco by ferry to supply drinking water to refugees.

attempts to control what were perceived to be the lower classes.

By noon, firefighters with dynamite obtained from a Southern Pacific Company railroad construction site had begun to make a stand on the east side of Eighth Street. Other fires were moving south along Fifth and Sixth Streets, and soon reached the ruins of the California Wine Company's warehouse on Brannan Street. Here the vats had collapsed, and wine flowed in the street. No trains could leave San Francisco if the fire line could not be held here, on Townsend Street. Heat, cinders falling everywhere, debris from collapsed walls drove most refugees back from the Southern Pacific Company yards.

As the refugees turned back, they found the fires had jumped Eighth Street – as much from amateurish dynamiting as the steady wind from the west that later brought the Hayes Valley fire with it. By one o'clock, South of Market had become a single raging fire, driving west and south, toward the Mission District. Several thousand people were trapped near the Southern Pacific Company yards, on filled land over what had once been Mission Bay. They were without food or water.

Eyewitnesses, newspaper reporters, fire department and Navy personnel all gave gritty descriptions of the desperate fire fighting and rescue work. There were ten fire stations in the South of Market area before the earthquake. The fire department stables at 534 Tenth Street and Fire Engine Station No. 29 at 1305 Bryant Street were severely damaged by the earthquake, but were outside the eventual fire line. Chemical House No. 1 at Second and Natoma Streets and Fire Engine Station No. 9 at Main and Folsom Streets were the only facilities near the south waterfront and Rincon Hill – the third major area of the conflagration. Six other engine houses were in the heart of the South of Market district, but, as with Captain Cullen and Fire Engine No. 6, the combination of earthquake damage to firehouses, runaway horses, multiple fires and the necessity to rescue trapped people, overwhelmed the resources of these stations. They had lost centralized communications and could not call for assistance, even if it was available.

But the battle against the fires approaching the waterfront was not yet lost. A new force was about to enter the scene: the United States Navy.

From Mare Island, across the Bay near Vallejo, the destroyer "U.S.S. Preble" steamed for San Francisco under the temporary command of 31-year-old Navy Lieutenant Frederick Newton Freeman. This crew, the fire boat "Leslie" and the tug "Active," represented the first outside help to come to San Francisco.

Dr. Edward Topham, the chief surgeon of St. Mary's Hospital at Bryant and First Streets climbed to the roof of the building at about 6 a.m. He counted 13 fires in the downtown area. Even though the hospital had not been damaged to any great degree by the earthquake, he was alarmed "by the many injured people streaming into the hospital."

He and another doctor walked north on Second Street as far as Mission and quickly discovered the magnitude of the disaster. Firefighters trying without success to pump water from a sewer – overhead wires down, fallen buildings and – strangely – several steers shot between the eyes lay in the intersection.

As fires grew more intense in a broad area from the Ferry Building to the South of Market flatlands, St. Mary's staff elected to evacuate the entire hospital. Considering the demands on the hospital and the fragmented transportation system in the city, the result was miraculous. Wells, Fargo and Company stables on Second Street provided horses for the hospital's wagons; the captain of the Sacramento River steamer "Modoc" was persuaded to bring the vessel to the Pacific Mail Dock at the foot of Brannan Street. As patients were carried downstairs their mattresses were dropped to the wagons below.

Finally, at 1 p.m., when the surrounding blocks had begun to burn, Dr. Topham closed the front door of St. Mary's Hospital for the last time. Refugees fleeing the fire joined the hospital evacuees as the caravan made its way to the Pacific Mail Dock.

A baby was passed aboard; then along came an eight-year-old boy, "rapping the fence pickets with a stick, saying he had gone out to see the fire and upon his return found his home burned down and his parents absent." He was pulled aboard the "Modoc" with the rest of the refugees. The old steamer paddled toward Oakland at 5 p.m. From the deck the Sisters of Mercy watched as flames burst through the windows of the hospital, and by the time the "Modoc" berthed at Oakland the building was gutted by fire.

San Francisco burning was a fearsome scene from the vantage point of Oakland, but its horror could not be fully understood at that distance. Governor George Pardee arrived by train from Sacramento in the late morning to, in his words, "assess the situation close at hand."

His telegrams to President Roosevelt show the governor did not fully comprehend the actual conditions behind the billowing clouds of smoke rising from the great city.

Governor Pardee was at the mercy of hit and miss reports gathered from refugees arriving by ferry, but he did understand that resources of the state were inadequate and telegraphed President Roosevelt, "Mayor of Los Angeles and Chairman of the Los Angeles Relief Committee request use of war ships at Long Beach to transport supplies to San Francisco. If this can be done, it will be of the greatest benefit."

Even Lieutenant Freeman and the crew of the "U.S.S. Preble" were in no position to fully evaluate the scope of the disaster as their vessel pulled into San Francisco docks at 10:30 that morning. He first sent the Navy hospital party ashore where hundreds of wounded had overwhelmed the Harbor Emergency Hospital at the foot of Mission Street, near the Ferry Building. There were so many injured that a triage point was set up on the Howard Street pier, and the most seriously wounded were stabilized and evacuated from San Francisco to a hospital at the Naval Training Station on Goat Island, now known as Yerba Buena. Less seriously injured people were taken by ferryboat to the Navy Hospital at Mare Island and to a

Frederick Newton Freeman, U. S. Navy.

Earthquake wreckage of Butchertown piers near Hunters Point.

General Funston conferred with his chauffeur, believed to be William P. Levy, Vice President of Joseph Levy Bag Company. Captain Wildman of the Signal Corps origi- *nally hired Mr. Levy from in front of the St. Francis Hotel on the morning of April 18 to act as his driver at a salary of $100 per day.*

temporary hospital established at the YMCA building in Vallejo.

Lieutenant Freeman also wanted to make contact with members of the San Francisco Fire Department to find out what help was needed. The "Active" and the "Leslie" were docked at Pier 8 at the foot of Howard Street. The lower Market Street fire had spread to Spear and Fremont Streets and several fires near the waterfront had joined in the early afternoon. Navy pumps were able to draw an endless supply of salt water from the bay for the firefighters on shore, and these boats could condense fresh water necessary to keep the boilers heated on the fire department's engines.

Close collaboration between the Navy and the fire department, forged in the first hours following the earthquake, resulted in some of the most dramatic moments in saving San Francisco from complete destruction. But it was mainly a Navy victory. Midshipman John E. Pond complained, "From that Wednesday morning until the fire was under control the following Saturday, April 21, we worked almost steadily with little rest. The city firemen worked with us all of the first day and night. After that very few of them were to be seen

in the waterfront district. Many of them left to look after their own families, while our men, most of whom had no kin in the city, stuck to their posts until they almost collapsed."

The Navy tug "Sotoyomo," just back from Goat Island with a tankful of fresh water, positioned herself off Pier 8, while Lieutenant Freeman directed the hookup with the fire engines on shore. Fifteen-hundred feet of hose from the "Leslie" ran as far as the base of Rincon Hill at the foot of Brannan Street.

Two State of California fireboats, the "Governor Irwin" and the "Governor Markham," berthed at the Ferry Building and pumped salt water to Fire Engines No. 1 and No. 9 attempting to save the Ferry Building, Harbor Emergency Hospital and government buildings in the vicinity from fires along Steuart and Fremont Streets. Fire Engine No. 20 at the foot of Washington Street drafted directly from the bay to keep the wholesale district fires from attacking the Ferry Building from the north. This battle to protect the northern flank was later assisted by two Oakland Fire Department engines brought to the city by ferryboat.

Fires which Dr. Topham and the Sisters of Mercy saw burning through St. Mary's Hospital threatened to come down to the piers. On Spear Street, the Mutual Electric Light Company, one of the few undamaged electric generating plants in the city, and Folger's Warehouse were still untouched by fire.

Navy personnel took a stand at the Sailor's Home at First and Bryant Streets. Revenue Cutter "Golden Gate" joined the three other vessels in the fight, pumping the only water that reached into the southeastern section of the city. By 10:30 that night, they had beaten back the flames and saved the old Sailor's Home, the Pacific Mail Dock, and everything east of Spear Street to the waterfront.

As soon as this one battle was over, firefighters reported their boilers out of fresh water in the Mission Creek area, and the Southern Pacific Company freight sheds along Townsend Street were again threatened by fire. Lieutenant Freeman immediately abandoned his hose on Spear Street and took the "Leslie" and the tug "Sotoyomo" around to the Fourth Street channel.

He was fortunate that he was able to navigate as far as Fourth Street. The earthquake had jammed the Third Street bridge

Detailed map of major structures in the fire zone published with a report on structural damage authored by Richard L. Humphrey.

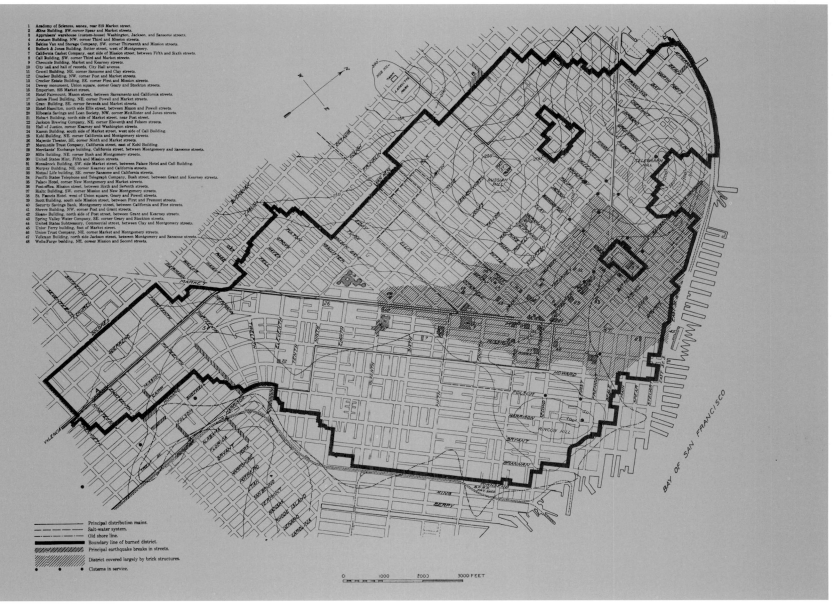

Andrea Sbarboro, President of the Italian-American Bank and member of the Committee of Fifty, and Horace Hudson of the San Francisco Chronicle, witnessed the shooting of an unidentified man at Battery and East Streets. Mr. Sbarboro told the committee that National Guard "Captain Ernest Denicke . . . pulled out a pistol and cried to the man to stop. The man continued to run toward the waterfront. Captain Denicke fired his pistol, then he cried 'Stop' again, and fired again. As the man continued to run he [Denicke] again cried 'Stop,' and fired a third time. Then the man fell." The man had grabbed the bayonet of a drunken U. S. Marine who had tried to arrest him for stealing chickens. The man lay in the street for several hours, then his body was weighted with iron and thrown into the Bay by Lt. Charles Herring of the U. S. Army.

Soldiers from Fort Mason looted boxes of shoes on Market Street between Seventh and Eighth Streets as the Hayes Valley fire jumped San Francisco's main thoroughfare. Note the severe earthquake damage to buildings on both sides of Market Street.

General Funston ordered all available troops on the West Coast to San Francisco. Here, fresh troops from The Presidio of Monterey march along Van Ness Avenue.

in the up position; the Fourth Street bridge was also damaged, but locked in the down position.

Lieutenant Freeman pumped 5000 gallons of fresh water from the "Sotoyomo" into a shallow boat and moved it under the disabled Fourth Street bridge and then pumped it to fire engines working to save the Southern Pacific Company freight sheds. He also left 200 gallons of fresh water in barrels for the refugees in the area, who "were piteously crying for water."

The lieutenant was also appalled at the human vagaries exhibited in the calamity. "The crowds rushed to saloon after saloon and looted the stock," he reported, "becoming intoxicated early in the day."

There was nothing he or his men could do. "My force was unarmed, with the exception of the officers who carried revolvers, and the police, of whom I saw only two, were utterly helpless." He reported that "in my opinion great loss of life resulted from men and women becoming stupefied by liquor and being too tired and exhausted to get out of the way of the fire.

"During this whole day we needed unarmed men to rescue women and children in the neighborhood of Rincon Hill, the fire having made a clean sweep of this poor residence district in about an hour's time. The most heart-rending sights were witnessed in this neighborhood, but with my handful of men we could not do as much for the helpless as we wished.

"Able-bodied men refused to work with the fire department, stating that they would not work for less than forty cents an hour, etc. Men refused to aid old and crippled men and women out of the way of the fire and only thought of themselves."

Midshipman Pond was sent by Lieutenant Freeman to Rincon Hill to urge people to leave. "During the operations on Howard Street we had stopped the bayward progress of the fire within a block of the Embarcadero [then known as East Street], when a shift and slight increase in the breeze started the flames sweeping toward Rincon Hill at a terrific pace. Seeing the danger, the Captain [Freeman] sent Boatswain [Daniel E.] Moriarty and me to warn the poverty-stricken residents of that section to get out. The fire was sweeping up the hill at such a rate that it seemed impossible that any one on the hill could escape its path. The scene there was heartrending. Those who heeded our warning escaped to the waterfront, but many who delayed to gather personal belongings became panic-stricken when they found escape in one direction cut off by flames and smoke, and ran screaming in all directions like a hive of ants whose hill had been disturbed. The old and crippled, taken out of their houses on mattresses, were carried a little way and dropped, then picked up by someone else, carried a little further and dropped again. The whole section was swept clean in less than an hour, and many must have perished."

Other eyewitnesses felt the calamity developed slowly, like a stock market crash: a sudden fear, then reassurances, growing panic and finally full-blown retreat.

This is how Roland M. Roche, a letter carrier living at 527 Castro Street, saw the disaster. First came the panic of the earthquake and a survey of the damage in his flat. Then, reassurance that the damage was not that bad, then the growing realization that the city was severely damaged by the earthquake and was about to be destroyed by fire.

On his way to report to work at the Ferry Building Post Office, Mr. Roche saw that the tall brick smoke stack of the Market Street Railway on the southeast corner of Market and Valencia Streets had snapped near the top. Between Franklin Street and Van Ness Avenue, Market Street's sidewalks were buckled, and blocked by fallen fire walls and cornices of two large lodging houses. At Van Ness Avenue and Hayes Street the assembly hall of St. Ignatius Church had fallen halfway into the street.

Passing the rubble of City Hall, Mr. Roche could see down Sixth Street, where "a great fire was raging on the west side. We were beginning to realize that grave things were happening. Never had such a jumble of traffic been seen on the streets of San Francisco before. Horses, men, women, and children were filling the streets, and it was not yet 7 a.m."

He pressed down to Fourth Street on Market, noting all the damaged buildings. "Here it became a difficult job to make our way through the blocked roadway and crowded traffic: buggies, autos, saddle horses, baby carriages, everything on wheels had been pressed into service for the emergency. . . ."

Turning in to New Montgomery Street, under the second story walkway that connected the Grand and Palace Hotels, he could see the fires coming out of Minna and Natoma, as well as Mission toward Third Street. Then, turning left down Mission street he was startled to find the east side of Fremont Street "a seething furnace." It was then Mr. Roche chanced upon what he called "one of the most extraordinary catastrophes of the day" – a cattle stampede in the heart of the city.

Police Officer Henry F. Walsh was drinking coffee with a watchman named William Beatty at the Meese and Gottfried Company machine shop at 167–169 Fremont Street, on the east side of the block between Mission and Howard Streets, when the earthquake rocked the building. Next door was the Martel Power Company at 149 Fremont Street. The Martel and the Meese and Gottfried buildings collapsed and began to burn with the first earthquake shock. Officer Walsh escaped, but Mr. Beatty was trapped and killed.

As Officer Walsh ran from the building he saw a herd of longhorn steers in full stampede up Mission Street charging everything

Post Office employee Roland M. Roche.

Governor James Budd (at left) and Abe Ruef (second from left) in court defending Ernest Denicke (second from right). The Socialist Voice *reacted with indignation when Mr. Denicke was released on bail. The newspaper wrote that* "when bail was asked for National Guardsman Denicke, who is held on a charge of murdering a defenseless sailor, this charge being sworn to by several of the most reputable citizens of San Francisco, eyewitnesses to the hired assassination, bail was granted. Why? Well, Abe Ruef, a lawyer with no reputation and a politician with no character, asked for it, aye, demanded it. Who is Abe Ruef? Well, he is the man that the big capitalists allow to own the city government. He is the owner and manipulator of a certain puppet known as Mayor Schmitz; he has become wealthy through Tammany Hall methods of city deals, special grafts, inside information, holdups, and other forms of high finance and public looting."

Captain Denicke was tried, and later acquitted of the murder charge.

U.S. Navy on patrol in the Western Addition where hundreds of wood-frame homes fell from their foundations during the earthquake. Note the man with the peg leg at the far right.

and everyone in its path.

He was amazed. "While a lot of them were running along the sidewalk of Mission Street, between Fremont and First Streets, a big warehouse toppled out into the thoroughfare and crushed most of them clean through the pavement into the basement, killing and burying them outright. The first that I saw of the bunch were two that were caught and crippled by falling cornices, or the like on Fremont Street, near Mission, and they were in great misery. So I took out my gun and shot them. Then I had only six shots left, and I saw that more cattle were coming along and there was going to be big trouble.

"At that moment I ran into John Moller [Moeller], who owned the saloon at the southeast corner of Fremont and Mission Streets, almost across the street from where we met. I asked him if he had any ammunition in his place and if so to let me have some quick. He was very scared and excited over the earthquake and everything, and when he saw the stampeding cattle charging and bellowing, he seemed to lose more nerve.

"Anyhow, there was no time to think. Two of the steers were charging right at us while I was asking him to help, and he started to run for his saloon.

"I had to be quick about my part of the job, because, with only a revolver as a weapon, I had to wait till the animal was quite close before I dared fire. Otherwise I would not have killed or even stopped them.

"As I shot down one of them, I saw the other charging after John Moller, who was then at the door of his saloon and apparently quite safe. But as I was looking at him and the steer, Moller turned, and seemed to become paralyzed with fear. He held out both hands as if beseeching the beast to go back. But it charged on and ripped him before I could get near enough to fire.

"When I killed the animal, it was too late to save the man. We got a hose wagon from the fire engine that came along, and could do nothing in its own line of business for lack of water. It took Moller down to the Harbor Emergency Hospital on the wharf at the foot of Mission Street, where he died very soon afterward.

"Things were then moving very quickly. A dozen or more of the wild cattle came tearing into Fremont Street, and my revolver was empty.

"Then a young fellow came running up to me carrying a rifle and a lot of cartridges. . . . We probably killed fifty or sixty out of that herd. Some of them were running wild, others crippled or wounded. We were going to shoot a horse that we saw standing up, half-buried in masonry, on Mission Street between First and Fremont; but when we got near the poor creature, we found it was already stone dead. It was near there that the big warehouse had fallen out and crushed a number of cattle clear through the sidewalk

Refugees hurry by the carcasses of longhorn steers on Mission Street near First Street. Most of the cattle were shot by Police Officer Henry F. Walsh, or were killed by falling walls.

On Mission Street lay a dozen steers, in a neat row stretching across the street, just as they had been struck *down by the flying ruins of the earthquake.*

– Jack London

and into the basement."

Some cattle ran as far as the Palace Hotel, and a single terrified steer careened through Chinatown and caused panic among the terrorized Chinese, who considered the appearance of the beast a bad omen.

Meanwhile, Mr. Roche continued up Fremont Street, even though he might have reached the Ferry Building via Mission Street where a three- story brick machine shop was burning furiously at the corner of Howard Street.

Despite this circuitous route, he managed to arrive at the Ferry Building Post Office Station D at 7:30 a.m. So had a dozen other letter carriers, out of a possible 16. Howard Street had sunk about two feet east of Fremont Street; the Ferry Building tower verged on collapse and fires were – more than two hours after the earthquake – out of control to the north of the Ferry Building in the wholesale district and in the South of Market district. The postal employees were told to go home.

To go north on East Street [now the Embarcadero] was impossible; the Wellman and Peck grocery warehouse was an inferno just two blocks away. Market Street was blocked with debris, bystanders and firefighters. Going back south on East Street, Mr. Roche noted that lower Mission Street "had risen in waves and stayed that way." The freight shed of the Mission Street Wharf had collapsed for a length of two hundred feet.

Plume of smoke in the center of the picture was the beginning of the Hayes Valley fire that broke out in late morning. Two smaller earthquake-caused fires extinguished by the fire department – at Fell and Octavia Streets, and Golden Gate Avenue and Buchanan Street – can be seen at the left.

Refugees removed belongings from the shattered Strathmore Apartment Building on Larkin Street as the Hayes Valley fire attacked City Hall.

The streets were bumped into ridges and depressions, and piled with the debris of fallen walls.

– Jack London

Mr. Roche was deep into the South of Market district when the large aftershock hit at 8:14 a.m. "Regardless of the swaying ground and the panic all around them," firefighters at Clementina, Tehama and Howard Streets kept playing water on the burning shops and factories typical of the area; the water came from abandoned and nearly-forgotten cisterns lying under city streets.

Fires along Market near Third Street seemed to be growing more intense; along Fourth the flames had already reached Folsom Street. Police and army troops drove the crowds south toward the Southern Pacific Company freight yards. Mr. Roche saw "a great stream of autos, buggies, patrol wagons, express wagons and other vehicles along Market Street carrying wounded to Mechanics' Pavilion" at Grove and Larkin Streets, across from City Hall.

The so-called "Ham and Egg" fire in Hayes Valley is said to have been started by a woman cooking breakfast or lunch in a building with an earthquake-damaged chimney. There was no subsequent investigation by either the fire department or insurance underwriters to establish the true cause of the blaze, but it is known to have broken out shortly before 11 a.m. at 395 Hayes Street on the southwest corner of Hayes and Gough.

Pushed by a fresh westerly wind, this fire rapidly worked its way east toward Van Ness Avenue and caught the giant spires of St.

Ignatius Church at Van Ness Avenue and Hayes Street. Firefighters mopping up two earthquake-caused fires farther out in Hayes Valley responded to this new blaze, but it had gained too much headway.

Fire Department Second Assistant Chief Engineer, Patrick H. Shaughnessy, tried to stop this fresh fire with the few fire engines available in that part of the city. First, firefighters used dynamite at Octavia and Gough Streets and were successful in stopping the northward spread of the blaze. Chief Shaughnessy also had 700 feet of hose stretched from a functioning hydrant at Buchanan and Eddy Streets, and with three engines working in relay, was able to keep the fire from moving southwest toward the Mission District.

The Hayes Valley fire caught Battalion Chief John J. Conlon by surprise. He was supervising the unsuccessful fire department effort to blast a firebreak along Eighth Street, from Market to Harrison Streets, to keep the South of Market conflagration from sweeping into the highly combustible Mission District. The new fire, if it jumped Market Street, would defeat his containment plan.

But there weren't enough firefighters or fire engines to stop this new conflagration from its relentless movement toward City Hall and Mechanics' Pavilion, or onward to Market Street.

Mechanics' Pavilion was a great wooden structure on the block bounded by Hayes, Grove, Polk and Larkin Streets, and was the city's unofficial civic auditorium. In 1903, President Theodore Roosevelt had addressed several thousand people there when in San Francisco to dedicate the Dewey Monument in Union Square.

Across the intersection at what is now Market and Grove Streets, behind the James Lick Monument at Marshall Square, was the immense triangular configuration of City Hall. Central Emergency Hospital comprised the western tip of the triangle, and had been wrecked by the earthquake.

Central Emergency Hospital's staff began the transfer of all salvageable medical equipment and supplies to the barn-like Pavilion shortly after their rescue. Within a few minutes after the earthquake the first South of Market injured began to arrive. Other victims were carried to Mechanics' Pavilion from fallen apartment buildings in the blocks immediately north and west of City Hall.

Rabbi Jacob Voorsanger of Temple Beth Emmanu-El was among the first to arrive at Mechanics' Pavilion to offer his help. "I can scarcely describe," wrote the Rabbi, "the motley crowd that came rushing into the improvised hospital" to be helped by an "army of physicians, nurses, clergymen, monks, nuns, . . . and Sisters of Mercy." The rabbi also watched automobiles bring the dead and wounded to the Pavilion by the carload.

Lucy B. Fisher, a nurse, made her way to (Continued on page 57)

A soldier guarded California Street near Taylor Street as the fire crept up Nob Hill. The Tobin Mansion at 1021 California Street is on the left.

Mayor Schmitz issued this infamous and illegal proclamation shortly after the earthquake. The mayor also issued the following order to Chief Dinan of the police department:

"As it has come to my note that thiefs are taking advantage of the present deplorable conditions and are plying their nefarious vocations among the ruins in our city, all peace officers are ordered to instantly kill any one caught looting or committing any other serious crimes. E. E. Schmitz, Mayor."

Editors of the Socialist Voice newspaper were horrified, and wrote shortly after the disaster, "Mayor Schmitz and not General Funston, gave the order in San Francisco to the military to 'shoot and shoot to kill' wherever private property was in danger.

"Schmitz is so fond of private property that he has been caught in the act of changing a whole lot of public property into private property for the benefit of himself and his friends. Of course, while he was in the act of looting, none of the military forces that should protect public property took a shot at him.

"Why should the poor little looter, who is scraping something together to live on for a little longer, be shot to death, and yet the big looter, the Schmitzes and the Ruefs of public plunder, who loot simply to lay by a store of luxury, are allowed to go free? This is one of those questions that must be answered sooner or later. Law for the little looter may very soon become law for the large looter."

Captain Orrin R. Wolfe (center of photograph) and Companies B and C, 22nd Infantry.

General Funston posed with military officers who directed the Army relief in San Francisco.

Bottom row, left to right. Lt. Col. G. W. Dunn, Col. C. L. Heizmann, Gen. Funston, Col. William A. Simpson, Col. E. E. Dravo, Col. J. L. Clemm.

Second row, Capt. O. P. M. Hazzard, Capt. William C. Wren, 1st Lt. R. K. Mitchell, aide to Gen. Funston, Lt. Col. W. H. Comegys, Capt. Leonard D. Wildman, Capt. Aristides Moreno, 2nd Lt. Samuel E. Patterson.

Third row, Capt. Lawrence B. Simonds, Capt. Frederick R. Day.

(U.S. Army Signal Corps photograph.)

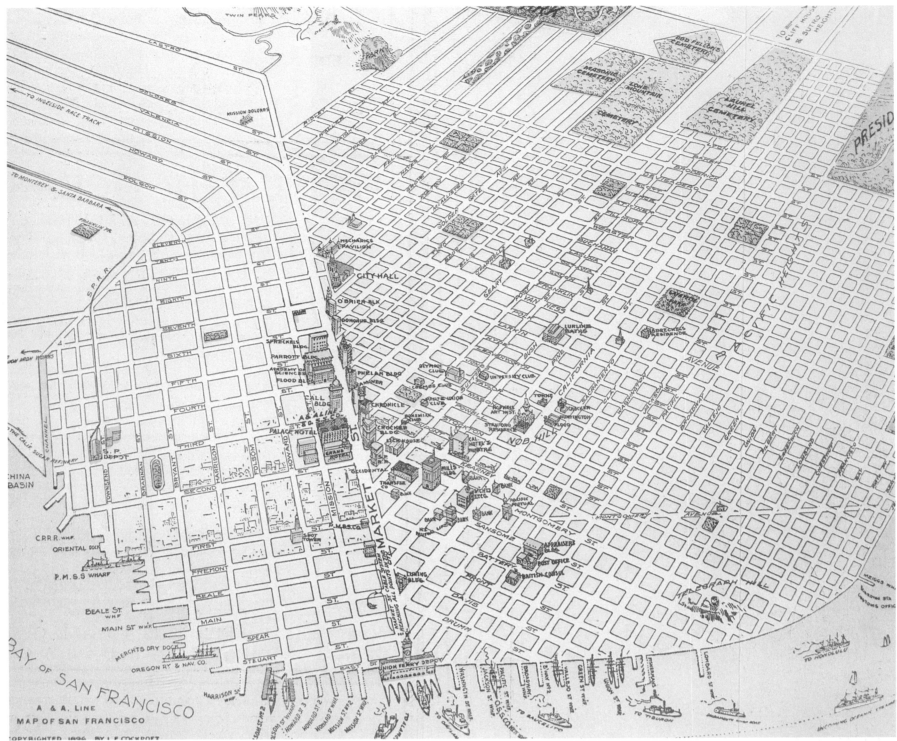

1905 tour map of San Francisco.

(Continued from page 55)
the Pavilion after hearing it had been opened as a hospital. She wrote in *The American Journal of Nursing*, "We found on our approach to the Pavilion that its entrance was surrounded by a cordon which was guarded by a force of policemen. We asked to be passed through the line but were refused until we said we were nurses. Instantly at the mention of the word 'nurse' we were directed to the entrance.

"What a scene that huge building presented as we entered it; a building of such large dimensions that its area covered an entire block! The floor was strewn with mattresses, which were nearly all occupied by patients even at that early hour. Near the entrance to the building, where the patients were received, an improvised surgery had been established; it was surprisingly well

equipped under the circumstances and seemed to lack nothing in the way of operating-room tables, dressings, instruments, enamel pans and basins, and even quantities of hot and cold sterilized water. Some days later I learned that most of this outfit had been carried over from the Central Emergency at the City Hall opposite, immediately after the earthquake, when Dr. McGinty, the surgeon on duty that night, had ordered the policemen to open the Pavilion for the new emergency hospital; the rest of the supplies had been appropriated from the surrounding drug-stores."

To keep the temporary emergency hospital supplied with bedding and medical supplies, volunteers stripped abandoned hotels of mattresses and sheets. Other volunteers, some from the Salvation Army, worked their way along Market street, smashed windows of drug stores and carried away all available

supplies. Hot water and coffee were brought from the nearby St. Nicholas Hotel, which had been severely damaged by the earthquake.

Nurse Fisher's graphic eyewitness account continued. "Patients were being brought in constantly and rapidly moving groups of physicians and uniformed nurses were gathered around the operating-room tables. There was great danger in the confusion that the drugs administered would be duplicated, so as a precaution each one who gave a hypodermic injection pinned a tag on the patient on which was written the quantity of the drug and the time when it was given.

"Considerable perplexity and delay was caused in losing the location of patients. The arrangement in itself was confusing – mattresses lying without any attempt at regularity all over the floor and constantly being rearranged by kindly-disposed people...."

DISASTER AS ART
This collection of paintings executed after the disaster clearly conveys the vivid impressions as seen by an unknown artist. The original oil paintings were on cardboard.

the injured woman's sister, a Salvation Army lassie. I held the woman's poor crushed leg while the surgeon put on a temporary bandage after deciding that an amputation was necessary. The surgeon told me later in the week that the woman had at the time I saw her a chance for recovery, but she was moved twice on account of the fire and subsequently died from shock."

As the Hayes Valley fire crossed Van Ness Avenue, wind-blown sparks and cinders fell onto the roof of the Mechanics' Pavilion. The word quietly spread through the building that the roof was on fire. "I went up to the men near me," she wrote, "and passed the word on to them in a low voice and directed them to pull the patients on the mattresses to the rear entrance beginning with those nearest the exit, as there was no passage way to drag the further mattresses until those in front were removed."

A police officer climbed to the roof of the giant structure to put out the fires. He managed to knock some of the flames down, but the Hayes Valley fire roared on.

To move all 354 patients from the building volunteers were called from the street and passing automobiles and wagons commandeered by the police. Dr. George Blumer described how the injured were taken from the immense building: "Three men would get on each side of a patient, two at each end and two at the middle, push their arms under the mattress, clasp hands, and carry out the patient who was deposited in an automobile. We managed to get all the living patients safely out before the fire got too hot, but about twenty dead in one corner of the building could not be removed and were cremated."

Crushed and burned bodies of the dead had been stacked in the rear of the Pavilion to keep them out of view. A young doctor named Asa W. Collins had a horrifying experience as he tried to escape from the burning Pavilion. "One corner of the building had already caught fire and I had to run before I was overcome by smoke. Keeping close to the wall, I stumbled over a row of dead bodies and fell to the floor. As I rose I noticed two of them resting side by side, a man and his wife. It seemed unbelievable that of the few patients I had in this city of half a million population, these two should be mine. The woman, a young German girl, was to have been a mother in a month."

Reporter James Hopper of *The Call* was at the Hayes Valley fire when it had already covered a four-square-block area southeast of Gough Street. "We went before it and stopped at the Mechanics' Pavilion," he wrote, "just in time to observe the last of the injured carried out a side door and loaded onto wagons. Some victims went to the U. S. Marine Hospital, others to Golden Gate Park and some to damaged Lane Hospital."

Across the street, window frames, doors and furniture of City Hall had now reached

"Among the many heartrending scenes that I witnessed the one that touched me most deeply was a story that in one short sentence told of a grief that made physical injuries seem slight in comparison. I saw a woman weeping and knelt beside her to offer my assistance. She seized my hand and told me in a broken voice that she had lost her three children. My own overwrought nerves almost gave way when she told me this, and I was compelled to leave the woman to hide from her my distress."

Lucy Fisher also watched police stop volunteers and patients from fleeing the building when the big earthquake aftershock rocked Mechanics' Pavilion at 8:14 a.m. She was also struck by another event that, like a photograph, would stay in her mind for years. "One of these pictures is of a group standing around a cot on which lay the unconscious and mangled form of a woman. In the group were physicians and nurses and the combustion point. While rare Shake-spearean folios, incunabula, and irreplaceable volumes of English law from the Sutro Library burned with bodies of the dead in the Mechanics' Pavilion – the property and tax records in City Hall and the books of the Law Library produced a bonfire of equal proportions.

Orders to Federal troops to protect $7,000,000 in the municipal treasury collided with common sense at City Hall just a few hours after the earthquake and effectively established who was in charge of San Francisco. The orders also guaranteed that the shattered city communications systems could not be restored to allow the police and fire chiefs to re-establish tactical control of their departments.

After the first earthquake, William R. Hewitt, chief of the Department of Electricity for the city, had gone immediately to his department's fire alarm office at 15 Brenham Place, near the Hall of Justice. Wet-cell batteries for the fire department's alarm system were scattered on the floor and the alarm wires inoperable. A small fire started by hot coals thrown from the hearth by the earthquake was, ironically, extinguished by the mixture of water and acid from broken batteries.

From the vantage point of his small Portsmouth Square building, Mr. Hewitt could see fires starting to spread around the city. He set about the impossible task of restoring the fire telegraph system. By 9 a.m., the wholesale district fires were so threatening that he decided he might have to abandon the Central Fire Alarm Station.

Mr. Hewitt somehow secured a wagon in Chinatown and set out for City Hall "to remove the departmental records and such instruments and material as might be necessary in re-establishing our signal office in a new location entirely removed from the reach of the fire; but, unfortunately, we were prevented from entering the building by a guard of Federal troops, who refused to listen to any argument or supplication whatever for permission to remove such records and instruments as we might be able to save, telling us their orders were without exception to permit nobody to enter the city hall building. This is very much to be regretted, since it was quite possible, with the time and means at our disposal, to save nearly all of our equipment. . . ."

The Department of Electricity chief and his men returned to the badly damaged Central Fire Alarm Station at Brenham Place just in time to salvage the equipment there and pile it in Portsmouth Square. Records and valuable equipment needed to restore the fire department communications system burned in City Hall and there was no chance to re-establish the fire department's communications system for the rest of the Great Fire.

While the main course of the South of Market fires was west and south, they had

found vulnerable targets in the narrow streets immediately behind Market Street. South of Market fires now had to be fought on four sides.

Federal troops and firefighters had begun to dynamite along Market Street. By mid-morning, Lieutenant Freeman and the State fire boats were supplying water to firefighters along East Street. Southern Pacific Company personnel and firefighters were backed up along Townsend Street on the south, and a retreating band of citizen volunteers and

firefighters abandoned their makeshift fire-break along Eighth Street and began their retreat into the Mission District, dragging the fire engines and hose with them as the sweeping Hayes Valley fire jumped Market Street between Eighth and Ninth and roared into the South of Market district from the north.

There were four unburned outposts within the South of Market fire zone: the U. S. Post Office and Court House at Seventh and Mission Streets, the U. S. Mint at Fifth Street, the California Electrical Works at Second and Folsom Streets and the Long Syrup Warehouse at Eighth and Brannan Streets.

Three sons of Colonel J. M. Long – Herbert, Harry and Matt – together with three employees, saved the huge factory when the conflagration attacked. The fire sent tongues of flame shooting across Brannan Street, setting the cornices of the building ablaze. The Long brothers used sacks wet in buckets of water filled from a nearby broken water main to slap at the flames attacking the structure. When they ran out of water they used hammers to beat at the fire. For 36 hours the Long brothers and their employees protected the warehouse. At the end of this ordeal their eyes were swollen closed by the intense heat and long hours of labor.

All morning, employees at the U. S. Mint had awaited the assault by fire. Those inside were joined by troops from the Sixth Infantry. When fires began to converge from Lincoln School across the street and from Sixth Street the Superintendent of the Mint, Frank Leach, ordered tar roofing stripped away and thrown into the buildings' interior courtyard. Roof beams were kept wet with chemicals and water drawn by hand from an artesian well behind the structure.

The thirty-year-old U. S. Mint was built on a massive scale, with steel shutters for the windows and two giant smokestacks for the pumps and furnaces. Though embers from the very center of the fire cascaded like incoming shellfire into the courtyard before noon, the U. S. Mint was saved by sheer manpower and intelligent fire fighting counter measures.

The new U. S. Post Office and Court House was also carefully defended. It had suffered severe damage in the earthquake and eventually required several hundred thousand dollars in repairs, but at least it remained standing.

Unlike the U. S. Mint, the U. S. Post Office had only 10 employees inside to fight the fire, and they used mail sacks dampened with water from hydraulic elevator tanks to beat out the flames. Fire did manage to invade the court chambers of Judge John J. DeHaven on the upper floors, but was beaten back by mail clerks.

North of Market, another major Federal building defied the flames. The Appraiser's Building was a squat, aging structure on the southeast side of Sansome between Washington and Jackson Streets, precisely where its handsome successor is today. This building was directly in the path of the wholesale district fires that broke out with the first shock of the earthquake.

Just after the earthquake, the men of Fire Engine No. 1 extinguished a fire at the southeast corner of Clay and Davis Streets. Fire Department Captain Walter A. Cook's engines stopped two fires around Davis Street and

Impressionistic view of the destruction of the Fish Market District on Merchant Street.

Broadway. He then moved the fire apparatus to East Street to protect the docks and freight cars. The Appraiser's Building was also shielded on one side by the excavation for the new Custom House, which had filled with water from broken mains. The real test of the building and its occupants would not come until the third day – from the opposite direction.

Earlier in the day, Second Assistant Chief Patrick H. Shaughnessy turned his attention to the fires along lower Market Street: the quake-wrecked Martel Power Company plant at Fremont and Mission Streets, Alice's rooming house and Brown's store on Steuart between Market and Howard Streets, and the Mack & Company drugstore at the northwest corner of Market and Fremont Streets. Fires in all these buildings began just after the earthquake and had joined into a conflagration.

Fire Engine No. 38 had been unable to find water here earlier, and Chief Shaughnessy feared these fires would jump Market Street and join the blazes running through the wholesale and financial districts. Fire Engines No. 1 and No. 9 were a few blocks away near the Ferry Building pumping salt water to stop the lower Market Street fire from spreading to the Ferry Building and Harbor Emergency Hospital. Fire Engine No. 20 and two Oakland fire units remained near the Washington Street pier to keep the wholesale district fires from attacking the Ferry Building from the north.

Fire from the Chinese laundry at Third and Howard Streets was making headway to the east and north. Fire Engine No. 4 was drawing water from Fire Engine No. 10 stationed at the cistern at Second and Folsom Streets, but Captain Charles Murray could not rescue the Chinese employees trapped in the rubble.

A saloon at the northwest corner of Third and Minna Streets, just around the corner from Fire Engine Station No. 4, collapsed in the earthquake and began to burn. A house collapsed and caught fire at 282 Natoma Street, near Fourth. Fire had broken out in another Chinese laundry on Howard Street, about a block west of the Brunswick House blaze, and the Prost's Bakery and Girard House fires had joined and were moving east. Another blaze was creeping out of the wreckage of the SFG&E plant on Jessie Street behind St. Patrick's Church. This fire in the electric plant was of immediate and overriding concern because it threatened to spread to the Call [or Claus Spreckels] Building at Third and Market, and the rear of structures that fronted on Market Street. Overtaxed firefighters weren't able to reach most of these fires as they began to spread north and east.

Fire from the Brunswick House was now opposite the U.S. Mint, behind Lincoln Grammar School at Fifth and Stevenson Streets,

(Continued on page 64)

Sheet music could be published quickly and publishers found "instant songs" quite profitable. Turn-of-the-century publishers were quick to capitalize on sensational real-life events or disasters.

A Beautiful Song-story descriptive of the Earthquake at San Francisco on the morning of April 18th 1906.

THE SWEETHEART THAT I LOST IN DEAR OLD 'FRISCO

Words by
HELEN OSBORNE
Music by
WALTER POTTER

5

THE PACIFIC PUBLISHING CO
214 W. 42ND ST
NEW YORK

SAN FRANCISCO - FALLEN
—APRIL 18TH 1906—

DRAWING BY
COURTESY OF W.R. HEARST

ONLY TO RISE AGAIN

5

WORDS AND MUSIC BY
ALMA A. CROWLEY.

PUBLISHED BY
ALMA A. CROWLEY
1164 Alice St., Oakland, Cal.
Copyrighted

Lurid flames sweep across San Francisco in William Alexander Coulter's (1849-1936) panorama of the largest maritime rescue effort in United States history where more than thirty thousand people were taken from the shoreline between Fort Mason and the foot of Lombard Street. Mr. Coulter's painting depicts the flotilla of rescue vessels ferrying between the burning city and Sausalito.

Mr. Coulter painted from sketches drawn as he helped during the Dunkirk-like evacuation, and he took certain liberties with the San Francisco skyline to give this magnificent picture balance. The eye is first drawn to the large sailing ships highlighted against the thick, black smoke which obscured the downtown area. He moved the Hall of Justice near Chinatown to just left of center, the Call Building to just right of center, and depicted the burning of Nob Hill on the far right. True perspective would place almost all of these landmarks within the ominous smoke cloud.

This painting, executed on a 5x10 foot window shade, hung for many years in San Francisco's Commercial Club and was later sold by Maxwell Galleries, Ltd.

W.A.COULTER
SAN FRANCISCO
APRIL 18 1906

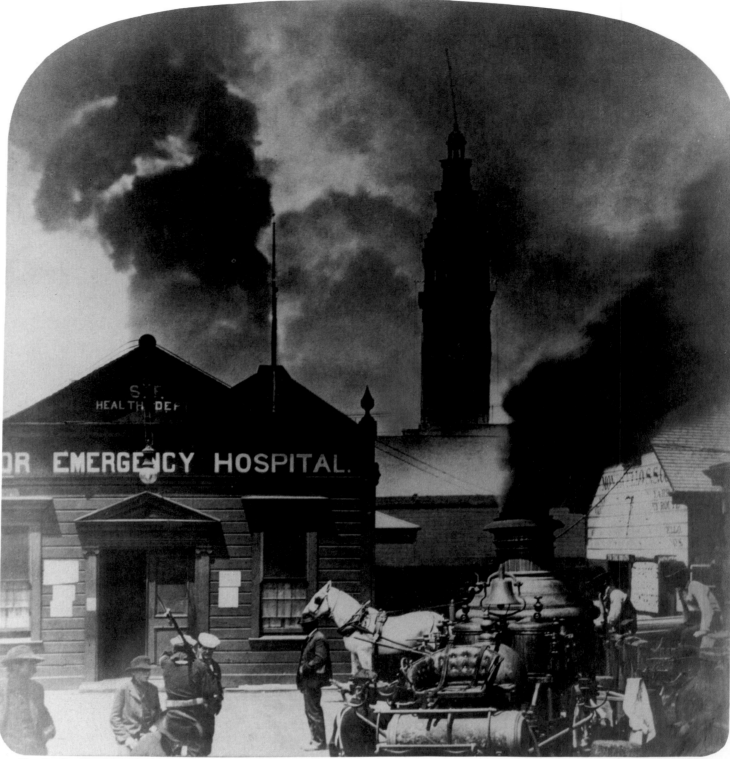

Fire Engine No. 1 pumped water from the bay to protect Harbor Emergency Hospital as Navy guards from Mare Island stand by. The small hospital at the foot of Mission Street was beseiged by the wounded after the earthquake and doctors were forced to remove the most seriously wounded by ferryboat to Navy hospitals at Goat Island and Mare Island. Note that an artist has airbushed away the damage to the Ferry Building tower.

(Continued from page 61)
and working its way down behind the Emporium.

There were only three sources of water protecting Market Street by noon: a single hydrant attached to a main that brought sea water from Ocean Beach to downtown bath houses, the Palace Hotel's independent fresh water supply, and water pumped from the bay by two State fireboats to fire engines at the foot of Market Street.

Before noon, fire department personnel, with the Army's help, dynamited the Hearst Building at Third and Market Streets. The adjoining Monadnock Building was also dynamited to keep the fire in the wreckage of the San Francisco Gas and Electric works

from jumping Third Street and attacking the Palace Hotel. It had become critically important to protect the Palace's functioning water supply, if not the hotel itself.

William Ralston started construction of the world's largest hotel in the late 1860s. He plunged millions into 3000 tons of "earthquake-proof" iron banding for the brick walls and a major self-sufficient fire protection and water system. The Palace's 358,000 gallon sub-basement reservoir beneath the Grand Court and six roof tanks, as shown on the 1905 Sanborn insurance maps, were filled by two of the hotel's four artesian wells.

The hotel's roof was covered with iron; several large boxes of fire hose were placed there for further protection. Each floor had

two carts with 250 feet of 2½ inch hose to allow bellboys to fight any blaze. As far as fire was concerned, the Palace Hotel was the best protected building in San Francisco. This had been William Ralston's lesson from the Great Hayward Earthquake of 1868 that caused so much damage in San Francisco.

Mr. Ralston had also the foresight to install 12 hydrants on the curb-front of the structure along Market and New Montgomery Streets, connected to the roof tanks. He had anticipated the need for the hydrants should a major fire break out in or around the hotel. He could not, however, foresee the possibility that the hotel's water supply might be used elsewhere.

The battle for the Palace Hotel was waged

Fire from the nearby SFG&E plant was drawn up the elevator shaft of the Call Building which then burned from the top floor down. The Palace Hotel is on the left.

Soldiers watched the Palace Hotel burn on the afternoon of April 18.

A spectacular photograph of the fire burning in Breuner's Rug Store at 261 Geary Street shortly before the flames attacked the St. Francis Hotel.

in the late morning and early afternoon of the first day. Hotel employees fought off the fires converging from the south and west. The southern flank came from fires in the district between the waterfront and Third Street. The western flank attacked the hotel after the Natoma and Minna Street fires joined with the blaze from the San Francisco Gas and Electric Company plant.

Eyewitness James W. Byrne watched as clerks and bellboys fought the conflagration with hand-held hoses. "The heat on the fire escapes was at times terrific, and the boys were often compelled to hold an arm up to protect their faces while trying to manage the hose with only one hand. Nevertheless they stuck to their job manfully, and they

fought off the fire on the west and south sides of the hotel that it seemed to me at this time – I suppose it was somewhere about 9:30 o'clock (a.m.) – that no menace to the Palace any longer existed unless the fire came up from the east side and through the Grand Hotel on the east side of New Montgomery Street. . . ."

"While I was standing on the corner of New Montgomery and Market Streets I saw a Fire Department hose cart come up Market Street from the eastward. It stopped at one or two hydrants on the way, and came on again. Then it stopped at the Palace Hotel hydrant, screwed on a hose and went off with the water into Sansome Street."

Mr. Byrne was watching Captain Thomas

Magner and the crew from Fire Engine No. 3. Captain Magner picks up the dreadful story of the end of the Palace Hotel. "I received orders from Second Assistant Chief Shaughnessy to take members of [the] Company and man [a] relief engine opposite [the] Palace Hotel. I then led a line of hose from there down Market to Sansome Street and worked on the corner of Market and Sutter Streets until the Palace Hotel caught fire and caused our water supply to be shut off."

Mr. Byrne was appalled "when the city fire department tapped the hotel hydrant and took the water away to Battery and Market. Of course, that ended it; the power plant in the Quartermaster's Building took fire from the Crossley Building [on the southeast corner of New Montgomery and Jessie Streets] and the hotel was soon in flames. I am convinced in my own mind that the Palace would have been saved if its water had been left alone."

The Hayes Valley fire had moved in a broad front toward Market Street by early afternoon. In a dramatic account by the National Board of Fire Underwriters' in May 1906, this part of the conflagration was accurately described as the turning point of the first day.

This fire swept east over the Mechanics' Pavilion and City Hall, overran the firefighters and jumped Market between Ninth and Twelfth Streets to join the slower-moving but relentless South of Market fires.

Three main fires were striking on at least nine fronts by early afternoon. In Hayes Valley, firefighters were holding the northwest and southwest sides of the triangle. In the wholesale district, the fire lines were falling along Sansome Street to the north and Bush Street to the west.

South of Market, the coffin-shaped firestorm was held along the waterfront and the Southern Pacific Company yards, but burned in the direction of the Mission District. And it turned on the prized "skyscrapers" along the south side of Market Street after the Palace Hotel water supply was lost.

At 11 a.m., General Funston's staff abandoned the U. S. Army's Department of California headquarters in the Phelan Building across from the Palace Hotel. Sergeant Earle Binkley of the Signal Corps had been able to string a telegraph line into the building from the Presidio just before it was abandoned; he would later save most of the records there by impressing a wagon hauling whiskey. The lone telegraph operator at the Postal Telegraph-Cable Co. in the Hobart Building at 534 Market Street transmitted his last message at 2:20 p.m., as the Army ordered him out of the structure because of the approaching fire.

Loss of the Western Union and Postal Telegraph offices forced the Signal Corps to shift operations to the Ferry Building at 3 p.m., and communication with Washington was maintained from there, via Oakland, for the rest of the fire period.

The Fire Underwriters' report of 1906 is the most damning indictment of the weakness of fire protection in the downtown area. Building-by-building, this report detailed how supposedly "fireproof" structures were invaded along the south side of Market street: the Emporium from unprotected windows facing its Mission Street warehouse; the 18-story Call Building at Third and Market Streets from broken windows facing the burning SFG&E plant to the southwest; the Palace Hotel from the narrow rear and side streets.

The report also condemned the use of dynamite to fight the fire, concluding that dynamite "has been proved in all modern

(Continued on page 69)

An enumeration of the dead will never be made. All vestiges of them were destroyed by the flames.
— Jack London

Crowds gathered to watch the successful effort to stop the Hayes Valley fire on Golden Gate Avenue near Franklin Street. Water for the fire engines was relayed *from a functioning hydrant at Buchanan and Eddy Streets. Below, firefighters stopped the southwest flank of the Hayes Valley fire.*

The Emporium Department Store at 825 Market Street before it was attacked by the fire. Photographic evidence suggests that the interior of the structure had been wrecked by either the earthquake or the falling of the store's powerhouse smokestack. The Emporium Building also housed the chambers of the California Supreme Court before the earthquake The James Flood Building at Powell and Market Steets is to the left.

The facade of The Emporium after the earthquake and fire. The building was supposed to have been demolished after the disaster, but Superintendent of the Mint Frank Leach objected to dynamiting wrecked buildings so close to the U. S. Mint at Fifth and Mission Streets. Crews tore down the building by hand and left only the facade, which remains today.

Interior of The Emporium rotunda after the fire.

LOS ANGELES RAZED BY THE GREAT EARTHQUAKE!

EXTRA

Berkeley Reporter

Last Edition

VOL. IV.   BERKELEY, CALIFORNIA, WEDESDAY, APRIL 18, 1906.   No. 133

CITY A ROARING FURNACE

Palace Hotel Burns---Cliff House Topples Into Ocean

Weather Forecast for Friday and Saturday:
FOR WESTERN PENNSYLVANIA AND OHIO-FAIR AND COOLER FRIDAY SATURDAY FAIR, LIGHT TO FRESH WINDS BECOMING VARIABLE. FOR WEST VIRGINIA-FAIR FRIDAY, COOLER IN WEST PORTION, SATURDAY FAIR.

The Pittsburgh Post.

LAST EDITION.
ALL THE LATEST NEWS.

SIXTY-FOURTH YEAR.   FRIDAY MORNING, APRIL 20, 1906. •:• SIXTEEN PAGES.   ONE CENT A COPY.

FLAMES RAGE IN 'FRISCO AND ENTIRE CITY SEEMS DOOMED.

A BIRDSEYE VIEW OF SAN FRANCISCO TAKEN FROM THE TOP OF THE SPRECKELS BUILDING.

THE ABOVE SHOWS AT THE LEFT ST. FRANCIS HOTEL, AT THE EXTREME RIGHT TELEGRAPH HILL. THIS ENTIRE SECTION IS SUPPOSED TO BE A MASS OF RUINS.

THE WEATHER
Washington, April 20.—For eastern New York; Slightly cooler to-night; Saturday fair; light to fresh winds, mostly westerly. For western New York; Partly cloudy to-night and Saturday.

Utica Herald-Dispatch

1 CENT.

GAZETTE ESTABLISHED 1793.   **AND DAILY GAZETTE**   DISPATCH ESTABLISHED 1898.
HERALD ESTABLISHED 1847.

VOL. LVIII.—NO. 134.   UTICA, N. Y., FRIDAY EVENING, APRIL 20, 1906.—TWELVE PAGES.   ONE CENT.

GENERAL FUNSTON REPORTS FIRE IS PARTIALLY UNDER CONTROL;
CITY OF SAN FRANCISCO NOW ONLY A BLACKENED RUIN

AT LEAST ONE SECTION OF STRICKEN TOWN LIKELY TO ESCAPE DEVOURING FLAMES

work with patience. The great story of the San Francisco disaster is yet to come. It will never be all told. There will be as many versions of thousands of tragedies as there were people in the stricken city.

AS THE DESTRUCTION GOES ON.

Pitiful Scenes Witnessed Amid Ruins of Wrecked City.

Oakland, Cal., April 20.—San Francisco is apparently gone. To the west, across the bay, there is nothing but a great cloud of smoke, shot with streams of fire and shaken now and

ing rooms. Shelter seems to have come more easily than food. Not an ounce of supplies, of course, has come in for two days, and most of the permanent stores are in the hands of the soldiers, who dole them out to all comers alike. But the hungry can not always find the military stores and the news has not got about, since there are no newspapers and no regular means of communication.

An Italian tells me that he was taken in by a family living in a three-story house in the fashionable Pacific avenue. There were twenty refugees who passed the night in the drawing room of that house whose mistress took down hangings to make them comfortable. In the morning all the

far out of town that it must be spared, is crowded, even to mattresses on the floors. Many bodies were left in the ruin of the Valencia Hotel on Seventeenth and Valencia streets, and were consumed in the flames. In fact, this must happen all over the city. Anyone who knows San Francisco must realize that in the first tumble of Market street many little, crazy structures must have gone by the board. Each of these probably buried its two or three victims, and now the hot rush of flames has come over the district, so that bodies will be consumed utterly. For this reason it is unlikely that anyone will ever know just how many people were killed. An estimate of

GRAPHIC DESCRIPTIONS OF EVENTS THAT FOLLOWED THE UPHEAVALS IN RUINED CITY

Gas main explosions caused streets to collapse and made automobile passage hazardous.

Shattered 16-inch water main at Seventh and Howard Streets.

Army Captain Le Vert Coleman and members of the dynamite squad reconnoitered Van Ness Avenue on the morning of April 19.

(Continued from page 66)
conflagrations to have been useless, and, in the opinion of prominent fire chiefs and experts, even harmful." But without water, the firefighters had no other weapon, and dynamiting along fire lines continued to the end of the conflagration.

Early in the day, the fire had been blown across Eighth Street by dynamiting. Battalion Chief John J. Conlon and his men had never used the explosive, and a railroad foreman brought the first sticks from the Southern Pacific Company yards from Baden, near San Bruno, where construction of the Bayshore cutoff was underway. Chief Conlon wrote, "My experience with dynamite did not prove entirely satisfactory, due to the fact that up to this time I had never been called upon to use high grade explosives; therefore I relied upon the [Southern Pacific] foreman who represented himself as having had experience in this line, to do the necessary dynamiting. I recall in one instance, that after dynamiting the two frame buildings facing Eighth Street, next to the northeast corner of Harrison Street, we placed a case of dynamite on the east side of each floor, of the three story frame building [next door] . . . and attempted to fall this frame house into the premises previously dynamited. We failed in this however, the building was blown in the opposite direction into the street."

Mayor Schmitz, Acting Chief Engineer Dougherty and Police Chief Dinan maintained headquarters at the Hall of Justice opposite Portsmouth Square through the morning. It was here that the mayor assembled a group of prominent citizens later called the "Committee of Fifty" at 3 p.m.

In the next hour it became clear that further meetings had to be held elsewhere because of the approaching fires. A block and a half from Portsmouth Square in narrow Leidesdorff Street, lodging houses and print shops were dynamited in an attempt to create a firebreak, but this only started another blaze.

The San Francisco Fire Department had appealed to the Army for help almost immediately after the earthquake and before General Funston's handwritten notes reached either Fort Mason or the Presidio.

Captain Le Vert Coleman of the Artillery Corps at the Presidio wrote: "About 6:30 a.m. the morning of the earthquake April 18, 1906, the Fire Department of the City of San Francisco sent a messenger to the Presidio requesting that all available explosives with a detail to handle them be sent to check the fire as the earthquake had broken the water mains and the fire department was practically helpless. I reported with the messenger to the Commanding Officer Colonel Morris, A. C., who ordered me as Ordnance Officer to provide the necessary explosives. I then sent about forty-eight barrels of powder in field battery caissons under the charge of 1st Lieu-

Harried refugees pushed and pulled trunks along Van Ness Avenue, as the Army prepared to blow up buildings.

Refugees at Golden Gate Avenue and Leavenworth Street at 8 a.m. on April 19.

Nearly-starved horse pulled a wagon filled with refugees to the Ferry Building. Local entrepeneurs began private transit service between the refugee camps and the ferries because of the destruction of the streetcar and cable systems. Twenty-five cents was five times the normal fare.

tenant Raymond W. Briggs, A. C., to the Mayor.

"As the caissons were not suited to carrying large amounts of explosives I procured two large wagons, and, having loaded them with the remaining powder and with about 300 pounds of dynamite procured from the civilian employees of the Engineering Department – the only dynamite procurable at that time – reported to the Commanding Officer Colonel Charles Morris, A. C., on O'Farrell Street. By his orders I immediately proceeded to the Hall of Justice and reported to the Mayor.

"Here I found Lieutenant Briggs with the powder I had sent, and also a large supply of dynamite provided by Mr. Birmingham [John Bermingham, President] of the California Powder Works. General Funston, and the Mayor, who were both present at the time, placed me in charge of the work of handling all the explosives.

"At this time Lieutenant Briggs had begun dynamiting buildings on Montgomery Street under orders from the Mayor, and a Captain of the Fire Department who was also dynamiting buildings on Montgomery Street. Mr. Birmingham was ordered by the Mayor

to report to me – he was a civilian expert on explosives – unfortunately he was so far under the influence of liquor as to be of no service, and lest he should be in that condition cause serious accident, I sent him away."

Mayor Schmitz left the Hall of Justice and patrolled the scene, while Lieutenant Briggs placed the charges. Lieutenant Briggs later complained that the dynamiting was doomed from the beginning because the expected firebreaks were too close to burning buildings. But Mayor Schmitz was still not convinced that such desperate measures were necessary. Some of the buildings along Montgomery and Kearny Streets near Bush were owned by his political supporters and he didn't want to destroy them unless absolutely necessary.

The mayor chose to compromise. Lieutenant Briggs was allowed to dynamite buildings only if they were "about to burn."

By 5 p.m. Portsmouth Plaza was a ghastly scene of desolation. Graves had been dug by police for the fifty or more corpses of earthquake victims haphazardly stacked in the morgue and the police pistol range, and

more bodies arrived as they dug.

Troops of the 22nd Infantry garrisoned around the Appraiser's Building on Washington Street were pulling down frame buildings with ropes to create a firebreak and were, at the same time, looting liquor and grocery stores around the Montgomery Block. Remarkably, the officers of the 22nd Infantry saw little of the looting. Captain Orrin R. Wolfe and Company D were detailed to the nearby Custom House to fight the fire, and the transcript of his testimony in one looting case is illuminating. Questions were asked by Colonel J. L. Chamberlain, Inspector-General of the Department of California:

Q. "What was the character of your orders on the morning of April 18th?

A. My orders were to proceed to the Custom House and use my discretion; I understood these orders to mean that my duty was to protect the Custom House and any United States property; there was also an adjoining sub-post-office station on Jackson street a few doors from Sansome and I placed a guard over that.

Q. Was there much drunkenness among your men during the period that you were on

A young man demonstrated how refugees used any conveyance to transport precious posssessions away from the fire.

Refugees fled to Jefferson Square Park on the afternoon of April 18. The Lutheran Church at Gough and Eddy Streets is in the background.

Soldiers in front of tents pitched in Jefferson Square Park on Eddy Street near Gough Street.

duty at the Custom House?

A. Very little indeed – one or two men were under the influence; there was more or less drinking as was natural since the whole community was a bar-room and liquor was flowing like water, but I saw no man of my company, nor of Captain Berry's company [D. G. Berry of Company K], that was so drunk that he could not walk, and only two or three who were not able to perform their duties at all times. . . ."

"On April 18th, when I went to the Custom House it appeared that we were marching into a wall of fire and there were crowds on the street, everybody was panic-stricken and people were backing away from the fire and carrying things in wagons, rushing here and there loaded down and I particularly noticed, as I was standing on the corner of Washington and Sansome streets, that wagons were backed up to the sidewalks on each side and the people were loading stuff into them and hurrying away."

Colonel Chamberlain's questioning of James Willway Treadwell, an eccentric banker who stayed in the Montgomery Block through the entire fire, brought a different perspective to the looting charges:

Q. "Did the soldiers and others continue to enter these buildings by the windows right on from day to day for some time?

A. They were going in and out at all times except when the officers were coming to pass the word along to post the guard – then they would skip out like rats from a trap – I don't think that the officers ever saw them.

Q. Did you see the soldiers carrying goods out of Rinaldo's store [300 Battery Street at Sacramento]?

A. I saw the soldiers carrying out cigar boxes, loaded under their arms, 10 or 20 boxes, as much as they could carry.

Q. Did you see them coming out [of] any other specific store?

A. Yes, out of Raggi's [James Raggi, 624 Montgomery Street] – that place was a regular pandemonium – the floor was covered with broken bottles, champagne bottles, etc."

Mr. Treadwell's memory was refreshed by entries from a diary he kept during the fire.

He lived in a room in the Montgomery Block, and during the earthquake he wrote, "I had stood at the window of room 310 on the 3rd floor and saw 7 horses and 3 men killed dead" in the shock.

Later, he noted a man "with his arms and hands burned in the fire, his skin hanging down like rags. Man sat down on Washington Street and I went down to Garbini's store to get some oil for his hands . . . I bandaged his arms and oiled them."

At about 8 p.m., Mayor Schmitz was still confident that a good part of downtown could be saved. The north side of Market, from Kearny to Taylor Streets, was untouched by the inferno across the street. Behind this stretch of mainly steel-frame buildings lay the theater and shopping districts, Union Square, and the apartment-house district beyond. Here were large shops, clothing stores, and several major hotels.

But two events occurred that effectively ended any possibility of controlling the spreading fires. First, evening breezes picked up and came in from the south. Worse, a new, possibly man-made, fire erupted near the very center of the supposedly protected area.

Fire at Market and Taylor Streets at 3 o'clock on the morning of April 19.

Fire has laid waste to Market Street in this photograph taken 24 hours after the earthquake.

Fire from the electric generating plant behind St. Patrick's Church burned through the Winchester House at Third and Stevenson Streets. The small wood-frame restaurant on the corner collapsed in the earthquake and several occupants were killed. The earthquake-damaged Hearst Building is on the right, the Call Building on the left.

One contemporary account places the blame on soldiers cooking in the wreckage of the Delmonico Restaurant, housed in the four-story Alcazar Theater building; the front of the Alcazar had been sheared away by the earthquake. Another account has it that the fire was deliberately set by an enemy of building owner M. H. de Young, publisher of the *San Francisco Chronicle*. Like a parachute attack behind enemy lines, the Delmonico Restaurant fire immediately disorganized resistance around the perimeter.

In the financial district to the east, the huge Merchants' Exchange Building was burning from the upper floors. Across California at Montgomery Street the lower floors of the Kohl Building, perhaps the best modern "fireproof" structure in the city, were ablaze. Further west on Montgomery Street, the Mills Building was about to catch fire after its windows were blown out by dynamite.

At Goldberg, Bowen's on Sutter Street, wagons lined up under the protection of troops to remove the store's vast assortment of groceries for relief use.

Shortly after the Delmonico Restaurant ignited, reporter Hopper made a survey of the eye of the fire burning across Market Street, at the Palace Hotel. "There was a lull in the wind," he wrote, "and before me the Palace and Grand Hotels were burning with a sort of quiet mournfulness. Suddenly, the great Crocker Building on the north side of the street began to burn, slowly, one window-shade here, one window-shade there, with a sort of flippant deliberation. Then, with a roar, the flames poured out all the openings."

Unknown to Mr. Hopper, this last holdout of the major downtown buildings had been attacked from the west and north. The Hayes Valley fire was about to join with the Delmonico Restaurant fire.

At 9 p.m., firefighters tried to make a new stand on Powell between Sutter and Pine Streets where there were several empty lots. For a few hours this seemed successful. The Delmonico Restaurant fire was kept from spreading up O'Farrell Street. Union Square in front of the St. Francis Hotel was a natural fire barrier, and at midnight, firefighters held the inferno somewhat in check.

The firefront ranged from Montgomery Avenue (now named Columbus Avenue), to the Hall of Justice, along Dupont Street (Grant Avenue), and to the western slopes of Nob Hill. Ornate wooden mansions on those slopes were abandoned in the early hours of Thursday.

Mark Hopkins Institute of Art, formerly the home of one of the "Big Four" railroad magnates, was the object of a rescue party of students from the University of California led by its president, Benjamin Ide Wheeler. Many important paintings were saved, cut from their frames. But many others left in front of the Flood mansion diagonally across the street were destroyed by the fire the next day.

As the Fire Underwriters' report noted, the growing wind from the south and the upward slope of Nob Hill created ideal conditions for the further rapid spread of the fire from Union Square. There was no further chance of using Powell Street as a firebreak. Fire jumped Powell Street at O'Farrell after midnight, and then burned the apartment houses on Bush Street an hour later. At 2:30 Thursday morning, the St. Francis Hotel finally caught fire. There was now nothing to stop the inferno from burning all the way to Van Ness Avenue, seven city blocks away.

Acting Chief Engineer John Dougherty tried to hold out at Mason and California Streets with what water was left in the Spring Valley water tank at Clay and Jones Streets. The Committee of Fifty met again at the Fairmont Hotel before midnight and then left Nob Hill because of the fire danger.

Mayor Schmitz remained to watch the defense of Nob Hill for another three hours. But the fire rising from Mason and Powell Streets threatened the Hopkins mansion from two sides, despite a steady stream of water played on the huge structure. U. S. Marines and sailors helped exhausted San Francisco firefighters in the vain hope that at least the stone Flood mansion and the granite Fairmont Hotel could be saved.

Water supplied to hydrants by the Spring Valley tank at Clay and Jones Streets finally ran out. Mayor Schmitz and Captain Magner of Fire Engine No. 3 found a cistern at the Hopkins mansion in the early morning, but that water, too, was soon exhausted. At 4 a.m., Lieutenant Freeman arrived with a party from the "Active" to find the hill deserted and the Stanford home next to the Hopkins mansion beginning to smoulder.

Thursday's dawn brought a greater shock to the earthquake survivors. The future of San Francisco hung in the balance if the conflagration could not be stopped at Van Ness Avenue. Further, there were rumors circulating that if home owners had earthquake damage no insurance money would be paid unless the building burned. Signal Corps Captain Wildman heard from a firefighter on the waterfront that people along Howard Street had torched their quake-damaged houses in hopes of collecting fire insurance.

To Mayor Schmitz and the Army, the only way to stop the conflagration was with the drastic use of dynamite. There were many dynamiters at work. Captain Coleman and Lieutenant Briggs headed the Army squads; the National Guard of California was assisting the fire department's effort to blast another firebreak along Fourteenth Street; the Navy had its dynamiters working along the waterfront and the Mission District.

With the mayor's approval, the intoxicated John Bermingham carted a load of explosives through Chinatown and the Barbary Coast and had, as he later testified in court, managed to start 60 fires with dynamite. Lieuten-

Hopkins Institute of Art on fire at 11 a.m. on April 19.

Wreck of the Fairmont Hotel after the fire. Nearly all of the interior steel frame was replaced because of severe fire damage caused by lack of adequate fire-proofing.

ant Freeman, working his way up to the top of Nob Hill, told an *Oakland Tribune* reporter "at least 20 Chinese, opium fiends and drunks were blown up by dynamite." Several mangled bodies were found in Chinatown's ruins and, "in at least one building 5 or 6 bodies were thrown 50 feet into the air and back into the flames." And there were vague, disquieting reports of building owners who wanted to dynamite their own structures.

J. Dalzell Brown, vice president and manager of the Safe Deposit and Trust Company at California and Montgomery Streets had systematically embezzled from his bank for some years before the earthquake. During the fire, Mr. Brown went to the waterfront to find Thomas Crowley, founder of Crowley Maritime. In a 1967 oral history interview with Karl Kortum and Willa Klug Baum, Mr. Crowley said, "He wanted me to go up and get three or four cases of dynamite. I tried my damnedest to keep away from doing it. He kept after me and there was nothing that I could do because I was banking with him. . . ."

The nearest available dynamite was at the powder works at Pinole or Hercules, and Mr. Crowley dispatched a tug to run Mr. Brown's errand.

When the dynamite was delivered two days later, Mr. Crowley went to Mr. Brown's home at 2231 Washington Street. "I told him I had the dynamite. He said, 'Well, you got it in too late.' I said, 'I told you that beforehand.' I said, 'What am I going to do with dynamite?' He said, 'You can do whatever you want with it. It is your funeral.' I said, 'No it isn't. It's your funeral.' He said, 'How do you mean?'"

Mr. Crowley told Mr. Brown, "If you don't pay me for the trouble that I have gone to and you don't take the dynamite . . . I know what you wanted to use the dynamite for. You were going to blow up this building. Then your records would have gone with it and you would have been in the clear. He damn near died when I told him that. Then he made some kind of deal with me; I forget what it was."

J. Dalzell Brown, a member of Mayor Schmitz' Committee of Fifty, was later indicted by the Grand Jury after bank examiners found that the Safe Deposit and Trust Company had been looted by its officers.

A second significant problem confronting Mayor Schmitz on Thursday morning was how to coordinate the overall response to the catastrophe. General Funston had brought troops from every Army garrison in the West, and Governor Pardee had called up the entire National Guard of California. And the mayor had been persuaded to swear in private citizens as special police, which effec-

tively turned what was left of San Francisco into an armed camp.

But decisions about the very fate of the city had to be made. After a quick meeting at the North End Police Station at 1712 Washington Street, the mayor's Committee of Fifty was sure of only one thing: they had to retreat even farther from the advancing fire lines. The inferno had already engulfed the Fairmont Hotel on the crest of Nob Hill, only a few blocks from the police station. The seat of government moved again, this time to Franklin Hall, a mile west into the Western Addition at Bush and Steiner Streets.

There was some good news. The Navy's Pacific Squadron was also enroute to San Francisco, after Admiral Caspar Goodrich was notified of the disaster by the operator of an experimental De Forest wireless station near San Diego. General Funston, Colonel Charles Morris and Captain Coleman had also prepared a drastic plan to stop the fire: cut a 50 yard-wide swath along the east side of Van Ness Avenue from Sacramento Street to Golden Gate Avenue. General Funston argued this drastic measure was not only necessary to stop the fire from burning into the Western Addition, but also protect the Army's Fort Mason and the Presidio beyond.

There were also incessant complaints to the mayor about the conduct of the troops,

Buildings at Third and Market Streets are attacked by the fire. This photograph looks south from about Bush and Montgomery Streets. The San Francisco Chronicle

Building in the center of the photograph was badly damaged during the earthquake when Linotype machines fell during the shock. The structure to the left

of the San Francisco Chronicle Building is the new Monadnock Building.

who kept residents and merchants from their homes and businesses. Photographer Arnold Genthe bribed a soldier with a bottle of fine wine to rescue a few possessions from his Sacramento Street apartment – several hours before it was in danger of fire. R. B. Hale, owner of the famous Hale Brothers department store, railed at the mayor for depriving citizens of the right to salvage their own belongings or protect them from fire.

Panic began to spread among the refugees as one avenue of escape after another began to close. Dazed refugees moved away from the expanding fire lines and thousands of them dragged their pathetic belongings to Golden Gate Park and the Ocean Beach. Others went out the Mission Road in the direction of the peninsula. Other refugees camped around the Southern Pacific Company yards and still thousands of others went to the military reservations in the Western Addition. Drayage men and boat owners seized upon the helplessness of the population to extract the highest prices they could. The privileged had family and relatives taken from the burning city by special boat. Boatman Thomas Crowley ferried the parents of Abraham Ruef to the German steamer "Uarda," where they stayed for the duration of the fire.

Though the Ferry Building tower was in imminent danger of collapse, the threat of fire was over by Thursday morning. But the sheer number of refugees, who jammed against the gates along the docks, panicked even the ferry operators. Men strong-armed anyone in the way – women, children, the sick, the injured. Some men waved guns and demanded to be let aboard the ferries.

Panic and confusion at the Ferry Building was further compounded by horrendous stories of atrocities – of fingers cut from the dead for their rings, of the bayonetting of looters, of executions of innocent people by the military. There were rumors of pestilence, of hordes of rats rampaging from Chinatown's ruptured sewers, of drunken soldiers running amok in abandoned saloons.

Even before his impromptu meeting with the Committee of Fifty on Thursday morning, Mayor Schmitz had the common sense to appreciate the danger of thirst and hunger.

In the desolate stretches of the Southern Pacific Company yards, women gave liquor to children to quench their thirst, and members of the 22nd Infantry began systematic looting of the freight cars. An Army inspector-general's report said, "It appears that some of the men under Sergeant E. G. Mundorf, 61st Co., Coast Artillery, obtained whiskey from the cars guarded by the infantry men of Lieutenant [Russell V.] Venable's company,

but the special policemen and other employees of the S. P. Co. also looted the whiskey cars and furnished whiskey to the enlisted men."

This report also pointed to "the energetic work of Captain D. E. Aultman, Artillery Corps, commanding 67th Co. Coast Artillery . . . in protecting cars and S. P. Co. property, in preventing looting and arresting the artillery detachment of the 61st and 68th Companies, Coast Artillery, deserves commendation."

Twenty members of the National Guard of California were also caught looting Chinatown and arrested by the Army, and Thomas P. McGinn, of the guard's Company A, was arrested for attempting to assassinate Chief of Police Dinan and later adjudged insane.

Lieutenant Freeman reported about Thursday morning's situation, "At this time there was no water on the waterfront and the suffering was intense." Tens of thousands of other refugees were huddled in Golden Gate Park, public squares, school yards, on sand dunes at the Ocean Beach, and at Fort Mason and the Presidio. All were virtually without food, water or shelter.

Refugees further panicked when soldiers and Marines in the Western Addition and Marina suddenly entered closed saloons and grocery stores and began to smash barrels

Fires burned along both sides of Market Street on the afternoon of April 18.

and bottles of liquor. They went from saloon to saloon. kicking in doors and breaking windows to get at the liquor. To the refugees, this was an example of a military out of control, and they were frightened.

These soldiers were armed with *General Orders No. 1*, issued by Colonel Charles Morris from his district headquarters at 2000 Broadway. This unusual order read: "All liquor, except beer, shall be immediately seized and poured into the gutter of the ground so that it cannot be imbibed. The Commanding Officers shall send details of men under Commissioned Officers for this purpose to places where liquor can be found." Morris' explanation for this order was elegantly simple and pragmatic. "I ordered the destruction of intoxicating liquor 'Wherever it could be found,' or words to that effect," he wrote, "it being, in my judgement, an imperative necessity to do so in order to safeguard the lives of homeless and defenseless men, women, and children. Rioting and drunkenness by a turbulent element were already rife at places where liquor was procurable, and it was only through prompt and energetic action that such disorders were quelled in their incipiency.

"As a district commander I was expected and required to preserve order in my district; to do so I was compelled to remove every discovered cause that would logically result in disorder. The police had vanished from the streets. . . .

"Furthermore, I could not risk the incapacitating of my soldiers through drunkenness, for this would seriously have weakened the only available power for preserving order, nor could I hope to deal effectively with widespread drunkenness among civilians, there being no place to confine unruly persons. Moreover, prevailing intemperance would unquestionably have precipitated street fights and riots, involving the certainty of much bloodshed, for those were days when if shots were to be fired, they must have been fired, not to intimidate, but to kill. . . .

"An incident occurring but a few hours after the publication of my order, will serve to indicate, at once, the feeling of unrest and insecurity prevailing among the most prominent and highly respected residents of the Western Addition, and likewise the satisfaction occasioned by my order among this most reputable class of citizens.

"I was waited upon at my headquarters on Broadway by a committee of highly respected residents of the district, who stated they had learned on good authority that the poor who had been burned out, felt that the rich had not suffered losses as had the poor, and were therefore determined to invade the Western Addition and lay it waste by incendiarism and attendant acts of spoil, looting and violence. I completely reassured this committee by informing them of the precautionary measures, particularly as regarded

Burned body of a looter lay at the intersection of Post Street and Grant Avenue. According to police department records, the man had attempted to burglarize Shreve's Jewelers just before the troops arrived down-town. He was caught by the crowd and turned over to a soldier who then shot him. The body was left to burn in the intersection.

Temporary graves in Washington Square. Below, a fresh plot is prepared by a gravedigger.

Before the flames, throughout the night, fled tens of thousands of homeless ones.
— Jack London

Dead body of a fire victim huddled in the ruins.

Anxious family on hillside keeps an eye on the progress of downtown fires.

Graveside service for Anna Alemany Butler of the Salvation Army who was killed in her home at 913 Natoma Street. The big smokestack of a former United Railroads powerhouse fell upon several houses on the south side of the 900 block of Natoma Street and killed or injured most of the residents.

the destruction of liquor, adopted to safeguard the lives and property of the people residing in my district.

"I am convinced, that the spirit of the poorer classes being as represented, prevalent drunkenness would have led unavoidably to the gravest disorders. When it became known that no liquor was to be had, it is a notorious fact that this intelligence occasioned universal satisfaction and gratifying reassurance to all concerned, except, of course, to the intemperates. Prohibition, pure and simple, was my unqualified aim and object. I certainly intended to convey this idea when my order, or its context, was telephoned to Department Headquarters for authority to use it."

General Funston seemed genuinely taken aback when he found out what had been done in the name of the Army, and wrote that Colonel Morris had committed a grave error of judgment.

"On the night of April 19th, during the progress of the fire, I was at Fort Mason and received a telephone message from Colonel Morris, asking if I would authorize the destruction of liquor. I did not go to the telephone myself, but the message was brought to me by some officer whom I cannot now recall. I replied in the affirmative; but took it for granted that Colonel Morris meant liquor that was in the streets or being used or in saloons that were open and it never occurred to me that he would construe my message as indicating that he could break into saloons or groceries and destroy liquor found therein. I was astounded when I learned that he had taken the view that he evidentially did."

U. S. Marine Corps 1st Lieutenant Sidney W. Brewster, one of those officers detailed to enforce Colonel Morris' order, was aware of the need of *General Orders No. 1.* In his report to the Commandant of the Mare Island Naval Station, he wrote, "A squad of men under my command entered the saloon of P. Boragni, 1840-1846 Union St., seized whatever liquor there was there and destroyed it. The saloon is divided into two portions, storeroom and bar, I entered the storeroom first and then went to the bar, where I found a number of soldiers and civilians drinking liquor, had them ejected from the saloon and placed a sentry over the door until all liquor was destroyed. . . ."

"Saloon of Miller and Peterson, 1942 Filbert St., this place was entered and looted, the proprietor stating, by members of the California National Guard, who took most of the liquor. What liquor was left was destroyed by the detail under me, estimate value of liquor destroyed, $50.00 to $75.00.

"Saloon of C. Barner, 3001 Laguna St. This place was entered and looted, the proprietor stating, by enlisted men of the U. S. Army, members of the National Guard and Municipal Police. What liquor was left was destroyed

(Continued on page 80)

Some people stood on the roof of the Fairmont Hotel (left) to watch the sweep of the fire. An artist has retouched this photograph, taken from the Hopkins Institute of Art, to remove much of the evidence of the earthquake, and to highlight the clouds of smoke. The Hall of Justice tower was redrawn in this picture.

Panorama of the burning city as seen from the roof of the Mills Building on the northeast corner of Montgomery and Bush Streets.

View of the fire as it burned toward California Street. This photograph was taken from the Merchants' Exchange Building at 431 California Street near Sansome Street.

Within an hour of the earthquake shock the smoke of San Francisco's burning was a lurid tower visible a hundred miles away.
— Jack London

The smoke-pall viewed from beneath, was a rose color that pulsed and fluttered with lavender shades. There was no sun. And so dawned the second day on stricken San Francisco.
— Jack London

An oil tank at Meiggs Wharf burned on the last day of the Great Fire.

(Continued from page 77)
by detail under myself. Estimate value of liquor destroyed, $250.00 to $300.00.

"Saloon of P. Fraysee, 2300 Union St. This place was entered, the proprietor stating, by members of the California National Guard, who took most of the liquor. What liquor was left was destroyed by detail under me, estimate value of liquor destroyed $250.00 to $300.00.

"Saloon of L. Macroit, 2154 Filbert St. This place was entered and looted, the proprietor stating, by members of the California National Guard and Municipal Police. . . ."

Seizure and destruction of liquor and beer was of grave concern to Major-General Greely, who later investigated the hundreds of damage claims against the U. S. Army. He wrote Secretary of War Taft to say, "While not versed in the intricacies of the law yet I am of the opinion that the destruction of liquors under lock and key was illegal and improper. As to the destruction of liquors in open grocery and liquor stores or indeed elsewhere, it appears questionable as to whether the destruction of such liquors was justified by the emergencies unless the dealer had been formally notified to close his stores and saloons, in which cases action might properly have been taken by the officers in charge."

Refugees crowded into the Mission District also began to panic. After the Southern Pacific Company managed to repair its main track out of San Francisco, the first passenger cars were mobbed as they rolled through the Mission District along Harrison Street. Thousands of refugees crawled in and onto the cars; every inch of every piece of rolling stock was occupied by human beings who wanted to flee the burning city.

By the time the fire was over, the Southern Pacific Company train and ferry service alone would carry away 225,000 refugees from San Francisco in 96 hours, the largest peacetime evacuation of any American city.

The question of "who was in charge" was still a problem a day and a half after the earthquake. This was underscored by Lieutenant Freeman's uncertainty of his, and General Funston's, constitutional authority in the disaster. "From rumors which reached me I learned that the military was in control," he wrote.

To find out the exact line of authority, Lieutenant Freeman took the "Active" to Fort Mason and reported to General Funston on conditions along the waterfront. General Funston placed the Navy lieutenant in charge of a contingent of U. S. Marines and instructed him to continue his authority over the waterfront.

To Midshipman Pond, the general had no alternative. "For four days and nights following the 'quake I did not see a single uniformed policeman anywhere in the entire waterfront district of San Francisco. From the time of our arrival Wednesday morning until early Saturday, our small force, which consisted mostly of the crews of the Perry, Active, and Leslie, and a handful of Marines, had not only to fight fire, but to police and patrol the districts in which we worked. With the exception of the officers, who carried revolvers, our force was unarmed, although later during the week we obtained a few arms and organized a waterfront patrol."

After a morning of hesitation and distraction by problems of food and water shortages throughout the city, problems with the military and the terribly disorganized police and fire departments, the mayor and General Funston met that afternoon at Fort Mason where Funston convinced Schmitz of the desperate need to sacrifice Van Ness Avenue as the final line of defense.

This plan called for the Army to cut a firebreak using dynamite and backfires. Every soldier, every National Guardsmen, every member of the Navy that could be spared, and every fire engine available would be brought up to Van Ness Avenue to take the Great Fire head on.

Neither Mayor Schmitz nor General Funston were fully aware of what was occurring out in the Mission District; the defenders there were effectively on their own. For now, the last major part of the city, the Western Addition and the military outposts were threatened – everything from Fort Mason to the Presidio to Fort Miley on the way to the Cliff House, and from there to Golden Gate Park. General Funston's last telegram to the War Department that day expressed the opinion that the whole city would burn.

The search for more dynamite took on a renewed urgency when the fire swept over Jones, Leavenworth and Hyde Streets to the west as it crossed Sutter Street. Firefighters did find some functioning hydrants in this area, but the fire was too intense. They were driven out – barely saving the fire apparatus.

Lieutenant Briggs was aboard the tug "Priscilla," steaming to a dynamite plant at Pinole at the northeast end of the bay. Lieutenant Freeman diverted the launch "Independence," with a small supply of dynamite, to Meigg's Wharf at the foot of Powell Street, with orders to report to Mayor Schmitz who had been finally forced to accept the need to demolish and backfire the entire eastern stretch of Van Ness Avenue from Fort Mason to Sacramento Street.

The Great Fire descending on Van Ness Avenue had a wind-driven, mile-wide front. The day of waiting – of firefighters snatching sleep in the streets and on lawns – was over. As a contemporary account put it, the fire "came on, an angry, terrible power, before which men bowed their heads and trembled."

From every vantage point west of Van Ness Avenue – the steps of St. Mary's Cathedral, at Jefferson Square Park, at Lafayette Park – citizens whose homes were in flames, or in danger, watched as the head-on battle against the Great Fire began.

Block by block, Eddy to Ellis Street, to O'Farrell to Geary Street, the Army demolition crews launched the counterattack with dynamite. Mansions and churches fell and torches of kerosene rags were hurled into the buildings to set back fires.

Another long relay of fire hose, this time from the Army tug "General Slocum," brought salt water nearly one mile up Van Ness Avenue, almost to Sacramento Street. From the south, hydrants were functioning at Golden Gate Avenue and Buchanan Street and firefighters were making efficient use of that limited water supply.

Now Post Street, now Sutter, now Bush, now Pine. Members of the Committee of Fifty watched impassively as their businesses or homes, or those of friends or enemies, were shattered by dynamite and burned. And still the fire moved north and west, running a race along Van Ness Avenue to outflank the dynamiters. Well into the night the fight continued, and the line seemed to be holding.

The running dispute over "who was in charge" between military and civilian authorities intensified as the battle of Van Ness Avenue went on. It was the classic turf battle, except the turf in this case was San Francisco and San Francisco was burning to the ground.

Though Mayor Schmitz and General Funston agreed on strategy at their Fort Mason meeting, now there was a breakdown in fire fighting tactics. After much haggling, it was decided that Acting Chief Engineer Dougherty was in charge of operations along Van Ness Avenue, according to Frank Nichols, captain of Fire Engine No. 4, who witnessed the heated discussion in the street.

National Guard of California Brigadier-General John Koster believed the mayor to be in charge, and he claimed that he, Koster, had received orders for dynamiting along Van Ness Avenue directly from Schmitz.

General Koster complained bitterly about the confusion. "During the time in which the [National Guard of California] troops were engaged in clearing streets, much opposition to the plan of action was interposed by the chiefs of the Police and Fire departments. I strongly urged upon these officials the advisability of presenting the objections to the Mayor, to enable him to modify or change his orders if such conclusion should be ar-

Wreckage of the Kamm Building at 716 Market Street. The rear of the structure was badly damaged by the *earthquake which caused a partial collapse of the interior.*

rived at. The time for the accomplishment of this was ample, but neither of these officials appeared sufficiently interested in my recommendation.

"When ready to proceed with the work of dynamiting, the wagon containing the explosive had been removed from the position assigned to it by me, and could not again be located. It is presumed that, being a portion of the equipment of the Fire Department, the same was withdrawn by direction of the chief of this department in order to prevent the carrying out of the Mayor's orders. After a lapse of considerable valuable time, during which the conflagration was rapidly approaching the [Van Ness] avenue, a quantity of dynamite was obtained from a quarry in the Mission District and the work proceeded with."

The report of Le Vert Coleman, the artillery captain in charge of dynamiting for the Army, criticized city authorities who refused to give permission for full-scale dynamite operations. "During the first day of the fire, and until the evening of the second day, the city authorities withheld their permission to blow up buildings except those in immediate

contact with those already ablaze. Consequently, although we were able to check the fire at certain points, it outflanked my party time and again, and all our work had to be done over. . . ."

"On Thursday night, the 19th of April, when the fire reached Van Ness Avenue, I received authority from Colonel Morris to use my judgment in the demolition of buildings in the burning district. After this we blew up buildings far enough ahead of the fire to make a clearing along Broadway, Franklin, Gough Street, etc., which the fire was unable to bridge, and in this manner the fire stopped after it had crossed the broad Avenue of Van Ness and the Fire Department seemed powerless.

"Had not this course been pursued in accordance with the authority from the District Commander, Colonel Morris, the fire would unquestionably have destroyed the present unburnt portion of the city, in the same manner and for the same reasons that it devoured the burnt districts, after crossing the broad thoroughfares of Market Street, Van Ness, and others, where authority was not granted to clear a bare space sufficiently broad to arrest the course of the flames."

From Captain Coleman's report it is clear that Colonel Morris resolved the turf war between General Funston and Mayor Schmitz. Colonel Morris, alone, was responsible for approving the tactics to be used to stop the Great Fire along Van Ness Avenue.

At 5 a.m. Friday, the fire invaded the Western Addition as far as Franklin Street and had circled south down Franklin rather than moving west against the wind. A single fire hose from the hydrant at Golden Gate Avenue and Buchanan Street was passed hand-to-hand as firefighters reeled in exhaustion and fell back. Again, the dynamiters came, this time backing up to Gough Street for one last desperate stand.

Even with the terrible damage to the distribution system within the city, the Spring Valley Water Company was able to pump Lake Merced water to the Western Addition within 14 hours of the earthquake. This was the water supply responsible for continued operation of fire hydrants along Buchanan Street in the Western Addition.

The Great Fire was stopped that morning at Gough and Sutter Streets, blown out by dynamite – smothered – shorn of its power. "The city tottered on the edge of a complete disaster," wrote reporter Paul Ditzel. In the end, firefighters tore shingles by hand from burning roofs, threw horse blankets over embers, to finally stop the progress of the in-ferno. Shortly after Friday's dawn, Mayor Schmitz sent a telegram to the War Department that said the city was no longer in danger from fire. It was a dreadful mistake.

During the night, the fire line along Green Street at Van Ness Avenue was broken when the Viavi chemical warehouse was dynamited. Later that morning, the winds shifted back to the west and all at once the fire was alive and moving back toward Russian Hill and beyond – all of previously untouched North Beach was in its path. This residential area had not been evacuated, and there was true and absolute panic.

The fire quickly swept up the eastern slopes of Russian Hill and all the way down to Meigg's Wharf at the foot of Taylor Street. Escape to the west was not possible.

To the east, Telegraph Hill was about to be overrun by the fire Lieutenant Freeman tried to stop the previous evening. He found that dynamite was insufficient against this new threat. One city block was burning every half hour, in spite of the two wagon loads of dynamite he had used along Broadway.

Lieutenant Freeman, along with members of his crew and the remnants of the San Francisco Fire Department, almost pulled off the impossible when they were able to run a one-mile stretch of hose line from the waterfront, over the crest of Telegraph Hill, and into North Beach. Plagued by damaged hose and the overwhelming fire, this near-miracle was too little, too late.

This band of firefighters retreated to the waterfront, loading wagons with food and goods from the many shops in North Beach that were about to burn and took up a fire line between Vallejo and Filbert Streets, under the bluff of the hill.

Here, a company of U. S. Marines, augmented by citizens impressed into service at gunpoint, invaded the cooperages and coal shops at the base of Telegraph Hill and tore them down.

When the "U.S.S. Chicago" arrived after a 500 mile trip up the Pacific Coast, Commander Charles J. Badger found Lieutenant Freeman and Navy tugs "Fortune," "Active," and "Leslie" together with "other State or private tugs fitted with pumping apparatus. Assistance was rendered this party by the 'Chicago' where possible. Food, hose, etc. etc. were furnished and men were detailed to take the places of those who became exhausted by hard and long continued work. In the early morning of the 21st the original party was almost entirely replaced from this ship."

Atop Telegraph Hill, citizens fended off evacuation orders given by intoxicated Army troops and saved a few houses with sacks and window curtains soaked in wine and a little water from an abandoned well.

Mother Superior Mary Josephine Hagarty, Superior General of the Presentation Order

Refugees gathered their belongings in front of the Ferry Building to await transportation out of the burning city.

Thousands of people jammed Clay Street as the conflagration jumped Sansome Street. The printing company of Phillips and Van Orden was located at 508 Clay Street.

in California, remained in the Order's convent at Powell and Greenwich Streets until it was almost too late to leave. "Throughout the day our friends and past pupils were coming into our garden to seek comfort in their terror of the advancing fire. We kept in the garden ourselves, especially those Sisters who had dread of earthquakes. We feared to go to bed as there were constant light quakes and the noise of the explosions in the burning stores, added to the dynamiting of the streets by the military to prevent the spread of the fire was terrifying."

Mother Superior heard from a neighbor that Abraham Ruef was on Stockton Street at the bay with a fire hose, and was told he said he would save North Beach. Mr. Ruef had taken the hose from one of the fire department hosecarts, much to the outrage of the firefighters. Lieutenant Freeman subsequently held the political boss of San Francisco at gunpoint and took the hose away from him.

Dynamite explosions rocked the convent and the Sisters prepared to leave. "The shock was terrific, explosion after explosion. It threw the Sisters off the chairs and brought the Reverend Mother down. She went out to see the progress of the fire. We went out also and took Father Cleary with us to look for a wagon or for the man who had promised us one. Father Cleary couldn't get one. We met the man driving fast up Powell Street. He shouted from the vehicle, 'I can't give you the wagon now, Sisters. They are burying the dead on the Plaza [Washington Square]. I must help remove people from there – the fire is on them.'" This rout of North Beach in the face of the firestorm left the streets littered with hundreds of dead, overrun by hot gases from the fire or by the fire itself. From Fort Mason to Pier 27, more than 30,000 people found themselves driven to the water's edge. Every ship, every scow, every rowboat was used to evacuate them off the piers and beaches. Lieutenant Freeman wrote, "people hysterically endeavoring to escape the flames" drove their teams at frantic speed across fire hoses and were restrained by armed sentries who had orders to shoot their horses.

"The city on the Fort Mason side of the harbor was, at this time, in full blaze," wrote Commander Badger of the "U.S.S. Chicago," "The buildings within the limits of the post were in danger. The air was filled with burning cinders which were blown by the wind far into the harbor and all the awnings on board had to be furled and the decks wet to prevent fire. Thousands of panic stricken, homeless and destitute people thronged the shore in the neighborhood of the Fort. Food was being supplied but there had not yet been time for any well organized system of distribution. Drinking water was difficult to find. All were eager to leave but no transportation was immediately available."

Historian Bailey Millard watched as tens-of-thousands of panicked refugees stood on the beaches, waiting for someone to rescue them from the sweeping firestorm. He wrote, "About us was every conceivable kind of craft, full-freighted with refugees, bound for Sausalito, Belvedere, Tiburon, Napa and other places, and many going our way. Tugs shrieked sharp warnings, boatmen called aloud from two junks, crowded with escaping Chinese, there was a hubbub of voices. We passed lateen-sailed fisher boats, loaded down with Italian voyagers, shouting to each other. We passed fire tugs on which dead-beaten firemen lay stretched in slumber, and so on down to Goat Island and across to Berkeley. . . ."

Sixteen enlisted men and two officers from the "U.S.S. Chicago" alone supervised the rescue of 20,000 refugees from the foot of Van Ness Avenue.

Major Carroll A. Devol wrote, "All the tugs in the harbor . . . including the Army Transport Tug Slocum and Army Tug McDowell, probably twenty all told, combined near the foot of Lombard street, stretching hose up to meet the fire and pumping salt water with all available power. The wind blew a hurricane, but the tugs stuck to their work heroically, the tug Slocum being obliged to play a hose on her own deck-house to keep it from catching fire from the intense heat and

Mother Superior Mary Josephine Hagarty, Superior General of the Presentation Order in California.

Globe Mills at Chestnut and Montgomery Streets, near Telegraph Hill, burned on the last day of the Great Fire. Company President W. E. Keller and his workmen stayed in the earthquake-damaged structure to fend off the fire. However, as he wrote, "On Friday afternoon, as the flames approached, we got ten of our men, and were confident of success in saving the mill. At four o'clock in the afternoon, soldiers appeared and ordered us out, threatening to shoot if we did not go.
Arguments and explanations were of no avail. We were ordered to go or be shot. We left the building, and late at night, after being exposed for many hours to the heat of burning lumber yards to the north and east, windows in the east front at length broke, and bins of wheat thus directly exposed to the heat, were ignited. There is of course no doubt whatever that one man could have saved the structure had he been permitted to remain. Our loss was $220,000."

falling cinders."

Army troops were driven to the water's edge and tug boats stood by to pull them from the beaches as they retreated ahead of the flames.

This firestorm sweeping across Bay Street destroyed General Funston's only communication link with Washington, and Captain Wildman and his Signal Corps crews worked through the day to stuff an insulated telegraph line into the cable slot of the California Street Railway between Market Street and Van Ness Avenue. This brought the Signal Corps telegraph line around in a big loop from the Ferry Building to Fort Mason.

One of General Funston's telegrams to the Military Secretary at the War Department said, "Some looters shot. Ft. Mason may be lost to fire; supplies handed out in parks and squares; Admiral Goodrich lands all available men from Fleet; Major Benson has Seventh Cavalry guarding all of the bank vaults. Most casualties in poor districts. Funston commanding."

Henry Anderson Lafler, a well-known San Francisco writer, worked his way down Telegraph Hill after participating in the fight to save some of the houses on the hilltop. "I went down the hill to the west toward a place where I had seen firemen working. As I approached I was amazed to see the hose, its nozzle pointed up by means of a box and two bricks, playing uselessly into the middle of the street. The firemen, a group of only fifteen or twenty, had looted a grocery store, and with cheese and olives and canned goods, and plenty of alcoholics to drink, were eating breakfast.

"I remonstrated. 'Well, if you had been dragging the hose around for two days,' said the fellow who appeared to be in command, 'and it hadn't done a damn bit of good, you'd be wanting some breakfast, too,' and he fell again to his can of salmon.

"Further along I came upon a squad of soldiers. They were just finishing two kegs of beer from a corner grocery. Meanwhile the fire was burning on toward perhaps sixty square blocks which it ultimately destroyed without a single hand lifted to stop it."

At 3 p.m. Friday, the Appraisers' Building was again attacked by fire, this time from the rear along Broadway and Pacific Street. Lieutenant Freeman found that winds created by the firestorm swung around and pushed fire at him, and he lost 2000 feet of precious hose. He also tried to pump salt water to the Appraisers' Building, but found that San Francisco Fire Department hose connectors would not couple with those of the "Active," and he abandoned the plan. The fight against the fire went past midnight Friday and into the early hours of Saturday. On the Van Ness Avenue side of the fire, Army troops tore away fences around Fort Mason to create a firebreak and they helped pump water from

(Continued on page 89)

Collapse of the San Francisco Gas and Electric Company's gas works during the earthquake sounded like an explosion to the people in North Beach.

Crowds gathered at Clay and Kearny Streets to watch as the Wholesale District fire burned toward Chinatown and the Hall of Justice.

The tall smokestack of the United Railroads power-house at Oak and Broderick Streets collapsed and wrecked several cable cars inside the carbarn.

A string of burned cable cars along Pacific Avenue at Polk Street.

Order Governing Conduct of Civilians

HEADQUARTERS PACIFIC DIVISION,
FORT MASON, CAL., April 22, 1906.

GENERAL ORDERS NO. 12.

1. The regular troops, including the United States Marine Corps, on duty in the city of San Francisco, will control all of Golden Gate Park, all the territory north and east of Golden Gate Park along H street to Stanyan, along Stanyan to Oak, along Oak to Fillmore, along Fillmore to Bush, along Bush to Powell, down Powell to Market, along Market to First, along First to include the Pacific Mail dock.

2. This territory is divided into six (6) districts and troops assigned with location of districts, headquarters as follows:

FIRST DISTRICT.

To include all ground north of Golden Gate Park between the beach and Devisadero street, including the Presidio reservation, but not including Fort Miley.

Headquarters at the Presidio, San Francisco, California.

Commanding officer, Colonel Charles Morris, Artillery Corps.

Personnel of command, the Coast and Field Artillery on duty in the city of San Francisco and at the Presidio of San Francisco, California.

SECOND DISTRICT.

To include all ground north of Union street and between Devisadero and Hyde streets, including also all of Fort Mason reservation, except the post proper.

Headquarters at Fort Mason, California.

Commanding officer, Colonel Reynolds, Twenty-second Infantry.

Personnel of command, all that part of the Twenty-second Infantry now on duty in the city of San Francisco.

THIRD DISTRICT.

To include all ground bounded as follows: Hyde, from the bay south to Bush street, thence on Bush east to Powell, thence on Powell south to Market, thence on Market north east to First, thence on First south-east to water front, thence along water front to foot of Hyde street, not including wharves.

Headquarters at Portsmouth Square.

Commanding officer, Colonel Marion P. Maus, Twentieth Infantry.

Personnel of command, six (6) companies of the Twentieth Infantry.

FOURTH DISTRICT.

To include all ground bounded by streets as follows: Beginning at the corner of Devisadero and Union streets, south on Devisadero to Oak, east on Oak to Fillmore, north on Fillmore to Bush, east on Bush to Hyde, north on Hyde to Union, west on Union to Devisadero.

Headquarters at No. 1040 Broadway.

Commanding officer, Lieutenant-Colonel Lincoln Karmany, United States Marine Corps.

Personnel of command, all of the United States Marine Corps on duty in San Francisco.

FIFTH DISTRICT.

All of Golden Gate Park.

Headquarters at the Park Lodge.

Commanding officer, Major G. W. McIver, Fourth Infantry.

Personnel of command—Two companies of the Twentieth Infantry and one troop of the Fourteenth Cavalry.

SIXTH DISTRICT.

To include the wharves between Fort Mason wharf and the Pacific Mail Dock, both inclusive: in charge of the navy.

PROVOST GUARD.

Headquarters at Fort Mason Reservation.

Commanding officer, H. C. Benson, Major Fourteenth Cavalry.

Personnel of command—Two troops o fthe Fourteenth Cavalry.

Each officer designated in this order as a district commander will establish his headquarters immediately at the point designated and will distribute the troops under his command so as best to protect the property and keep order in his district.

The chief signal officer will as soon as possibe connect each district headquarters with division and department headquarters by wire communication.

At a conference with the Mayor of San Francisco, Callifiorinilia,l it was concluded that normal conditions should be established as soon as possible.

To accomplish this district commanders will instruct the troops under their command to prohibit the seizure of all vehicles of transportation by all persons within their district unless they have a written order signed by the Mayor or the division commander and dated April 23, 1906, or later.

Lights are authorized between sunset and 10 p. m. In case lights are burned after this hour sentinels will investigate quietly and inform the occupants that orders require lights to be extinguished at 10 p. m.

In houses no fire will be permitted in stoves, grates, furnaces or other fireplaces having exit through chimney flues unless the occupants of the household certificate issued by authorized inspector, showing the chimneys in proper condition. The importance of this provision is emphasized by the fact that no effective means are at hand for stopping fires. Oil stoves may be used.

4. All persons except suspicious characters will be permitted to pass sentinels without interruption, provided they are orderly and do not destroy or otherwise molest or misap propriate property not their own.

5. The division commander desires to impress upon troops the importance of temperate action in dealing with the unfortunate people who are suffering from the awful catastrophe that has befallen them. He desires also the assistance of the people for whom every possible effort is being made and whose forbearance already bespeaks their courage under circumstances impossible to fully comprehend without experiencing them. In spite of their unfortunate condition we must ask their co-operation and assistance.

Food supplies, tentage and blankets are beginning to come in very rapidly, and in a very few days, it is believed that sufficient supplies of all kinds will be regularly distributed daily for the absolute want of all.

It is particularly requested that no person permit himself to receive more of any kind of supplies than are absolutely necessary.

Our greatest danger in the future may be expected from unavoidable sanitary conditions, and every person is cautioned that to violate in the slightest degree the instructions of the sanitary officers would be a crime that could have no adequate punishment.

By command of Brigadier-General Funston.

S. P. JOCELYN,
Colonel, General Staff,
Chief of Staff.

Official:
S. W. DUNNING, Military Secretary.

General Funston's order divided San Francisco into three basic areas with the military policing one-third of the city, the National Guard one-third and the regular police one-third. This plan remained in effect until the withdrawal of the Army in June, 1906.

Water wagon provides drinking water to refugees waiting in line for ferryboats to take them to the East Bay.

The steps of the U. S. Mint filled with refugees at 6 a.m. on April 19.

Wreckage of flats on the northwest corner of Larkin and Turk Streets.

Sunday Mercury and Herald

SAN JOSE, CALIFORNIA, SUNDAY MORNING, APRIL 22, 1906—SIXTEEN PAGES.   NO. 112.

PLAGUE IS NOW THREATENING THE HOMELESS

The horrors of a plague threaten San Francisco. Typhoid fever, as a result of unsanitary conditions, has made its appearance. Four cases are now receiving medical attention. Smallpox and scarlet fever, too, are reported. General Funston has caused to be posted throughout the city notices of sanitary regulation. Water for drinking purposes must be boiled. All refuse and swill must be buried. These methods, with proper medical supplies and tents to live in, it is hoped, will check the threatened epidemic.

For Rebuilding
OF SAN FRANCISCO
See Page 3

The San Francisco Examiner

For information of your
friends and families
See Page 6

SAN FRANCISCO, SUNDAY, APRIL 22, 1906

STREET CARS START IN SAN FRANCISCO TO-DAY

Street cars will be in operation to-day from the Ferry Building, and construction of the entire transportation system will be begun.

An offer of $400,000 for a strip of Market-street property was emphatically refused yesterday.

Mayor Schmitz has issued a proclamation stating that after to-day no further seizures of automobiles or carts will be made. The condition of the homeless and shelterless who are camped in various points of the city is remarkably fine.

Offers of substantial financial assistance are being rapidly received from many cities in all sections of the United States.

FUTURE IS BRIGHT FOR SAN FRANCISCO

Considering the catastrophe that descended upon San Francisco without a moment's warning, conditions here are simply marvelous. Though from the water front to Van Ness avenue the city is laid waste, westward lie well-paved streets and solid houses, while the parks and squares are as green and inviting as ever.

There is absolutely no panic of any kind. Instead every one is

MARKET STREET CARS WILL BE RUN TO-DAY

Manager Mullaly of the United Railroads announces that cars will be operated to-day from the Ferry through the city to Turk, Eddy and Fillmore streets, and that within a few days the temporary

RELIEF FUND $4,154,000

The following is a tabulated statement of the amount of money raised yesterday for relief purposes. The grand total takes in all the moneys subscribed to date:
State of Massachusetts and

INSURANCE COMPANIES PREPARE FOR WORK

Several of the companies have already leased offices for a year in Oakland, and they will be down to business in no time. There is no limit to the liability of stockholders in the California company's

---

THE CHICAGO RECORD-HERALD.

TWENTY-FIFTH YEAR—NO. 299.   MONDAY MORNING, APRIL 23, 1906—TWENTY PAGES.   PRICE TWO CENTS

SAN FRANCISCO IN HEROIC RALLY; CHICAGO RELIEF TRAIN ON WAY

14 CARS ARE FILLED WITH SUPPLIES AND START ON FAST TRIP

Special Given Right of Way and Will Be First From East to Reach the Stricken City.

ANOTHER MAY GO TODAY

House-to-House Canvass by Police Planned and $1,000,000 Chicago Fund Is the Mark Set.

INSURANCE COMPANIES VIE IN EFFORTS TO MAKE QUICK PAYMENTS ON LOSSES.

THE San Francisco conflagration precipitated an unparalleled crisis upon the fire insurance companies of the country, and they are meeting it with wonderful courage and self-sacrifice. Succeeding several months of unusually heavy losses, it presented a sight draft upon them for more than $100,000,000. The response was prompt—indeed, in some instances heroic. The companies will meet their obligations in full, even though this, in some cases, will drain resources that have been built up in scores of years, and in others will wipe out all accumulations, and force the stockholders to assess themselves, often to the full amount of their holdings. It means sacrifice and self-denial in hundreds of cases, and perhaps the mortgaging of homes to meet these unexpected demands. But they are being met with courage and fidelity. Men give $100,000 to the relief fund, and are applauded. A hundred stockholders of fire insurance companies will lose $100,000 each because of the calamity and to relieve its suffering and replace its loss, and will never be heard of.

+ + +

Never before were the companies called upon to pay so enormous an amount in so short a time, but they have risen to the emergency. They are no longer mere financial machines, collecting premiums from the many to pay the losses of the few. They are actually striving to relieve distress as rapidly as possible at great cost to themselves. Under their contracts they have sixty days in which to settle, but every company covets the honor of paying the first claim, and they are racing their men and money across the continent. The insurance companies will be called upon to

THE DAWN AT SAN FRANCISCO.

PEOPLE OF RUINED CITY TAKE HEART; COURAGE SUBLIME

Rising Superior to Disaster, and Inspired by Spirit of '49, They Determine to Build Anew.

PRAY IN THE OPEN AIR

Clergymen, Ignoring Denominational Lines, Urge All to Unite in Repairing Effects of Calamity.

Fire burns on both sides of the 800 block of Sutter Street.

The conflagration as seen from Mission Dolores Park. Refugees from the South of Market District have begun

to put up makeshift shelters. Note man pulling wagon in the lower right of the photograph.

One of the early earthquake-caused fires burned on Golden Gate Avenue near Buchanan Street when this

photograph was taken about 8 o'clock on the morning of April 18. This blaze was put out by the fire department.

Author Henry Anderson Lafler wrote articles for Collier's Magazine *on his portable typewriter salvaged from his home at 612 Clay Street. He worked on a small table amid fresh graves dug in Portsmouth Plaza across from the Hall of Justice.*

Collapsed wood-frame buildings along Golden Gate Avenue near Hyde Street.

(Continued from page 84)

the bay to the few fire engines on the west side of the firestorm.

The Navy saved the Merchant's Ice and Cold Storage building at Lombard and Sansome Streets, the Gibraltar Warehouse at Sansome and Filbert Streets, the Italian Swiss Colony warehouse at Battery and Greenwich Streets and several other buildings on the east side of the fire. On the north and south sides, the firestorm ran out of fuel when it hit the perimeter of the areas already burned. This battle saved the piers and kept the fire from spreading to the all-important Ferry Building. By late Saturday morning the progress of the fire was stopped at Pier 27. Saturday afternoon, wagons from the Coroner's office slowly moved along North Beach streets to pick up the burned remains of the dead.

The firestorm had turned southwest and roared into the Irish working-class Mission District on Thursday. With a simultaneous thrust, it tried a sneak attack on the Potrero District, burning in the direction of the United Railroads' power house at Eleventh and Bryant Streets. This building had a fresh water well and tank, and a salt water supply drawn from the bay for the building's own fire protection system.

URR pumps were a godsend to Captain Cullen. With water from the power plant, the crew of Fire Engine No. 6 stopped the penetration of the blaze working its way south and west and held it to an irregular line along Folsom and Howard, where those streets curve into the Mission District.

Refugees filled every corner of the URR power plant, much to the concern of Thornwall Mullaly, assistant to the president of United Railroads, and a member of Mayor Schmitz' Committee of Fifty. "The Bryant Street plant was a very valuable one," he wrote, "and as it lay obviously in the path of the conflagration we spent a lot of time there.

"People in the district were filing by in the thousands during the earlier period of the fire; driven from their homes they wandered about not knowing where to go. Some camped in vacant lots; scores sought shelter in the car barn. One fellow, I remember, came along with a weeping jag and accosted me outside the plant. 'Well,' said he, 'I've lost a wife and five children; would that worry you?'

"I told him to go inside and sleep.

"You could scarcely keep these poor refugees out of the place. They seemed to permeate it like rats."

Thursday at 11 a.m., wrote Captain Cullen, "The fire being beyond danger at this point we again picked up the remaining hose in our possession and proceeded to 17th and Howard Sts. there being considerable water in a large hole in the middle of the street owing to a broken main, with stones and sand we dammed the water that was running to waste and put our Engine to work after

Members of Fire Truck Co. No. 10 and Fire Engine No. 7 in 1906.

stretching our hose as far as Capp St. near 16th St."

Without the political interference of Mayor Schmitz or the Committee of Fifty, without the rigid and authoritarian hierarchy of the U. S. Army, the fire department battalion chiefs were able to develop a brilliant, ad-hoc, sectional defense plan to save the Mission District.

Battalion Chiefs Edward F. McKittrick, John J. Conlon and William D. Waters had few fire fighting resources available. Exhaustion and fatigue had taken its toll on firefighters, horses, hose and engines. Most fire companies were out of action after the fiftieth hour of the conflagration, and some firefighters were delirious from fatigue, injuries and hunger.

The chief officers' plan called for creation of a firebreak north and west of the Mission District. This, they hoped, would force the conflagration to move in the direction of the two-block-wide park bordering Dolores Street between Eighteenth and Twentieth. If the plan worked, the broad thoroughfare of Dolores Street from Market to Eighteenth would hold the fire on the west, if all combustible wood-frame homes on the east side of the street could be removed. The fire chiefs also wanted to keep the fire in the flatlands

to avoid another upslope run that produced such disastrous results on Rincon, Telegraph, Nob and Russian hills.

A Navy dynamite squad from the submarine "U.S.S. Pike" and the Mare Island Navy Yard found its way into the Mission District and somehow connected with Colonel Walter Kelly's dynamite crew from the First California Regiment, National Guard of California.

Earlier, the National Guard tried to dynamite a fire line along Fourteenth Street to stop the southwesterly swing of the conflagration into the Mission District. Fire Engine No. 25 was with the National Guard dynamiters as they started blasting near Folsom Street. Joseph E. Finn, engineer of Fire Engine No. 25, wrote, "After they had dynamited about five buildings, they retired, and we connected up to the hydrant at the Southwest corner of Folsom and 14th Sts., but on account of the fierceness of the fire in the dynamited buildings, and the small volume of water in the main, we were compelled to retreat after about an hours hard struggle. . . ." This dynamiting forced the evacuation of both the Southern Pacific Company and St. Francis hospitals on the south side of Fourteenth between Mission and Julian Streets. Dynamiters fell back to Six-

teenth and Mission Streets and again tried to create a firebreak. They demolished a furniture store and started more fires. Dynamite-caused blazes began to spread ahead of the main conflagration roaring in from South of Market.

Fire Engine No. 27 did have one stunning success when firefighters stopped the conflagration at Market and Guerrero Streets, and saved a row of Victorian homes along Guerrero between Clinton Park and Duboce Street. This victory anchored the fire line on one side of the Mission District, and kept the fire from sweeping upslope along Market Street and into the Castro District.

Twentieth at Dolores Street at the far end of the park was to be the anchor point of the firebreak to be created on the north side of Twentieth, stretching to Mission Street. Another was to stretch from Twentieth and Mission Streets north and east back toward the South of Market district. This, they believed, would cut the fire's fuel supply and, simultaneously, force the fire toward the large open space of the park. This plan was flawed only by the lack of water on the Twentieth and Dolores Street side.

What was left of the San Francisco Fire Department, together with thousands of refugees, had retreated, block-by-block, into the

Fallen stones in the cemetery lean against Mission Dolores. The newer, larger, Mission Dolores Church is in ruins.

Mission District, where nearly every structure was built of wood. Firefighters worked along the east and west flanks of the fire, and opened each hydrant in an unsuccessful search for water.

The battalion chiefs had briefly toyed with the idea of rolling water-filled Southern Pacific Company tank cars on spur tracks through the Mission District, but that idea was abandoned because of the immense logistical difficulties of coordinating the movement of fire apparatus with the movement of Southern Pacific Company engines.

With the fire in front of them and the new fires spreading from Sixteenth and Mission Streets in back of them, the refugees retreated to the camp that had sprung up at Eighteenth and Dolores Streets. The camp was a hellhole. Weeks before the earthquake, horse manure had been spread in preparation for the planting of a vast lawn in the Mission Dolores Park. Refugee men, women and children sat, ate and slept in this combination of manure and dirt, and tried to protect themselves from fist-sized cinders and ash thrown at them by the fire, and they felt the strong winds that were sucked into the center of the firestorm.

National Guard and Navy personnel began to dynamite along the east side of Dolores from Market to Eighteenth as well as along the west side of Howard from Twentieth back to Fourteenth Street. Dynamite-caused fires were suppressed with water from the private water works of John Center at 2828 Sixteenth Street and the broken Spring Valley Water Company main at Seventeenth and Howard Streets. There was also some water in abandoned cisterns at Nineteenth and Shotwell and Twenty-second and Shotwell Streets.

On the south line of the perimeter, thousands of volunteers from the Mission District and the refugee camp worked to dismantle every structure along the north side of Twentieth Street. Navy personnel and National Guardsmen dynamited the larger structures as men with four-by-eight wooden beams battered the smaller out-buildings into kindling. Smaller houses were demolished by ropes attached to four corners of the structures; 100 men would pull simultaneously to tear the outer walls apart and cause the inward collapse of the roof and floors. There was simply no other way to save the Mission District.

Here again, Navy and Guard personnel ran low on dynamite needed to create the fire lines. At Twenty-fifth and Valencia Streets, five blocks from the southern line of the perimeter, a man jumped in front of car carrying

James D. Phelan.

The man identified himself as a firefighter and demanded the former mayor surrender his automobile. Mayor Phelan wrote, "When I asked him what he desired to do with my car he said, 'To carry dynamite to the firefighters at the front!' My chauffeur, John Munford, afterwards employed by James L. Flood, nudged me vigorously not to consent; but considering the demand a legitimate and important one, I told the fireman to get aboard and direct the car.

"We drove over a rough part of the city to the Kentucky Street carbarns of the United Railroad Company [on the south side of Third Street between Twenty-third and Twenty-fourth Streets], where men began noiselessly to fill the tonneau with sticks of dynamite. They evidently expected transportation. Not being familiar with dynamite, I asked the fireman, who had perched himself on top of the cargo, whether there was danger of its explosion by the jarring produced by the rough roads, and he said he thought not; that it could only be ignited by the caps, which he held aloft in his hand, and which he promised to hold aloft until the end of the journey! Hearing explosions in the distance, I asked if a pistol or gunshot could ignite dynamite, and he thought 'probably.'

Intersection of Eighteenth and Valencia Streets. The large corner building sank at least one story and trapped an unknown number of people. The Valencia Street Hotel is seen in the background. Below, all that remained of the area after the fire swept along Valencia Street.

Damage illustrative of that reported throughout the Mission District. This structure sank into Lake McCoppin at Nineteenth and Lapidge Streets.

"He directed the car to the corner of Twenty-first and Dolores Streets, and when we drove there – the crowd separating – the curious asked what was going on, and when I informed them that I had a load of dynamite, they dispersed as if by magic."

If ever the Reverend Philip Andreen of the Swedish Evangelical Lutheran Ebenezeer Church needed God, this was the time. There was nothing left of San Francisco between his church on the southwest corner of Fifteenth and Dolores Streets and the Ferry Building. With the greatest conflagration in the history of the world aimed directly at his small church, Reverend Andreen and his neighborhood volunteers gathered every possible water container, old-fashioned milk cans and buckets for the fight. They were also ready with mops, brooms, blankets, burlap sacks and what appeared to be sublime faith and courage. His line of defense was the dynamited rubble across the street, and he and his volunteers were alone; there were no more San Francisco firefighters left to help.

Most of the neighbors, not sharing the Reverend's faith and vision, had taken the more practical approach and had gone with their precious personal belongings to the park to sit out the conflagration.

The need to save the Swedish church was not necessarily symbolic. It was the largest structure at Fifteenth and Dolores Streets and its steeple was tin-covered to reduce fire hazard. If the church did burn, it was feared the steeple would become a conflagration breeder and spread fire into the Castro District. To blow up the church was too great a risk with no water to put out any dynamite-caused fire. So, what the Reverend Mr. Andreen proposed to do was, in reality, eminently practical.

The Swedish church was one of three large structures on the west side of Dolores Street between Market Street and the park. Mission Dolores at Sixteenth and Dolores Streets was an adobe structure that had not fallen during the earthquake, but its adjacent parish church had been wrecked. The National Guard dynamited the large, wooden Notre Dame Academy across the street to form a firebreak to protect the Mission. Mission High School at the northwest corner of Eighteenth and Dolores Streets sat well back on the block and was also protected by volunteers with sacks and blankets.

Discovery, or rediscovery of a functioning fire hydrant at Twentieth and Church Streets was made by John Rafferty, a blacksmith at the City Corporation Yard, who lived at 1714 Church Street. The hydrant had been used to fight a big fire in the Mission District on the morning of the earthquake. For some reason, it was not checked again until Mr. Rafferty gave the hydrant valve three turns and found water.

There was a rush to get two fire engines up the Twentieth Street hill to the hydrant, and another rush to find enough undamaged hose to get the water down to the Twentieth Street firebreak. Battalion Chief Waters ordered Fire Engines No. 19 and 27 to the hydrant. Engine No. 19's horses did not have the strength to pull the huge Metropolitan steam engine up the steep part of Dolores to Twentieth Street. The exhausted horses tried, but there was no forward movement. Refugees in the park rushed to the assistance of the firefighters. Two or three hundred hands grabbed Fire Engine No. 19 and began to push.

"Push–Push–Push" they shouted in unison, "Push–Push–Push." Fire Engine No. 19 began to move, slowly at first, then faster as the horses strained against the harness. The engine began the slow climb up the steep Dolores Street incline, then the turn on Twentieth toward Church Street and the hydrant. A hundred more sets of eager hands grabbed Fire Engine No. 27, and with the same rhythm began to push it up the hill, too. Fire Engine No. 19 was "first in" at the hydrant. Both engines pumped in tandem to Fire Engine No. 26 which, in turn, relay-pumped to Fire Engine No. 7.

Police officers and refugees tore away street lamp poles to allow the hose to stretch as far as it could; there was just enough to reach Fire Engine No. 7 on Mission Street.

Cinders and ash falling on the miserable refugees in the park became thicker with the approach of the conflagration. People took cover under umbrellas and blankets for protection from the fiery shower. As the fire rolled closer, larger firebrands began to fall on them and into the manure that surrounded them.

Larger cinders and firebrands thrown out well ahead of the fire fell on houses along Dolores Street and on Reverend Andreen's church and started numerous small fires. A bucket brigade lifted heavy milk cans upstairs and into the loft of the steeple. The radiant heat blistered and bubbled the paint and, when the ignition point was reached, a can of water was poured down the side of the church.

Three hundred people on the street ran after firebrands and attacked them with mops, burlap sacks, blankets and even their own clothing. Then the fire came with a power that was beyond the description of any eyewitness. First, the fire tried to breech Dolores Street on the west. Firebrands and cinders roared into the neighborhood like artillery strikes, but scores of people on rooftops beat out each incipient fire.

Unseen poisonous gases from the fire rolled over the volunteer firefighters along the Dolores Street perimeter and knocked them down. Doors were taken from buildings for heat shields. Volunteers ran forward in little squads, hiding behind doors held lengthwise, and for two or three minutes at a time two men attacked the firebrands with damp sacks, then retreated from the intense

The disorganized rescue efforts behind the Valencia Street Hotel.

Laguna de Manantial and its tributaries drawn over a latter-day street map of San Francisco. This was the area that saw such frightful damage to wood-frame homes and apartment buildings in the Mission District.

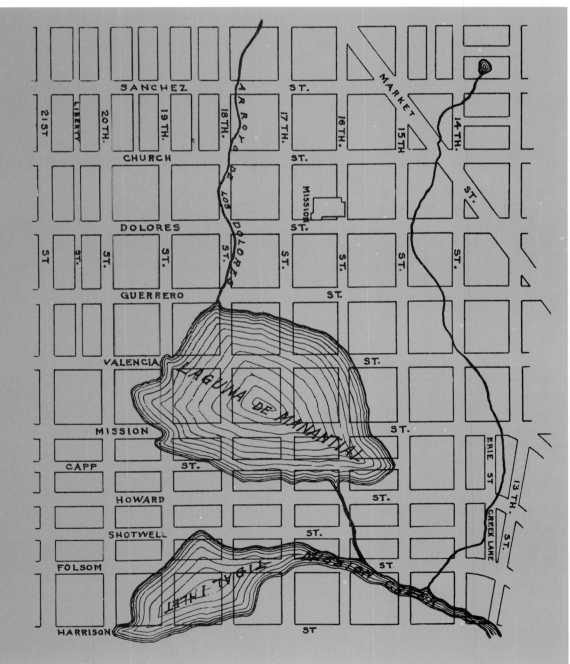

Fire from the Wholesale District jumped Battery Street and swept toward Chinatown and the Hall of Justice.

heat; their places then taken by other volunteers.

Others lugged heavy milk cans filled with water from the New Method Laundry wells at Sixteenth and Sanchez Streets to the fire line to keep those sacks and mops damp, or to pour down the front of any number of the Dolores Street houses exposed to the intense heat. Refugees dragged their pitiful belongings deeper into the park and away from the fire.

Along Twentieth Street, the battalion chiefs stood ready to direct the frontal attack on the conflagration. Firefighters and volunteers here experienced the same shock as Reverend Andreen's band of volunteers. First, cinders and firebrands rocketed ahead of the fire, then came the hot, rolling, invisible gases that nearly suffocated them or threw them to the ground. The Great Fire could actually be felt: vibrations like the rumbling of a steam boiler or the passing of several streetcars. No firefighter in San Francisco had ever before heard or felt anything like this.

Three thousand volunteers faced this four-block-wide fire. Heat shields charred and grew too hot to hold for more than a minute or two, but they held. Burlap sacks and mops caught fire and were replaced with bedsheets and blankets from abandoned houses, and refugees brought more blankets from the park when those burned. On rooftops throughout the Mission District small blazes created by huge firebrands thrown from the conflagration were smothered.

The battle to save what was left of San Francisco would last seven hours. Delirious firefighters collapsed in the street, only to be dragged from danger by refugees. Others rolled in the gutters to keep melted rubber turnout clothes from sticking to their bodies. From somewhere, said Captain Stephen Russell of Fire Engine No. 27, a doctor or nurse moved along the fire line, injecting strychnine, an alkaloid poison used for killing vermin, into the firefighters in the belief that a mild dose would ease the pain of burns and act as a stimulant.

The fight continued into the late night hours of Friday, when the fire managed to jump Twentieth at Lexington Street and began to burn along both sides of this small street. The fire hose was wrestled around into Lexington Street where the firefighters and volunteers blocked this new threat. Fire also jumped Mission and roared toward Howard Street, and as Captain Cullen put it, "Here we had a hard fight as the wind was blowing the intense heat of the fire in our direction. Soon it became unbearable and as the fire was gaining on us we could not stop it from crossing Capp St. but after fighting every inch of the ground we succeeded in getting it under control at 20th St."

Then, ever so slowly, the fire began to darken, so slowly at first that it was barely noticed on the fire lines. But refugees on the hills and in the camps saw it. The exhausted volunteer firefighters who had been carried to the refugee camp again picked up tattered sacks and blankets and went back to attack the fire. At 7 a.m., Saturday, April 21, 1906, the Great Fire ran out of fuel, in the middle of a block of wood-frame buildings, and in the face of 3,000 San Franciscans. History's greatest conflagration was over.

The fire as seen from Alamo Square at Fulton and
Scott Streets in the Western Addition.

A fire hose line was laid from the State fireboats at the
Ferry Building to Fire Engine No. 1 and two Oakland
fire engines, hidden by smoke, as they attempted to keep
the fire at Market and Steuart Streets from spreading.

South of Market refugees formed this camp on the grounds of the Protestant Orphans Asylum at Market and Laguna Streets a few hours after the earthquake. The building at the left still survives.

Fire insurance company photograph of earthquake-damaged structures in the area of Bush and Battery Streets. The large building at the bottom of the picture is the Occidental Hotel on the east side of Montgomery Street between Bush and Sutter Streets.

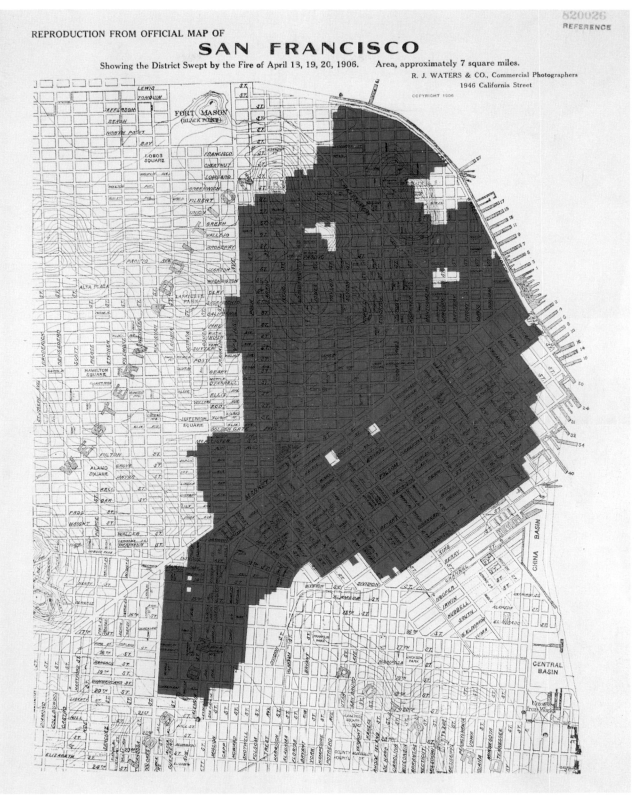

REPRODUCTION FROM OFFICIAL MAP OF

SAN FRANCISCO

Showing the District Swept by the Fire of April 18, 19, 20, 1906.   Area, approximately 7 square miles.

R. J. WATERS & CO., Commercial Photographers
1946 California Street

COPYRIGHT 1906

The official map showing the area burnt in the Great Fire of 1906.

This letter to Edward F. Moran is one of the few surviving known documents gathered by the Committee on History. City Engineer Thomas Woodward gave the official count

of the number of city blocks burned by the Great Fire. A vara is a Spanish measurement from the original survey of San Francisco and equals 33 inches.

Department of Public Works

BUREAU OF ENGINEERING
OFFICE OF CITY ENGINEER
2511 SACRAMENTO ST.

Brown & Power Co.

E. F. Moran -2-

San Francisco, Cal. _____ 190

  The 50-Vara and 100-Vara districts suffered the most. Of the total area of 1210 acres in the 50-Vara district 1088 were burned and of the 909 in the 100-Vara, 762.

  Enclosed herewith I also transmit copy of some suggestions in regard to our streets which I submitted to the Committee of Fifty on May 3d, and which were afterward acted upon by a sub committee; also of report on Sewers, to the Committee of Forty June 15th; which may be utilized by your Committee on History.

      Very Respectfully,

      Thos P. Woodward

      City Engineer.

AREA BURNED.

DISTRICT.	ACRES.	SQUARE MILES.	BLOCKS.	
			ENTIRE.	PORTION.
North of Market St.				
50-Vara	1088	1.70	299	13
Western Addition	301	.47	76	5
South of Market St.				
100-Vara	762	1.19	69	5
Mission	442	.69	46	9
TOTAL	2593	4.05	490	32

The south of Market fires had joined together by noon on April 18.

Market Street looking east from Fourth. The fire hose in the center of the photograph is attached to a salt water hydrant at Fifth and Market Streets.

An artist has removed most of the earthquake damage from this dramatic photograph of the south of Market fires burning toward Market Street.

Wreckage along Kearny Street is a telling example of the cleanup task that faced San Francisco. Streetcar service in most of the city could not be restored until the streets were cleared of rubble.

San Francisco's City Hall was said to have been poorly built and fell in the earthquake because of shoddy construction. That was not true. Two engineering reports after the earthquake indicated that the building could be rehabilitated and occupied and many city offices remained in the structure until it was torn down in 1909. Most of the old City Hall lot at Hyde and Grove Streets has been vacant since the structure was razed.

From left to right: The James Flood Building, the Lincoln School site and the Metropolitan Temple as seen from Fifth and Stevenson Streets. Nordstrom Department Store currently occupies the Lincoln School and Metropolitan Temple site. The James Flood Building was rebuilt and Woolworth's now occupies the first floor.

Union Square after the fire. Breuner's Rug Store at 261 Geary Street is in the center of the photograph, the St. Francis Hotel is at right.

Building owners begin salvage operations on California near Battery Streets. The Merchant's Exchange building at California and Sansome Street is on the right.

Three of the landmarks that still survive in San Francisco. The Shreve and Sloane buildings bracket the Fairmont Hotel in the distance. This photograph was taken on Market Street looking toward Post and Grant.

Earthquake damaged buildings on the south side of Market Street as seen from Grant Avenue.

Photograph taken from Jessie and New Montgomery looking toward Market Street. The wrecked Palace Hotel is on the left, the Crocker-Woolworth National Bank of San Francisco is in the center of the picture. The bank site is now Crocker Plaza and a BART station entrance.

The newly completed Shreve Building dominates the intersection of Post Street at Grant Avenue after the fire. The building was rehabilitated after the fire and still survives. A crowd of refugees caught a man looting Shreve's after the earthquake and turned him over to a soldier who then shot him dead and left his body in the intersection.

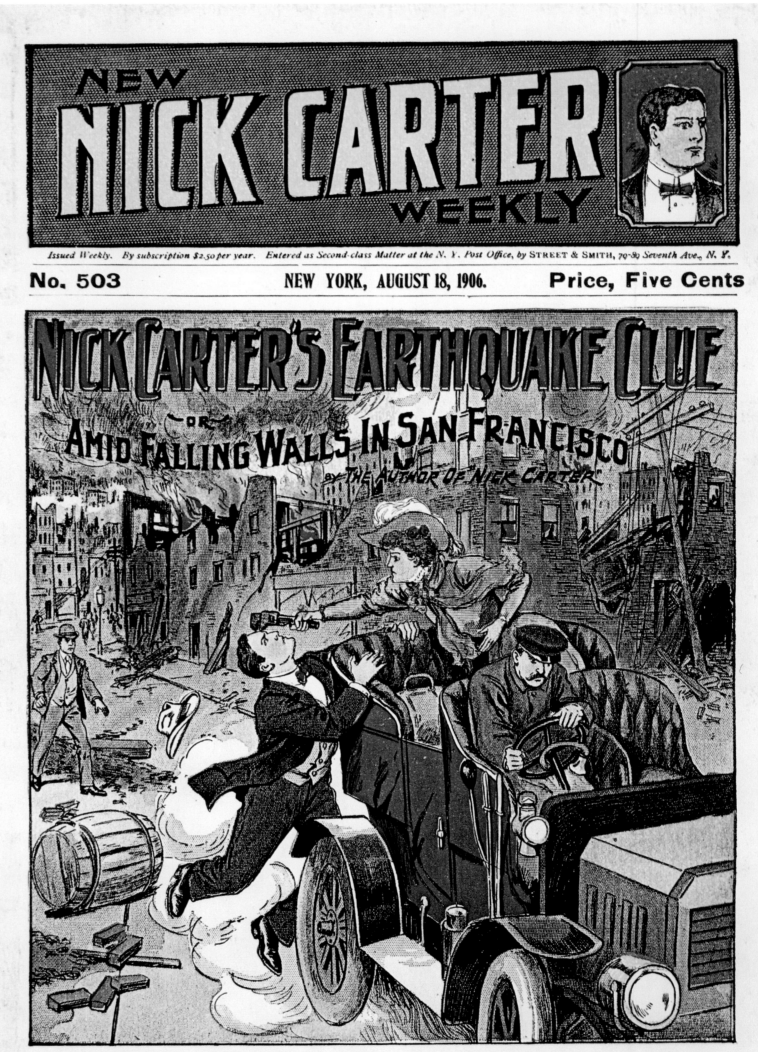

NEW

NICK CARTER
WEEKLY

Issued Weekly. By subscription $2.50 per year. Entered as Second-class Matter at the N. Y. Post Office, by STREET & SMITH, 79-89 Seventh Ave., N. Y.

No. 503   NEW YORK, AUGUST 18, 1906.   Price, Five Cents

NICK CARTER'S EARTHQUAKE CLUE
—OR—
AMID FALLING WALLS IN SAN FRANCISCO
BY THE AUTHOR OF "NICK CARTER"

The woman seized a wrench lying at her feet and, leaning over, struck the detective a savage blow.

The image San Francisco's business community did not want to project to the world is reflected by this cover of the New Nick Carter *weekly comic book.*

The 1907 money panic led to a shortage of gold currency in San Francisco. These Clearing House certificates were issued by the Associated Banks of San Francisco to ease the cash shortage as the city was being rebuilt.

The Ferry Building tower as reconstruction began. To stabilize the tottering structure, 5000 feet of wire rope from the cable car system were wrapped around the tower. The heavy Colusa sandstone exterior was removed, steel struts and rivets replaced, and a new, lighter, concrete exterior was added.

United Railroads of San Francisco cable and streetcar transfers for April 18, 1906.

Program cover for a convention that was never held.

Pastel drawn by F. Dormon Robinson, who watched the burning of the Phelan and the San Francisco Chronicle Buildings from two blocks away.

Popular stereopticon view of earthquake damage along California Street.

5. California St., looking toward the ferry depot—Banking District.

Famed artist Maynard Dixon was commissioned to paint the cover of the Southern Pacific Company's Sunset Magazine, *thus signalling the birth of the "New San Francisco."*

Map of the plans for the San Francisco Fire Department Auxiliary Water Supply System showing earthquake-caused water main breaks reported by the Spring Valley Water Company.

A set of popular postcards printed after the earthquake. Thousands of these were sent to anxious relatives in the East by refugees to let them know "all is well."

The Politics of Disaster

San Francisco pictured from a Captive Balloon one month and eleven days after the Earthquake-Fire of 1906. This view is the best known record of the devastation of the City.

John Caspar Branner, writing in the March 1913 edition of the *Bulletin of the Seismological Society of America*, complained of the lack of detailed information on past California earthquakes. A Stanford professor of geology, Branner had been a member of the 1908 State Earthquake Investigation Commission, and within two months of publication of this article, would be appointed president of the university. "A major obstacle to the proper study of earthquakes was," in his words, "the attitude of many persons, organizations and commercial interests toward earthquakes in general. The idea back of this false position – for it is a false one – is that earthquakes are detrimental to the good repute of the West Coast, and that they are likely to keep away business and capital, and therefore the less said about them the better. This theory has led to the deliberate suppression of news about earthquakes, and even the simple mention of them.

"Shortly after the earthquake of April 1906 there was a general disposition that almost amounted to concerted action for the purpose of suppressing all mention of that catas- trophe. When efforts were made by a few geologists to interest people and enterprises in the collection of information in regard to it, we were advised and even urged over and over again to gather no such information, and above all not to publish it. 'Forget it,' 'the less said, the sooner mended,' and 'there hasn't been any earthquake' were the senti- ments we heard on all sides.

"There is no doubt about the charitable feelings and intentions of those who take this view of the matter, and there is a reason- able excuse for it in the popular but very

Dynamiters destroy tottering walls along Stockton Street near Geary Street. Union Square is at far left and the Dana Building is on the far right.

erroneous idea prevalent in other parts of the country that earthquakes are all terrible affairs; but to people interested in science and accustomed to the methods of science, it is not necessary to say that such an attitude is not only false, but it is most unfortunate, inexcusable, untenable, and can only lead, sooner or later, to confusion and disaster.

"To meet the practical problems of earthquakes," concluded Professor Branner, "we must find out about them; and we certainly cannot find out about them if we are not informed, or if we are misled or misinformed."

Two years before the publication of Professor Branner's article, Andrew C. Lawson, head of the geology department at the University of California, wrote in the premiere edition of the society's journal, "The commercial spirit of the people fears any discussion of earthquakes for the same reason as it taboos any mention of an occurrence of the plague in the city of San Francisco. It believes that such discussion will advertise California as an earthquake region and so hurt business." Professor Lawson had given the San Andreas Fault its name, and oversaw the publication of the State Earthquake Investigation Commission report (Carnegie Institute, 1908, two volumes).

The biggest business in California in 1906 was the Southern Pacific Company, and while Messrs. Lawson, Branner and other earth scientists and engineers from the University of California and Leland Stanford Jr. University cataloged the destructive nature of the earthquake for the Commission, the Southern Pacific Company used its enormous political and economic muscle to build a public relations offensive to offset bad publicity created by the earthquake disaster. The need for "damage control" became urgent with Southern Pacific's enormous bonded indebtedness, caused mainly by Edward H. Harriman's rapid expansion of the system in the early part of the century.

Panic selling hit the New York Stock Exchange when word of the earthquake was received in the East. This selling sparked an immediate fall in the price of railroad stocks and those of other large companies with major California holdings, significantly reducing their borrowing power.

Southern Pacific Company also suffered an enormous amount of earthquake damage to its rail facilities in Northern and Central California, as well as significant fire losses to its various properties in downtown San Francisco. The potential for financial trouble was further compounded by the extraordinary costs of Southern Pacific's work to contain the rampaging Colorado River in Southern California that had begun to form the Salton Sea. Moreover, long-term losses of revenue that might be fueled by fear of future major West Coast earthquakes, or the inability of San Francisco to again be the commercial hub of the West, clearly could have significant impact on the company's fiscal position.

The stock market also began a general downward decline triggered by the forced sale of blue chip stocks and securities by fire insurance companies to pay the enormous San Francisco losses. Some analysts at the time felt the constant movement of money away from the stock market and other investments was partly responsible for the money panic of 1907.

Southern Pacific Company was also in a political battle with President Roosevelt over the railroad's continued control of the National Republican Committee and of some U. S. Senators and members of the House of Representatives. President Roosevelt had accused Mr. Harriman and his corporate friends of raising five million dollars to defeat him in the 1904 presidential election.

As part of this public relations strategy, James Horsburgh Jr., General Passenger Agent of the Southern Pacific Company, wrote to chambers of commerce throughout the state to candidly detail the railroad's efforts to "set the record straight." Essentially, the Southern Pacific Company began to rewrite the entire history of the disaster – a simple and sanitized version – to diminish the impact of the earthquake, and to assure easterners that investment in California enterprises would continue to be good business.

The scope of the Southern Pacific Company's reworking of the history of the catas-

Ruins of downtown San Francisco as seen from Sacramento and Mason Streets.

trophe was, and is, breathtaking. The company's point of view was that there was barely an earthquake. "We do not believe in advertising the earthquake," Mr. Horsburgh wrote. "The real calamity in San Francisco was undoubtedly the fire."

He feared lecturers speaking about the earthquake and fire would dwell upon only the dramatic features of the disaster. "In so far as possible, I suggest your organization attempting to reach everyone of these lecturers and get them to make the story complete – that is, not only to represent the vivid details of the catastrophe itself, but to give over at least the latter half of the lecture to [lantern slide] views and data showing how quickly and wonderfully San Francisco and California recovered from the effects, and how thoroughly and systematically they began the work of reconstruction."

Control of newspaper coverage of the disaster's after-effects was of prime concern to Mr. Horsburgh, who asked the chambers' cooperation in convincing the press to " . . . call attention to the small area of the State that was affected by the earthquake and the relatively small results in the way of destruction, and point out the great buildings of the business section of San Francisco and the residence portion of the city that escaped burning as proof of the fact that San Francisco did not suffer greatly from the earthquake. I would plainly and accurately describe, without undue prominence, the area and strength

of the temblor, and remark that except for a few cities which happened to lie directly in its pathway, practically no damage was done."

Mr. Horsburgh further suggested the press be assured that violent earthquakes are "so infrequent that no city in the temperate zone has ever been twice affected in a serious way by an earthquake. If you desire, dwell upon the fact that the California coast is heavily timbered, making lumber inexpensive; that San Francisco, in part was an old city; that it was a wooden city outside of the business section, closely built, with narrow streets for the most part, and as a result was particularly susceptible to destruction by fire."

He also thought of a clean, simple and grossly inaccurate answer to the complicated question of the catastrophic failure of San Francisco's water supply system. "You might describe how the water supply came from a system established many years ago, which had one main line of connections up the peninsula. Now, this line being broke by the subsidence of an old swamp land, cut off the water supply. Then I would dwell upon the new city of San Francisco, explain how it is to be beautified, how, by a salt water system of reservoirs, it is to be made fireproof, and so on."

Mr. Horsburgh, in closing, wrote, "We stand ready to cooperate with you in every way practicable to keep California and San Francisco from being misrepresented by sen-

sation mongers."

Southern Pacific's Passenger Division also published the glossy and expensive looking *Sunset Magazine* as a public relations and promotion vehicle to encourage business and tourism to come to California. In the 1906-1908 period, *Sunset Magazine* published dozens of articles and hundreds of pictures – some by the nation's best and highest paid writers and photographers – to promote the company's version of the earthquake and fire, as part of this disinformation campaign. *Sunset Magazine* articles about the disaster were, and continue to be, a major source of material for books and articles memorializing the San Francisco disaster. (The *Sunset Magazine* referred to here has no relationship to the present day *Sunset Magazine*, except in the similarity of names.)

Continued use of this large collection of well-written and well-packaged data by authors and researchers has effectively placed the Southern Pacific Company's sanitized, simplistic and, in many cases, grossly inaccurate version of the earthquake's effects into nearly all subsequent books and articles about the San Francisco earthquake and fire.

It was very easy to become lost in the ruins of the city in the first few days after the fire was brought under control. The expected landmarks were gone. In many cases, even the layout of the streets was unclear. Without the towering buildings – the conjunction of decades of architectural legacy and huge amounts of cash – there was concern that San Francisco real estate prices would go into general decline.

While the relief programs raced ahead, sputtered, then adjusted to the necessities of bread lines, even people in those lines had concerns about the erosion of property values the catastrophe had brought.

Quietly at first, then more desperately, the newspapers, the magazines, the "instant books" echoed the sentiment of a great many property owners, businessmen and the Southern Pacific Company – San Francisco had survived the worst, and looked pretty good in spite of the ordeal by fire.

"It wasn't the earthquake – it was the fire," they said – at real estate conferences, at community meetings, and in the offices of the companies listed on the New York Stock Exchange. It was their position that the out-of-town press had presented an exaggerated picture of the disaster. The real problems were the tenements, the flimsy, poorly built rooming houses, old brick structures on made ground and the poor water supply.

Ernest P. Bicknell, head of the Chicago Bureau of Charities, heard this on the train coming to San Francisco a few days after the earthquake. He was acutely aware of conversations in the corridors of the train among people enroute to San Francisco for the first time since the earthquake and fire – people who weren't there when the disaster happened. "The second day out of Chicago," Mr. Bicknell later wrote, "some men on board began to discuss the harmful effects on San Francisco's future, of a widespread impression that the city was subject to destructive earthquakes. This thought caused consternation. In the afternoon as many men as possible were herded into a sleeping car for a mass meeting. After a half an hour of vigorous speeches, a resolution was adopted to great cheering and entire unanimity, announced as a fact beyond dispute that the disaster in San Francisco was due solely to fire, to such a calamity, in short, as might occur in any well-ordered city and that the slight tremor which preceded the fire had nothing to do with the tragedy beyond, perhaps, breaking gas mains or water mains here or there. I am, of course, not giving the language of this resolution, which I have not seen since that day, but describing the general atmosphere and spirit of it as was impressed upon my memory."

San Francisco had established a "fire limit" around the downtown area after the Great Hayward Earthquake of 1868 that encompassed the industrial, business and shopping districts. This zone was expanded in 1905 and nothing but brick buildings with steel girders would be permitted in this critical area, and all utilities eventually would go underground. Reinforced concrete was excluded because the Bricklayer's Union objected to the potential loss of jobs if the new

Washington and Stockton Streets looking east toward the Hall of Justice.

An earthquake-damaged wood-frame home at 326 Eighth Avenue in the Richmond district.

Fire Engine No. 5 and Fire Truck No. 2 at temporary quarters on the waterfront after the fire. After the disas-ter the Navy established a ship whistle system to alert the fire department of any waterfront blazes.

Polk Street and Pacific Avenue looking toward Van Ness Avenue. St. Brigid's Catholic Church at Van Ness Avenue and Broadway was severely damaged by the earthquake.

View of Washington Square Park after the fire. Telegraph Hill is in the background.

"Like looking into a doll house" is how some refugees described such scenes. This apartment house was on

Sacramento Street near the home of Arnold Genthe who took this photograph.

material was permitted to be used in new San Francisco buildings. Significantly, older wood-frame buildings within the fire limits were "grandfathered" and allowed to remain.

Much of the area within the fire limits burned in the first 24 hours of the conflagration. A great many of the original fires, especially in the wholesale district, were within this boundary. With few exceptions, the fire penetrated every building and destroyed everything flammable. In many cases, brick and even steel-frame buildings had wood-truss floors. Where steel columns and floors were not protected by fire-resistive covering, the steel buckled in the intense heat and was either warped beyond repair or failed completely. "Grandfathered" wood-frame structures within those limits also acted as conflagration breeders, and were partially responsible for the spread of the fire to newer, fireproof buildings.

Exactly one week after the earthquake, the *San Francisco Chronicle* wrote of a meeting of the San Francisco Real Estate Board where a resolution was passed that the phrase "the great earthquake" should no longer be employed. It would be known as "the great fire." Clearly, real estate in San Francisco would not be worth much if subject to periodic "acts of God" in the form of disastrous earthquakes. On the other hand, with adequate water mains, good foundations and properly constructed buildings the city would rise from the ashes, impervious to another catastrophe by fire.

At that same meeting the issue of the "relocation of Chinatown" was addressed. It was taken for granted by everyone but the Chinese that this blight had to go; its sixteen-square-block area covered some of the choicest real estate in the city. The plan advanced by capitalist John Partridge before the earthquake – to establish a new and sanitary "Oriental City" at Hunters Point – was resurrected and supported by Mayor Schmitz.

Before the earthquake and fire, San Francisco's Chinese population was estimated at roughly 60,000, or 12 percent of the population. On May 6, 1906, a Red Cross relief survey found only 186 Chinese in San Francisco, huddled at Relief Camp No. 3 above Fort Point in the Presidio. Most of the others had gone to Chinese-only relief camps in Oakland. This was a propitious time to force the Chinese out of the heart of San Francisco.

Abraham Ruef and his arch-enemy, the rabidly anti-Chinese James D. Phelan had been appointed by Mayor Schmitz to a committee charged with finding a new location for Chinatown. Remarkably, both Messrs. Ruef and Phelan urged that a temporary camp for the Chinese at the foot of Van Ness Avenue be immediately abandoned because Mr. Phelan felt it would be extremely difficult to get the Chinese refugees to leave if they established themselves in that location.

Influential attorney Garret McEnerney

(Continued on page 114)

Chinese vice-consuls and Chinese merchants call on General Funston at Fort Mason to discuss the future of Chinatown.

Chinese-only refugee camp.

Stylized drawing of the so-called "Oriental City" that was to have been built at Hunters Point after the fire.

Chinese houseboys in the employ of Miss Sarah D. Hamlin, principal of the Hamlin School, prepare a meal in the street.

公報

奉本埠管理公家花園委員之命曉諭居住災
後各公園所建木屋之難民須知自公報日起
至八月十七號止爾等災民無論諸色人等須
要於期限以前一律搬遷限期滿日爾等所居
之木屋盡要拆除爾災民等早自爲計毋違此
示

西歷一千九百零七年七月十七號　大埠紅十字架救濟會啟

Temporary Chinese camp in The Presidio of San Francisco.

"Jabbering and gesticulating" residents of Chinatown filled Portsmouth Plaza in front of the wrecked Hall of Justice shortly after the earthquake.

Earthquake damage along Washington Street in Chinatown.

PUBLIC NOTICE –

From the order of local Park Committee. Due to the disaster, all refugees who lived in the park no matter color or race, has (sic) to evacuate before August 17, 1907. All buildings will be torn down at that time.

This order will be in effect on July 17, 1907, therefore all refugees (sic) are involved should act upon it as soon as possible.

(This notice from the San Francisco Red Cross Association.)

This is the English translation of the Chinese proclamation above.

NOTICE
—

Occupants of Refugee Cottages in Public Squares are hereby notified that by order of the Park Commissioners all Refugees must move as soon as possible, and that no cottage will be allowed to remain in the City Parks after the seventeenth of August, 1907.

The Japs Have Invaded the Western Addition

An object lesson of buying a residence where there are no restrictions is being exhibited daily. Chinese and Japanese are gaining foothold in the best parts of the Western Addition. Saloons are running full blast at the threshold of Churches and homes. Residence districts are being ruined as such because there is no protection the law affords. There is only one spot in San Francisco where only Caucasians are permitted to buy or lease real estate or where they may reside. Only one where stores and saloons and flats cannot be built. That place is Presidio Terrace. There you will obtain protection from the many nuisances that are now making life in many portions of San Francisco unbearable.

Lots average 50 feet front
Prices average $120 per front foot   BALDWIN & HOWELL
Terms 1-5 cash, balance as long   1692 Fillmore Street
   as you want at 5 per cent

Baldwin & Howell advertisement for Presidio Terrace published in The Argonaut, *September 1, 1906.*

Japanese refugees at the Point Lobos refugee camp.

(Continued from page 111)

agreed that Hunters Point was ideal: "I think it will prove difficult for the Chinese to get building permits from the Mayor and the Board of Public Works for the erection of any permanent structures at the foot of Van Ness Avenue. I would like to buy a long pool on that."

Arrival of a delegation from the Chinese Legation to the United States changed the tone and tenor of the "relocation of Chinatown" rhetoric.

Two days after Mr. McEnerney's bet – April 29, 1906 – Chow-Tszchi, First Secretary of the legation in Washington, met with Governor George Pardee at his Oakland headquarters. Chow-Tszchi expressed to the governor the Empress-Dowager's displeasure with the San Francisco authorities and the relocation plan. He told the governor, "I have heard the report that the authorities intend to remove Chinatown, but I cannot believe it. America is a free country, and every man has a right to occupy land which he owns provided that he makes no nuisance. The Chinese Government owns the lot on which the Chinese Consulate of San Francisco formerly stood, and this site on [806] Stockton Street will be used again. It is the Chinese Governments' intention to build a new building on the property, paying strict attention to the new building regulations which may be framed."

Gavin McNab, another member of the relocation committee, was at a loss to understand why the Chinese delegation was so upset. "Only this," said Dr. Thomas Filben, Methodist minister and chairman of the committee, "that the Chinese have been hustled from one temporary camp to another without ceremony. After the fire they were gathered together and [taken to] a temporary camp near Fort Mason [the Van Ness Avenue site]. Then there was a summary conference of which it was decided to remove them to the Presidio golf links. They remained overnight and then were hustled out of there and hurried over to a location further away, where the few Chinese remaining in the city are now encamped."

Yet it was the San Francisco Board of Education's decision to build "separate-but-equal" schools for Asian students that created the biggest uproar and sparked an international crisis.

The board argued that Japanese students attending San Francisco public schools were several years older than their classmates. Young girls shared classrooms with 93 adult Japanese males, and the Board of Education agreed this was sufficient reason to require all "Orientals" to be placed in segregated schools as soon as new facilities could be built.

The Imperial Japanese Government pro-

tested to President Roosevelt. The president denounced the action and said San Francisco's racism might set off an international incident. Rarely in the history of the United States has a president reached into the politics of a city school board. It is this dimension of Roosevelt's action that is so striking.

Reaction around the country was immediate. Famed as a liberal city, San Francisco was trashed in print for this unseemly discrimination. Editorials and political cartoons capitalized on San Francisco's embarrassment. Humbled by the experience, Mayor Schmitz, now under indictment in the graft cases, was permitted a trip to Washington to confer with Vice President Fairbanks to plead San Francisco's case for separation of the races in public schools. While the mayor was in the East, Abraham Ruef confessed to extortion in an attempt to gain immunity from the graft prosecution. District Attorney Langdon, his deputy, Francis J. Heney and detective William J. Burns also squeezed confessions from most members of the Board of Supervisors.

By June 1907, Mayor Schmitz had been convicted of extortion for taking bribes from owners of "French restaurants" that were in reality houses of assignation. After much high drama, appeals, death threats and other violence, Abraham Ruef was sent to the State Prison at San Quentin, and Mayor Schmitz

Refugees wend their way through the rubble near City Hall.

Extraordinary use of water forced the Spring Valley Water Company to cut service to 400 blocks, with the exception of one tap per block, until enough of the system could be repaired to allow free use of water in the unburned district. Mayor Schmitz also complained that "information comes to me that the manholes of the cable system of the Telephone Company in the streets are being used as receptacles of refuse and garbage. This is not only against public health, but is also a breach of the law."

The earthquake caused thousands of water main breaks, and houses loosened from foundations tore away service connections. Spring Valley Water Company, in many cases, could not find leaks until major mains were repaired and water pumped through them. Then, of course, the lesser breaks and leaks could be found as water came up through the pavement. Repair of the water supply continued for three years.

spent a short time in the county jail. (His conviction was thrown out on appeal, and in 1915 he successfully ran for the Board of Supervisors.) The president's involvement in the School Board issue came at a crucial and sensitive time in U. S.-Japanese relations, and as San Francisco's municipal government tottered on the verge of collapse. Two major events at the beginning of the twentieth century changed the balance of power in the Pacific Ocean. Admiral Dewey's conquest of the Philippines in 1900 spread the westward expansion of the United States into areas the Japanese Imperial Government thought was within its sphere of influence. Then in 1905, the Japanese moved toward supremacy in the Pacific Basin with a stinging defeat of the Russian Navy. It is clear, from a reading of the president's correspondence with his Secretary of War, William Howard Taft, that armed conflict with Japan was considered inevitable. President Roosevelt was clearly buying time by placating the emerging Asian superpower.

Damage to government facilities from the San Francisco earthquake had reduced the ability of the United States to defend its western shores. Coastal batteries near San Francisco had been damaged by the earthquake, and the U. S. Army had committed a large number of personnel and a huge amount of supplies to the relief effort.

Resources of the Army poured into San Francisco, and its combat ability was severely affected by several decisions made by the War Department on the first day. Every tent in the United States Army, for example, was dispatched to San Francisco to house refugees and every available ration was sent by train to the burning city.

Enormous numbers of telegrams sent and received at the War Department overwhelmed both major telegraph companies, and the need for thousands of freight cars to move hundreds of thousands of tons of supplies across the country strained the resources of the railroads for months after the disaster.

War Department telegraph records give some idea of the size of the relief effort, its logistical complexity, and its impact upon national defense readiness.

"San Francisco, Cal., April 18, 1906
(Received 11:40 p.m.)
"The Secretary of War, Washington:
"We need thousands of tents and all rations that can be sent. Business portion of the city destroyed and about 100,000 people homeless. Fire still raging, troops all on duty assisting police. Loss of life probably 1,000. Best part of resident district not yet burned.
Funston"

"Washington, D. C., April 19, 1906
(Sent at 4 a.m.)
"General Funston, San Francisco, Cal.:
"Your dispatch calling for tents and rations for 20,000 people received. Have directed sending of 200,000 rations from Vancouver Barracks, nearest available point. Will give orders concerning tents immediately and advise you within an hour. Do you need more troops? Of course, do everything possible to assist in keeping order, and saving life and property and in relieving hunger by use of troops, material and supplies under your orders. House passes enabling resolution today and Senate will tomorrow. All railway and telegraphic facilities surrounding San Francisco reported badly damaged and demoralized. Officers will accompany supplies where necessary, in order to insure as prompt forwarding and delivery as possible, with orders to keep in touch with you when practicable.
Taft, Secretary of War"

"Washington, D. C., April 19, 1906
(4:55 a.m.)
"General Funston, San Francisco:
"All available hospital, wall and conical wall tents will be sent at once by express from Vancouver, [Forts] Douglas, Logan, Russell, San Antonio, Monterey, Snelling and Sheridan. Remainder will be sent from Philadel-

phia depot. Little definite information thus far received as to limits of burned districts or conditions. Wire details comprehensively as possible.

Taft, Secretary of War"

"Washington, D. C., April 19, 1906
"Depot Quartermaster, Pa.:
"Ship by express at once to depot quartermaster, San Francisco, all Gold Medal cots on hand at your depot. Acknowledge receipt. Report number shipped and when shipment completed. Follow through by wire and report arrival.

Humphrey, Quartermaster-General"

"Washington, D. C. April 19, 1906
"Governor of Nebraska, Lincoln, Nebr.:
"By authority of Secretary of War, you will ship by express to the depot quartermaster at San Francisco all tents and blankets now in hands of Nebraska National Guard.

C. F. Humphrey, Quartermaster-General"

"Washington, D. C., April 20, 1906
"Depot Quartermaster, Philadelphia, Pa.:
"All tentage of Army now enroute to San Francisco. Contractors have been urged to hasten deliveries of duck. Report what material you have on hand and how many tentmakers at work. Push manufacture of tents. What tents due to be manufactured on authorizations already given.

Humphrey, Quartermaster-General"

A memorandum for the Military Secretary from Brigadier-General J. Franklin Bell, Chief of Staff, is one of hundreds of orders transferring personnel and equipment from across the United States to San Francisco. "All available men and horses except the sick and prisoners who have three months or more confinement to serve, with full field equipment; 30 days' rations and short forage for the cavalry; necessary medical supplies and attendance.

11th Infantry, Fort D. A. Russell;
27th Infantry, Fort Sheridan;
28th Infantry (Headquarters, Band and 10 Companies) Fort Snelling;
1st Cavalry, Fort Clark and Fort Sam Houston;
2 squadrons 11th Cavalry, Fort Des Moines, Iowa."

It was estimated that nearly 10 percent of the standing Army was in San Francisco by June 1906, and the military response to the disaster was the largest joint Army-Navy operation in the history of the nation to that time. San Francisco was also the point of debarkation for supplies supporting the Army's actions in the Philippines, and millions of dollars worth of Army, Navy and Marine Corps supplies destined for Manila burned in the Great Fire. An editorial in the November 1906 edition of *Army and Navy Life* put the mili-

(Continued on page 119)

Temporary police station at Lobos Square.

TO THE PEOPLE OF SAN FRANCISCO: WARNING!

Our city is becoming rapidly infested by disreputable money brokers and loan sharks who are attempting to secure all bank book accounts and insurance papers at a ridiculously low percentage of their actual value. This disreputable class is inducing citizens to relinquish their claims to bank accounts and insurance papers and is circulating reports that all banks upon opening will pay but 25 cents on the dollar on all bankbook accounts and further that the insurance companies have decided to pay no insurance upon buildings damaged by the earthquake.

You are hereby warned against any such misrepresentations and we would further strongly advise that you keep your bank accounts and keep your insurance papers until such time as rules governing the same are definitely established by the proper authorities.

Most respectfully,

J. F. DINAN, Chief of Police

The fire-gutted Hibernia Bank at Jones and McAllister Streets housed the San Francisco Police Department's Harbor Station for a few months after the disaster. The bank building was reconstructed and the exterior re- *mains essentially the same today. Spire of St. Boniface Church on Golden Gate Avenue can be seen in the background.*

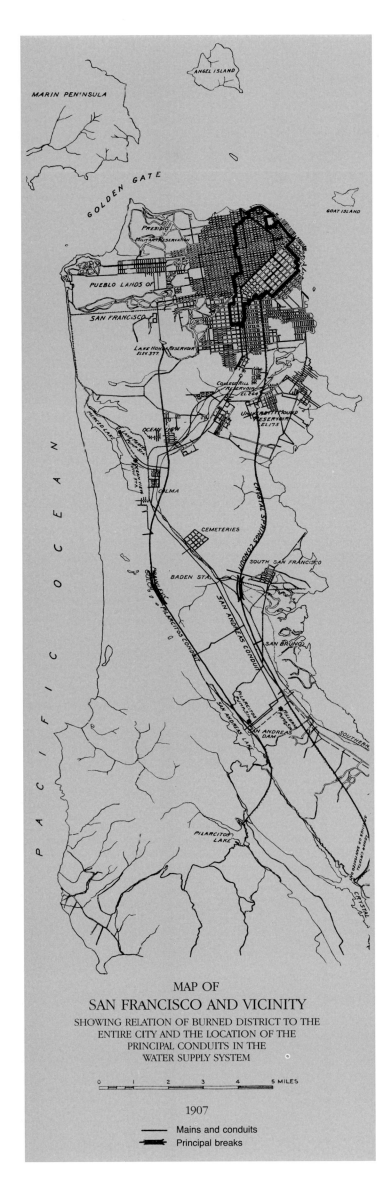

MAP OF
SAN FRANCISCO AND VICINITY

SHOWING RELATION OF BURNED DISTRICT TO THE
ENTIRE CITY AND THE LOCATION OF THE
PRINCIPAL CONDUITS IN THE
WATER SUPPLY SYSTEM

0   1   2   3   4   5 MILES

1907

— Mains and conduits
→ Principal breaks

Tents made of any available material appeared within a few hours of the earthquake.

Here a soldier guarded one of the temporary hospitals in Golden Gate Park.

Another temporary hospital established in the park to treat some of the hundreds of injured people. Doctors here said prostitutes from the Barbary Coast came to the hospitals to plead and beg for morphine because their supply of the narcotic had been destroyed by the earthquake and fire.

Sewer lines broken by the earthquake and raw sewage from hundreds of refugee camps polluted the entire underground water supply. The Army sent the largest hospital train in the world from Washington, D. C., to care for the injured and homeless. The hospital was packed aboard ferryboats at Oakland and brought across the Bay to Golden Gate Park. Here a purification plant provided water to Company A's Deer Park Hospital.

Military guards were stationed at the doorway of the California Bakery at the southwest corner of Fillmore and Eddy Streets, where free distribution of bread took place at various times throughout the day of April 18. "Men, women and children stood in line for blocks quietly waiting their turn but at the bakery door only the vigilance and firm bearing of the sentry maintained order. This baking company deserves special commendation for getting promptly to work to supply bread while rumors of approaching fire were rife. They began at once to repair the damage done by the earthquake and were an excellent example to the people who came to them for succor with or without payment," said a Navy report. The building was severely damaged by the earthquake but continued operation throughout the relief period. Photograph to the left shows the bakery before the earthquake.

Damage to the west side of the Memorial Museum in Golden Gate Park. This museum was built for the Mid-Winter Exposition of 1894. Every large structure in Golden Gate Park was heavily damaged or destroyed by the earthquake.

Sweeney's Observatory was one of the few reinforced concrete structures in San Francisco, and was completely shattered by the 8:14 a.m. aftershock. The observatory was atop Strawberry Hill in Golden Gate Park.

Broken water main on Stanyan Street near the entrance to Golden Gate Park. Nearby Park Emergency Hospital was also wrecked by the tremor.

The first business to open in San Francisco after the fire was this open-air barber shop on the Mission Street side of the U. S. Mint.

Mowry's Opera House at Grove and Laguna Streets served as the temporary City Hall after the earthquake and fire. This old opera house was destroyed by fire in 1970.

Temporary offices of the Sheriff, County Clerk and District Attorney at California and Webster Streets.

(Continued from page 116)

tary's concern into perspective: "The causes which are pressing Japan into an attitude of aggressive hostility toward us are many and potent. Not the least of them, of course, is commercial rivalry in the Pacific and our presence in Hawaii and the Philippines; but probably the most immediate and active are the pressure of her emigrant population; the existence of a large and victorious army and navy, restless, and self-confident; and the newly stimulated national pride and ambition, coupled with a supersensitiveness regarding any suggestion of racial inferiority which would be like a spark to tinder in its power to produce a war conflagration in her population.

"To have a powerful rival entrenched at the gate of Asiatic commerce," continued the editorial, "is intolerable to her national pride and conscience. She will undoubtedly fight it the moment conditions seem auspicious."

The *Army and Navy Life* editorial further suggested the San Francisco affair had become a terribly important incident in the relationship between the United States and Japan. "To preserve peace there is no alternative but an armament in the Pacific that will insure it. The more we apologize and yield the more certain will be oriental contempt and aggression. The sore spot in California will be kept irritated, or another developed elsewhere, until it is convenient to precipitate a crisis. In the meanwhile Nippon, wiping her sword with a grim smile, is preparing to whet it again upon the same grindstone which has served so well twice before; and as she feels its edge, she will continue to smile with courtesy and disclaimers until she brings it with sudden stroke upon our rear in Luzon."

On November 30, 1906, President Roosevelt discussed the urgent problem with President Benjamin Ide Wheeler of the University of California and U. S. Senator Frank Flint of California. The possibility of hostilities with Japan was talked about in the Cabinet, and Secretary of State Elihu Root said the situation was very grave and the United States should be considerate of the Japanese, at least until the Panama Canal could be completed. Thirty five years later, when Japan attacked Pearl Harbor instead of Luzon, the port of San Francisco was again the major West Coast supply point for military operations in the Pacific Basin.

Relief operations in San Francisco were racked by controversy, and riddled with corruption. There was a growing suspicion that many of the six million dollars contributed for the relief of the sufferers of the San Francisco earthquake were finding their way into the pockets of the grafters.

More than 80,000 barrels of flour had poured in from the Midwest, via Minneapolis, as part of the huge national relief effort. The flour was of relatively little use to refugees who were cooking on primitive street stoves.

The Relief Committee at first stored the flour, then decided to sell it for more usable supplies. Everyone was immediately unhappy.

The first auction of flour to commercial bakers at lower-than-market prices brought charges of graft. Indeed, the second auction brought prices closer to the market value.

In the meantime, with reports that 100-pound sacks of flour were being handed out at a relief center at Page and Gough Streets, a mob of angry women from Jefferson Square Park refugee camp stormed the warehouse and rioted.

In a personal letter to Secretary of War Taft, Major-General Greely wrote, "So far the entire relief system has been administered by the Army and so far no scandals or frictions have developed. Unfortunately a scandal is in the air connected with the selling about seven thousand tons of flour by the Red Cross Finance Committee but in this matter, the Army has had absolutely nothing to do as I carefully refrained from giving any assistance in the delivery of the flour in any way, stating that it was a commercial transaction which must be handled by the Finance Committee. It has been, I think, a case of bad judgment. . . ."

The *San Francisco Newsletter*, a strong voice in the city's politics for fifty years, suggested the six million dollar relief fund be distributed pro-rata – about $150 – to each man, woman and child in the relief camps.

Life in the camps was tough. U. S. Army and National Guard of California troops supervised most of the refugee camps in San Francisco, and when Major-General Greely wanted to withdraw the Army in May of 1906, Mayor Schmitz and the Relief Committee petitioned the War Department to keep the troops a while longer. Greely in a confidential telegram to Secretary of War Taft, wrote that "retention of troops here would be great mistake and request final decision. Await my report mailed today. Continued exercise of police power by troops and enforcement of military sanitary regulations on public parks and other city grounds must inevitably lead to clash of authority and consequent discredit of Army. During past fortnight have been frequently advised that political complications were developing and questions of public responsibility would be dodged by securing retention of Army and developing decisions on matters affecting municipality

and state or federal authorities through the Army."

Secretary Taft withdrew the Army from San Francisco on July 1, 1906, but left a few officers behind to oversee the relief operation.

Battles over fire insurance settlements, and the acrimonious controversy of the legality of paying claims on buildings damaged by earthquake or dynamite, began to reach their peak in mid- and late-1906, and there was the commensurate public relations effort to downplay the scope of the disaster.

Southern Pacific's *Sunset Magazine* pictured a city on the mend with "perfect order and harmony," in its June 1906 issue, and urged readers to send a souvenir copy of the magazine to family or friends in the East. The *San Francisco Newsletter* suggested the area burned in the Great Fire, though much larger than any other urban disaster in history, was "a mere fly-speck" compared to the total size of California.

Business and political leaders, at the same time, pressured geologists and engineers investigating the break in the San Andreas Fault not to publish any data that might damage the reputation of San Francisco or drive away

Refugees wait patiently in line at O'Farrell Street and Van Ness Avenue.

eastern capital needed to rebuild the city. The same business and political leaders also led political skirmishes with insurance companies about the adjustment of fire insurance losses.

So-called "scientific" management of charity advocated by reformers brought to San Francisco by the Red Cross was held up to ridicule as conditions deteriorated in the refugee camps. The summer of 1906 was mild, but there were fears that winter would bring additional hardships to the tens-of-thousands of refugees living in parks and squares throughout San Francisco and the East Bay.

Refugees became outraged when, in July of 1906, the American National Red Cross conducted a census of "unattached" women living in refugee camps. This census divided them into four types: (1) respectable women who desire to work, (2) respectable women who will not work as long as they are being fed, (3) unfortunate women desiring to reform, and (4) unfortunate women who are hopeless. The Red Cross petitioned the Relief Committee to separate the latter three groups into distinct camps "before the Army retires and the saloons are again opened."

Refugee activists were upset when the Red Cross and Relief Committee held expensive "business dinners" – such as the banquet on July 31, 1906 at the St. Francis Hotel. A band of 1500 homeless, calling themselves "United Refugees," passed out circulars in front of the St. Francis that read, "Let the whole world know that while we are starving they are feasting."

Thornwall Mullaly of United Railroads then created a major controversy when the St. Francis Hotel catered an expensive lunch aboard his private streetcar as he and his friends toured the ruins.

In the next three years, downtown San Francisco was overrun by researchers from engineering societies, universities and government agencies, who used the city as a vast laboratory to study structural engineering aspects of the earthquake and the following conflagration. Researchers attempted to decipher and separate the difference between damage caused by earthquake, by dynamite explosions or direct damage done by the conflagration.

It was a difficult task as Captain John Stephen Sewell of the United States En-

gineers Office found when he attempted to gather specific data about dynamite operations in San Francisco.

Captain Sewell came to San Francisco shortly after the earthquake and fire to document the failure of certain types of fireproofing materials in major structures. His report, titled *The Effects of the Earthquake and Fire on Buildings, Engineering Structures, and Structural Materials*, was published in Department of Interior Bulletin No. 324.

In a letter to Brigadier-General Mackenzie, Chief of Engineers, U. S. Army, Captain Sewell wrote, "To illustrate the importance of this, I stated in my report that for the first time in the history of fireproof buildings, the collapse of protected steel frames under the heat, owing to the inadequacy of fireproof covering, was a matter of common occurrence. Since writing this, I have seen in the technical press statements to the effect that certain buildings were dynamited. First and last, these statements have included practically every building upon which I based my statement above referred to. It was not possible, in the majority of cases, for me to get the debris out of the way, and satisfy myself

(Continued on page 124)

"The Wasp" wrote, "The refugee camps have been hotbeds of immorality and criminality, and it will be a good thing for San Francisco when the last lingering trace of them shall have been effaced." *The camps also became the hotbeds of socialism in San Francisco. Organizers of the short-lived Tammany Civic Federation charged* "The relief funds have not only been looted and stolen and the poor refugees humiliated, starved and reduced to a hapless condition by the conduct of their self-constituted guardians, but Rudolph Spreckels, as captain general of a horde of petty tyrants and camp commanders," *subjected refugees to* "indignities, the trails, the denials and the deprivations, which a people less forbearing would meet with arms and a heroic determination to take the lives of the thieves and overlords and petty tyrants that were degrading them. . . ."

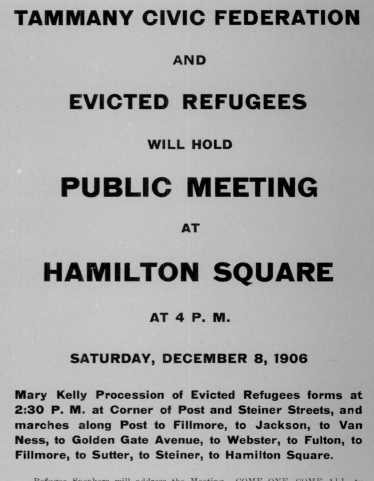

REFUGEES AND COMRADES
PAY NO RENT TO THE
RED CROSS

————

Extortion is the obtaining of property (such as rents) from another without his consent, induced by wrongful use of force or fear, under color of official right, and is a felony punishable by imprisonment in the State Prison, not exceeding five years. All persons concerned in the commission of the crime, whether they directly commit the act constituting the offense, or not being present, who have advised or encouraged its commission, are principals to any crime so committed.

This is the law of the case, as laid down in the Penal Code of California, and I am anxious to make such principals answer for their crimes in extorting money from you, whether such crimes be advised or encouraged or otherwise engaged in by James D. Phelan, Thomas Magee, Rudolph Spreckels, M. H. de Young, Henry Harrison "servant girl" Scott, or special police officers or other brutes engaged in extorting rents from you, with your consent induced by the wrongful use of force or fear, under color of official right.

When these reprehensible creatures, or any one of them, in the presence of reliable witnesses, threaten, under color of official right, to evict you from your homes, unless you pay rent for cottages built in the parks, or on other public lands, with relief funds, then pay the rent, under threats, and report the facts to me. It is the obtaining of the rents, or other money, from you, with your consent induced by wrongful use of force or fear, under color of official right, that constitutes the crime of extortion; and we want your assistance in bringing the criminals to account for their crimes.

ALVA UDELL,
Chairman of Provisional Committee,
Tammany Civic Federation.

Red Cross Thugs, Beware of Arrest!

Every person, who wilfully disturbs or breaks up a public meeting of electors or others, lawfully being held for the purpose of considering public questions, is guilty of a misdemeanor (punishable by a fine not exceeding five hundred dollars, or by imprisonment not exceeding six months, or by both.) Sec. 59, California Penal Code.

TAMMANY CIVIC FEDERATION

AND

EVICTED REFUGEES

WILL HOLD

PUBLIC MEETING

AT

HAMILTON SQUARE

AT 4 P. M.

SATURDAY, DECEMBER 8, 1906

Mary Kelly Procession of Evicted Refugees forms at 2:30 P. M. at Corner of Post and Steiner Streets, and marches along Post to Fillmore, to Jackson, to Van Ness, to Golden Gate Avenue, to Webster, to Fulton, to Fillmore, to Sutter, to Steiner, to Hamilton Square.

Refugee Speakers will address the Meeting. COME ONE, COME ALL, to consider public questions, and denounce the Red Cross Robbers.

M. R. Co.

Refugees on Guerrero Street in line for relief supplies.

Refugee Camp No. 13 at Laguna and Market Streets. The powerhouse of the Market Street Railway is on the right at Market and Valencia Streets.

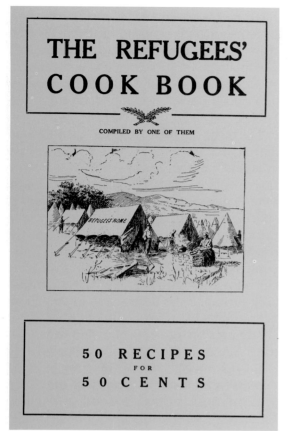

THE REFUGEES' COOK BOOK

COMPILED BY ONE OF THEM

50 RECIPES
FOR
50 CENTS

A cookbook for refugees featured the "Refugee Filter" for purifying water:

"Take a tomato can and perforate the bottom with holes; cover the bottom with a layer of cotton batting and place five or six tablespoonfuls of pulverized charcoal over it. Pour the boiling water in and let filter through. The water will be clear and free from sediment.

"To clear your house or tent of flies – Put a tablespoonful of cayenne pepper in a pan over the fire and let burn; open door, or window, and they will soon all disappear."

James Rolph Jr. used the relief program to build political support in the Mission District and was later elected mayor of San Francisco and then governor of California. Here Mr. Rolph (in straw hat) poses with his children and neighbors in front of his barn on Guerrero Street.

Dr. Rupert Blue of the U. S. Public Health Service was appalled at the shocking conditions he found in Mission District refugee camps. "A rapid tour revealed a deplorable state of affairs with regard to sanitary measures of the protection of these people against disease.

There must have been more than 30-thousand people living in shacks, tents and other temporary abodes in this district. Those whose homes were spared have to cook in the streets, as all chimneys, water and sewer connections have been destroyed by the earthquake."

Thousands of sacks of potatoes at Gough and Page Streets await transport to refugee camps throughout the city.

Thousands of loaves of fresh bread awaited distribution at Mr. Rolph's relief headquarters.

Typical refugee shanty in the Mission District.

Refugees paw through a wagonload of unsorted clothing donated to the relief effort.

Makeshift shelter dug out of the mud and manure in Mission Dolores Park.

(Continued from page 121)

by a personal observation, as to whether the damage was done by fire or by dynamite."

Captain Le Vert Coleman had not recorded specific addresses of dynamited structures, and the report was not as detailed as Captain Sewell had been led to believe.

The technical press, referred to by Captain Sewell, became a forum for acrimonious discussions between engineers debating earthquake versus dynamite versus fire damage. One engineer would write to detail how a specific building had been damaged by earthquake, while a second engineer, usually in the employ of the building owner or the company that built the structure, denied any earthquake or dynamite damage and invariably attributed the destruction to the fire or falling walls of surrounding structures.

Attempts by researchers to find why structures failed in the disaster further complicated bitter legal struggles between building owners and insurers over fire insurance settlements. Chairman Atwood of the Fire Underwriters' Adjustment Committee said, "The insurance companies are prepared with proofs where earthquake losses are in dispute. Abundance of photographic matter is in our hands. It will be used to insure fairness on both sides. Incidentally it may be considered as an extraordinary thing that in the first 2000 claims submitted to insurance men in San Francisco, after the earthquake and fire, every man filing a claim swore that his property was uninjured by the earthquake. I say, that is extraordinary."

One of the controversial aspects of the struggle, the "fallen building" clause, held insurance companies harmless for fire damage following the earthquake collapse of the building. The clause contained in the standard policy forms used throughout the United States and Canada read, "If a building, or any part thereof, fall except as the result of fire all insurance by this policy on such building or its contents shall immediately cease."

Theodore W. Letton, general manager of the Prussian National Insurance Company, said, "The point is that we do not consider we are liable for damage by earthquake and by the dynamiting of buildings. But we are prepared to pay every cent of damage resulting from fire. The trouble has been the difficulty in determining what damage resulted from one and what from the other. We have proposed a compromise, as a consequence, and as soon as an agreement is arrived at the damages will be paid."

This compromise was known as the "horizontal cut" – a percentage discount of the full value of the policy for dynamite or earthquake damage. Insurance adjusters at first wanted a one-third discount on the face value of the policy because of the inability to determine precisely the monetary damage the earthquake or the use of explosives had actually done. A compromise between the in-

(Continued on page 127)

Refugees in line for food at the Hamilton Square relief camp near Post and Steiner Streets in the Western Addition.

U. S. Army tents housed refugees in Jefferson Square Park.

Problems with relief distribution caused grave political troubles for Eugene Schmitz. Long lines and confusion at the Mission High School relief station caused activist priest Peter C. Yorke to interrupt a meeting of the Committee of Fifty and shout at Mayor Schmitz, "Mr. Mayor, you will be held personally responsible if with red tape you strangle American charity. If the present policy of administering assistance is continued, San Francisco twenty years hence will not be the greatest city of the Pacific Coast, but a fishing hamlet. I have no more to say."

Italian refugees near North Beach.

Kitchen crew of one of the relief camps at The Presidio of San Francisco.

Handbills in three languages were posted throughout San Francisco to warn people to properly dispose of garbage and to boil water because of the possibility of disease.

Horrific sanitary conditions in temporary refugee camps prompted health officials to take stringent steps to keep disease under control. When smallpox broke out at the Presidio refugee camps, the military enforced a quarantine and ordered 15,000 doses of vaccine from Parke-Davis Pharmaceuticals. At the same time, Lieutenant William P. White of the Navy said his detail of seamen was kept busy carrying bodies found in the streets, or taken from hospitals, to the fire for cremation. Dr. Regensberger, president of the State Board of Health also ordered medical inspectors to board ferryboats and look for people who exhibited symptoms of smallpox. Those who were found were quarantined at the old pest hospital at what is now Twenty Sixth and Army Streets.

Polluted water did spread typhoid through the camps and rats carried bubonic plague. Secretary of War Taft also took the precaution of sending enough medical supplies for 200,000 people for three months which were shipped in 30 railroad boxcars from St. Louis immediately after the earthquake.

The military's stringent sanitary measures and rigid enforcement of those measures in the camps averted what promised to be a smallpox and tyhpoid epidemic.

In mid-August 1906, the Board of Health condemned the Lake Honda and Lake Merced water supplies because of contamination by sewage from the refugee camps that dotted the sand dunes between Twin Peaks and the ocean. The plague, typhoid and smallpox scare was followed in 1907 by an outbreak of spinal meningitis, and this forced the Board of Health to burn or disinfect buildings or shacks that housed the victims.

1908 brought a troubling report from the San Francisco Board of Health that "insanity was increasing. On investigation it was discovered that the sale of cocaine, opium and other dangerous stimulants or opiates was also advancing at an astonishing rate."

Dozens of refugees killed themselves after the earthquake and fire, many left notes that said they had been despondent because of heavy financial losses. Others were adjudged insane and were committed to state mental hospitals.

Children at play in the refugee camp at Point Lobos Square near Chestnut and Bay Streets. The earthquake-wrecked gasometer of the San Francisco Gas and Electric Company can be seen in the far distance.

(Continued from page 124)

surance companies and a committee of policy holders worked that figure down to 10 percent.

This discount was the basis for future statistics which attributed 10 percent of the overall damage to the earthquake and 90 percent to the fire.

The *Report of the Committee of Five*, which adjusted most of the large claims, said, "The probable [fire] loss, including consequential damages of all kinds, will probably never be actually known, but it has been variously estimated at amounts approximating $1,000,-000,000." This billion dollar figure did not include losses outside of the fire zone or the cost for replacement or repair of water or sewer systems, schools, fire houses, police stations or private structures that did not burn or the cost of the huge relief operation. Rehabilitation of the city's infrastructure attributable to direct earthquake damage was, for the most part, financed by municipal bonds, some of which weren't paid off until the 1980s.

Insurance companies were taken to court over the fallen building clause and the horizontal cut. Victim's claims were almost always upheld after testimony was introduced that denied any earthquake damage. There were claims of perjured testimony and doctored photographs introduced as evidence in some of these insurance cases. The courts could not, however, force insurance companies to act faster or stay out of bankruptcy.

Truly big losers were those who simply had too little insurance. Of the 90,000 claims presented by individuals and companies, the largest by far was the Palace Hotel. For loss of building and contents it received the full value of its policies – $1,518,500 – believed to be the "largest loss on any single risk which was ever adjusted in the United States," according to the insurance report. Yet, this fell more than $300,000 short of the actual "salvage" value of the structure. The full loss, according to the manager of the Palace Hotel, was $6,000,000. This figure did not include $90,000 to pay to remove 15,000 wagon loads of rubble when it was decided to raze the building. Thirty-one-million bricks from Mr. Ralston's "earthquake-proof" Palace Hotel were carted away and used for land fill at Aquatic Park.

Most of the 90,000 claimants lost heavily, up to 90 percent of the value of their structures, even after the insurance payoffs.

A letter with no postage stamp sent from the destroyed city one week after the disaster. Postal service, even in the midst of America's greatest natural disaster, was better than today's. This letter took one day to go from San Francisco to Tracy, in the Central Valley.

Grove K. Gilbert of the U. S. Geological Survey, and a member of the State Earthquake Investigation Commission, wrote in August 1906 of the need for careful mapping of the relation of the isoseismals, or lines marking grades of intensity of earth shaking in the various areas of San Francisco, to underlying soil conditions. "The information contained in such a map should guide the reconstruction and future expansion of the city, not by determining the avoidance of unfavorable sites, but by showing in what areas exceptional precautions are needed, and what areas demand only ordinary precautions."

Mr. Gilbert turned to the seismic future of the West, and wrote, "Must the citizens of San Francisco and the bay district face the danger of experiencing within a few generations a shock equal to or even greater than the one to which they have just been subjected? Or have they earned by their recent calamity a long immunity from violent disturbance? If these questions could be answered in an authoritative way, or if a forecast could be made with a fair degree of probability much good might result; and even if nothing more shall be possible than a cautious discussion of the data, I believe such a discussion should be undertaken and published."

Panoramic views of the destruction left by the Great Earthquake and Fire. Below, the Fairmont Hotel as seen from the Spring Valley Water Company tank at Clay and Jones Streets.

Temple of Congregation Sherith-Israel underwent repairs after the earthquake. The temple became the temporary quarters of the San Francisco Superior Court, and Abe Ruef's graft trial was held there.

Wreckage of Girls' High School at Geary and Scott Streets.

The poem went:

"If, as some say, God spanked the town
For being over frisky,
Why did he burn the Churches down
And save Hotaling's Whisky?"

The A. P. Hotaling & Co. warehouse at 429 Jackson Street was saved from the fire. However, the Hotaling home at 1776 California Street appears to have been dynamited to save the surrounding structures. The building at 1735 Franklin Street, to the left in the picture, still stands.

The Humboldt Savings Bank on Market Street.

The Temple of Congregation Beth Israel on Geary Street near Fillmore Street was destroyed by the earthquake. It was rebuilt and was destroyed by fire in 1989.

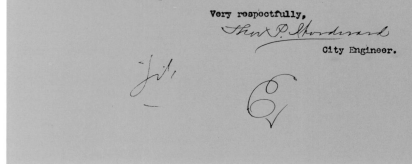

BOARD OF PUBLIC WORKS
BUREAU OF ENGINEERING
OFFICE OF CITY ENGINEER

Brown & Power Co.

San Francisco, Sept. 17, 1906.

Mr. Hugh H. Beggs,

2270 Market St.,

Oakland, Cal.

Dear Sir:-

It is impossible to give you even an "approximate amount of
iron and steel scrap there is in San Francisco as a result of the fire."
It is being "shipped, stored or thrown away." The iron brings about
$9.00 or $10.00 a ton. That from the City Hall was sold at auction
last week for $13.00, the purchaser to gather it and remove it. This
seems a very high price. The Insurance Companies are deducting as much
as they can for salvage on account of the scrap. If you were to write
to some of them, they could doubtless give you more definite information
than I have been able to give.

Very respectfully,

Thos P. Woodward

City Engineer.

City Engineer Thomas Woodward was nearly driven
to distraction by the thousands of letters that poured
into his office after the disaster. Mr. Woodward
answered nearly every one – no matter how trivial
the subject matter. Mr. Begg's letter addressed the issue
of recovery of scrap metal from the rubble of San
Francisco and Mr. Woodward's response indicates that
the amount was incalculable. Insurance companies
did try to sell as much scrap as possible to recover
some of the enormous fire insurance losses.

Scrap iron left over after the Great Fire.

*Wreckage of St. Dominic's Church and Monastary on
the northwest corner of Bush and Steiner Streets.*

Marcus Koshland Mansion at Washington and Maple Streets was a miniature replica of Marie Antoinette's Le Petit Trianon. The mansion was rebuilt and is still occupied.

The spires of the earthquake-wrecked St. Dominic's Church and Monastary at Bush and Steiner Streets.

Hahnemann Hospital on California Street near Maple Street, site of today's Children's and Marshal Hale Hospitals.

This 1905 panorama of the Richmond District (below) shows major buildings that were heavily damaged in the earthquake. The buildings include the Columbarium, the French, Children's and Hahnemann Hospitals, as well as the Richmond School, and the Geary Street, Park and Ocean Railroad Company powerhouse. Other buildings heavily damaged or destroyed included the Maria Kip Orphanage and St. John's Presbyterian Church.

1. E. O. Malley
2. G. Weilan
3. F. Flagecollet
4. J. Doherty
5. F. Kenny
6. F. Wells
7. J. Fitzimmons
8. W. O'Connor
9. W. Nicholas
10. C. Doherty
11. F. Klatz
12. B. Butler
13. D. O'Donnell
14. F. Myers
15. F. Woods
16. C. Maher
17. C. Bettelo
18. W. Conlin
19. P. Hunter
20. F. Carew
21. D. Farien
22. F. Jordan
23. T. McFlynn
24. O. O'Connell
25. J. Gilbert
26. J. Sweeneyh
27. W. Hanton
28. D. Coughlin
29. J. Pendergast
30. T. Flynn
31. W. W. Niefer
32. J. Quinn
33. A. Lafferty
34. W. Hellreigel
35. J. Tuites
36. F. Woods
37. Lt. A. Matlock
38. Capt. R. Woods
39. Lieut. F. Commings
40. J. Dolan
41. Lieut. J. Collins
42. Lieut. Christe Ward
43. Lieut. M. McLaughlin
44. Lieut. W. Otto
45. Lieut. T. Collins
46. Lieut. C. J. Brennan
47. Lieut. S. Rocco
48. Lieut. S. E. Kennard
49. Lieut. W. Farrell
50. Lieut. J. DeMeyer
51. A. Banker
52. A. Stoffer
53. Lieut. J. McGowan
54. J. Loretta
55. J. White
56. J. Leckie
57. Dr. G. E. Manning
58. Hon. W. W. Van Arsdale
59. M. Hale, Automobile Com.
60. Dr. E. R. Bryant
61. Hon. W. P. Lawlor
62. C. A. Bantel, City Treasurer
63. J. A. Stulz, Public Admin.
64. J. F. NIchols
65. H. E. Mulcrevy
66. Hon. C. T. Conlan
67. Hon. E. P. Shortall
68. Hon. M.C. Sloss
69. Hon. F W. Henshaw
70. Hon. W. H. Beatty
71. Hon. T. B. McFarland
72. Hon. F. M. Angellotti
73. T. B. Roche, Emergency Surg.
74. Rev. P. Murphy
75. D. R. Conniff, Asst. Sec. F.D.
76. Rudolph Spreckels, Finance Com. of Relief and Red Cross Funds
77. J. Kahn, Congressman
78. G. E. Middleton, Acting Chauffer for Chief Shaughnessy during fire
79. J. Holle, Automobile Service
80. Lieut. P. Shea, P.D.
81. T. F. Guest, P.D.
82. Sgt. H. H. Christiansen, P.D.
83. H. H. Dobbin, P.D.
84. B. Sanders, Acting Chauffeur for Chief Doherty
85. W. O'Keefe
86. T. Conran
87. J. Tickner
88. G. F. Bury
89. W. Belden
90. M. H. Severance
91. D. Lely
92. W. Willis
93. G. A. Crandall, P.D.
94. O'Connor, P.D.
95. P. McPartland, P.D.
96. J. J. Coughlin, P.D.
97. T. F. Burke, P.D.
98. Sgt. Detective A. Bainbridge
99. Sgt. J. W. Moffitt
100. P. H. Murphy, P.D.
101. G. J. Cashel, P.D.
102. A. C. Williams, P.D.
103. Sgt. J. T Donovan, P.D.
104. T. J. Dugan, P.D.
105. B. F Jones
106. W. DeLong
107. T. Walsh
108. H. Holmes
109. W. Shackleton
110. M. D. Wright
111. R. Powers
112. F. D. Hughes
113. E. J. Studdy
114. J. Maison
115. J. Koopman
116. J. Cowell
117. R. Cuneo
118. J. Mulligan
119. G. Clancy
120. F. Cassassa
121. W. Valente
122. W. Newman
123. H. S. McCormick, Asst. Chief Traub Agt. S.P. Co. Refugees' Transportation
124. P. P. DeGuire, P.D.

125. M. Lyons, P.D.
126. Sgt. J. R. O'Connor
127. Sgt. S. Campbell
128. T. F. Reagan, P.D.
129. Sgt. H. Hook
130. M. Shanahan, P.D.
131. Sgt. A. D. Layne
132. W. Moore
133. F. Franchi
134. C. Smith
135. A. Phelan
136. J. Brophy
137. W. Enright
138. E. Kelleher
139. T. J. Bean
140. S. S. Balk
141. J. W. Parry
142. J. Buker
143. V. F. Gernandt
144. J. E. Owens
145. L. Andrews
146. H. Welch
147. J. Cahill
148. M. Ryan
149. H. C. Mallen, P.D.
150. E. J. Thomson, P.D.
151. N. Miller, P.D.
152. J. C. Field, P.D.
153. J. J. Dow, P.D.
154. J. J. Hurley, P.D.
155. M. Judge, P.D.
156. Capt. L. B. Simonds, U.S.A.
157. Capt. W. C. Wren, U.S.A.
158. First Lt. O.P.M. Hazzard, U.S.A.
159. Col. W. A. Simpson, U.S.A.
160. Mrs. L. Ryan, Chief Matron, P.D.
161. Col. C. L. Heizmann, Chief Surgeon, U.S.A.
162. Capt. A. P. Buffington, U.S.A.
163. Capt. L. D. Wildman, Chief Signal Officer, U.S.A.
164. First Lt. B. J. Mitchell, U.S.A.
165. C. B. Kessing, P.D.
166. A. A. Hicks, P.D.
167. J. J. Doyle, P.D.
168. A. G. Hostetter, P.D.
169. J. B. Berrie, P.D.
170. A. A. Spingette, P.D.
171. B. Kaskell, P.D.
172. W. Flynn, P.D.
173. T. R. Walsh
174. E. Moran
175. C. Shemel
176. J. Meader
177. T. Barry
178. W. Walters
179. Lt. H. Speckman
180. W. Murphy
181. S. W. Horton
182. J. Nelson, Recorder
183. J. Mahoney
184. T. Hart
185. R. Jones
186. J. Herlihy
187. Lt. H. M. Smith, Surgeon, U.S.A.
188. Capt. W. T. Davidson, Surgeon
189. Capt. J. M. Kennedy, Surgeon
190. 2nd Lt. S. E. Patterson, U.S.A.
191. Lt. Col. G. M. Dunn, U.S.A.
192. Col. J. L. Clem, U.S.A.
193. E. E. Bravo, Chief Commisary, U.S.A.
194. Lt. J. H. Allen, Surgeon, U.S.A.
195. Lt. R E. Noble, Surgeon, U.S.A.
196. Lt. R P. O'Connor, Surgeon, U.S.A.
197. J. Buckley
198. D. Burke
199. T. Collins
200. J. Fay
201. T. O'Brien, F.D.
202. C. Strouse, F.D.
203. W. H. Middleton, Actg. Chauffeur, F.D.
204. E. Himmelright, Acting Chauffeu, F.D.
205. M. Brown
206. J. P. Reimers
207. J. Walsh
208. J. Lee
209. A. Florance
210. E. Toland
211. P. Gallagher
212. F. Johnson
213. Lt. F. A. Ellenberger
214. Capt. W. H. Byrnes
215. J. Sullivan
216. Capt. J. H. Dever
217. Capt. J. Mitchell
218. Battalion Chief M. Farley
219. Battalion Chief W. Cook
220. Battalion Chief E. McKittrick
221. Battalion Chief J. McCluskey
222. Battalion Chief H. F. Horn
223. Battalion Chief C. Cullen
224. Battalion Chief J. J. Conlan
225. Capt. J. Doherty
226. Capt. H. Schmidt
227. Capt. G. Brown
228. Lt. M. Hanna
229. J. Bridgewood
230. T. G. Logan
231. T. Hayden
232. A. McDonald
233. W. J. Conroy
234. C. F. Maguire
235. W. Shields
236. J. Timon
237. C. McDonald
238. B. J. McShane
239. F. J. Pope
240. M. J. O'Connell
241. L. Rudolph
242. H. Gelster
243. Sgt. W. H. Williams
244. H. Brown
245. Lt. A. Davis
246. Lt. Lerman
247. Capt. J. Layden
248. Capt. R. Allen
249. Capt. W. Carew

250. Lt. J. Reilly
251. Capt. W. Gallatin
252. Lt. M. Duddy
253. J. White
254. J. F. Collins
255. J. Flater
256. E. O'Neil
257. T. Reilly
258. W. Mullaney
259. W. Foley
260. E. Linderberg
261. J. McNamara
262. M. Norton
263. J. Finn
264. D. Leyons
265. H. Cull
266. C. Reinfield
267. J. Long
268. Lt. W. F. Curran
269. Capt. J. Matheson
270. Lt. J. Kenny
271. Capt. C. R. Murray
272. Capt. W. Shultz
273. Capt. Sayers
274. Capt. Sayers
275. Lt. J. Bolan
276. L. Kiehl
277. F. Reckenbiel
278. Dr. W. J. Walsh, Coroner
279. C. J. Molloy
280. G. Faubel
281. M. J. Rodriguez
282. J. Fitzpatrick
283. C. Kelleher
284. G. Lahnsen
285. W. Swanton
286. J. Crowley
287. J. Murray
288. H. Carter
289. R. E. Charlton
290. Capt. A. W. Welch
291. Capt. J. Capelli
292. Capt. P. F. Dugan
293. Capt. E. Skelly
294. Capt. J. Fitzpatrick
295. Capt. T. Magner
296. Capt. Kentzel
297. Lt. W. Conniff
298. H. E. Church
299. G. Dykes
300. J. Rogers
301. J. Conlan
302. J. Windsor
303. J. Driscol
304. T. McGovern
305. J. Woods
306. H. Newman
307. W. Sawyer
308. P. L. Raffestin
309. W. Hensley
310. C. Malloy
311. E. King
312. Lt. G. Hartman
313. Capt. E. J. Gillig
314. Capt. J. Fay
315. Capt. H. Mitchell
316. Capt. M. Boden
317. Capt. W. J. Bannan
318. Capt. J. Conniff
319. Lt. M. Drury
320. W. Roebling
321. J. Shaughnessy
322. W. Hopkins
323. P. DeMartini
324. C. Gill
325. W. Shade
326. T. Cashin
327. O. Pyritz
328. C. Brownell
329. J. Cannon
330. G. Hall
331. J. Heyden
332. F. Meehan
333. C. Haines
334. Lt. A. Engleke
335. Capt. S. D. Russell
336. Capt. D. Newell
337. Capt. F. Nichols
338. Battalion Chief M. O'Brien
339. Battalion Chief J. Wills
340. 1st Asst. Chief M.J. Dolan
341. Chief Engineer P. H. Shaughnessy (present)
342. Chief Engineer D. T. Sullivan, killed during the disaster
343. 1st Asst. Chief Engineer J. Doherty (retired)
344. 2nd Asst. Chief T. Murphy
345. Battalion Chief W. Waters
346. Battalion Chief J. Maxwell
347. Capt. J. Radford
348. Captain E. O'Connor
349. Capt. T. Murphy
350. Capt. J. O'Brien
351. H. Powers
352. T. O'Brien
353. W. Lane
354. D. Capilli
355. A. Isaacs
356. W. Spinetti
357. B. Brandon
358. Lt. J. Conroy
359. W. Crosby
360. J. Wales
361. M. O'Connell
362. Lt. T. Kelly
363. Capt. F. Grote
364. Lt. J. Feeney
365. W. D. Flinn, P.D.
366. P. J. O'Brien, P.D.
367. J. F. Cronin, P.D.
368. Sgt. H. Cills
369. Sgt. P. H. McGee
370. Lt. J. M. Lewis, P.D.
371. Lt. T. Tobin
372. Capt. M. O. Anderson, P.D.
373. Gen. A. W. Greely
374. Capt. H. H. Colby, P.D.
375. Lt. M. Carrol, P.D.
376. Sgt. W. E. Dinan, P.D.
377. Sgt. J. H. Moerissey, P.D.

378. Lt. D. W. Boyd, P.D.
379. Sgt. W. Ferguson, P.D.
380. J. Rainsbury
381. G. M. Greiman
382. Capt. D. Murphy
383. Lt. J. Hayden
384. Lt. J. Canley
385. R. McShane
386. J. Gavin
387. P. Creede
388. J. Tynell
389. J. Bohen
390. G. Bonner
391. D. O'Rourke
392. J. Stevens
393. Lt. W. Gill
394. Lt. J. Kelly
395. Lt. L. O'Neil
396. J. M. Brodt, P.D.
397. Sgt. P.M. Mahoney
398. Sgt. L. Shaw
399. Sgt. J. J. Farrell
400. Lt. H. J. Wright, P.D.
401. Capt. B. McManus, P.D.
402. Capt. T. F. Duke, P.D.
403. Capt. J. Kelly, P.D.
404. Capt. J. B. Martin, P.D.
405. Capt. H. Gleeson, P.D.
406. Lt. J. H. Lachman, P.D.
407. Lt. F. P. Green, P.D.
408. Sgt. P. E. Fraher
409. Sgt. W. F. Brophy
410. Sgt. M. J. Griffin
411. E. G. King, P.D.
412. Lt. E. McCormick
413. Lt. J. Pendergast
414. E. Daunet
415. F. Crockett
416. P. Hogan
417. G. Davis
418. T. Trivett
419. E. Crummery
420. D. McAuliffe
421. J. Titus
422. H. Reed
423. N. P. Brown, Relief Comm.
424. Garret McEnerney, Chairman Resumption of Civil Govt.
425. C. J. Heggerty, Relief Services
426. T. Kytka, Citizens' Police Committee
427. I. W. Hellman, Finance Com. of the Relief and Red Cross Funds
428. Dr. F. G. Canney, Board of Health
429. M. H. DeYoung, Finance Com. of the Relief and Red Cross Funds
430. R. C. Hill, Emergency Surgeon
431. R. J. Tillman, Emergency Surgeon
432. Dr. W. C. Voorsanger, Relief Committee
433. C. C. Bucher, Chief Steward, Emergency Hospitals
434. J. W. Raphael, Chairman Transportation Com.
435. T. Reagan, Police Commissioner
436. Hon. J. W.Ward, M.D., Relief of Sick and Wounded, President of the Health Commission
437. Hon. J. D. Phelan, Finance Com. of the Relief and Red Cross Funds
438. H. E. Law, Relief Com.
439. Col. G. H. Pippy, Relief Com.
440. H. H. Geertz, Relief Com.
441. F. W. Don, Relief Com.
442. C. C. Hopkins, Transportation Service
443. E. Ganvi
444. Lt. J. Crosby
445. M. O'Neil
446. W. F. Tracy
447. A. Swanberg
448. Lt. F. Murray
449. J. McFernan
450. E. P. Brennan
451. Rev. D. O. Crowley, Relief Com.
452. W. Hunt
453. Dr. C. B. Pinkham, Chief Surgeon, Emergency Hospitals
454. R. E. Lund, Chief Train Agt., S.P. Co.
455. Hon. G. C. Pardee, Governor of Calif. Relief Work
456. Rev. J. Voorsanger, Chairman Relief of Hungry
457. Hon. J. C. Hebbert
458. Hon. C. Cook
459. Hon. F. H. Kerrigan
460. E. F. Moran, Secretary History and Statistics
461. Dr. D. D. Lustig, Insanity Expert
462. Dr. E. T. Devine, Red Cross Society
464. F. A. Leach, Supt. U.S. Mint
465. J. Rolph, Jr. Chairman Mission Relief Comm.
466. C. H. Burks, Secretary S.F. Chamber of Commerce
467. T. Magee, Chairman Transportation of Refugees Com.
468. Hon. G. C. Perkins, U.S. Senator
469. R. P. Jennings, Relief Comm.
470. E. H. Harriman, President S.P. Co. Transportation of Refugees
471. H. J. Temple
472. C. Neil
473. M. J. Glennan
474. J. F. Fitzgerald
475. Brig. Gen. F. Funston, Commanding Dept. of California
476. J. F. Dinan, Chief of Police
477. Hon. E. E. Schmitz, the Mayor

Photo montage of "Heroes of the Great Calamity" published in 1907. The only woman "hero" listed is Mrs. L. Ryan (photo 160), Chief Matron of the San Francisco Police Department. She supervised the rescue of terrorized and hysterical prisoners from the shattered Hall of Justice after the 1906 earthquake.

The criteria for inclusion as a disaster hero is not clear. Only a fraction of the members of the police and fire departments are shown, and none of the U.S. Army dynamite squad is included. Also absent is Colonel Charles Morris who made the decision to dynamite a firebreak along Van Ness Avenue. The late Fire Chief Engineer Dennis Sullivan is number 342, Captain Wildman of the Army number 163 and General Greely number 373.

ROES OF THE GREAT CALAMITY.

COPYRIGHT 1907
L. MURAT, 1018 VALENCIA ST. S.F.

The Future of San Francisco

Panoramic view of high-rise buildings constructed in the 1960-1989 era.

Photo by Robert W. Cameron

"The Fire Made Its Own Draft. . . ."

"By Wednesday afternoon, inside of twelve hours, half the heart of the city was gone. At that time I watched the vast conflagration from out on the bay. It was dead calm. Not a flicker of wind stirred. Yet from every side wind was pouring in upon the city. East, west, north, and south, strong winds were blowing upon the doomed city. The heated air rising made an enormous suck. Thus did the fire of itself build its own colossal chimney through the atmosphere. Day and night the dead calm continued, and yet, near to the flames, the wind was often half a gale, so mighty was the suck."

Jack London, San Francisco
"The Story of an Eyewitness"
Collier's, The National Weekly
May 5, 1906

An engineering report published shortly after the 1906 earthquake and fire carried this prediction. "It is probable that the new San Francisco to rise on the ruins will be to a large extent a duplicate of the former city in defects of construction." Today, as a former fire chief of San Francisco and a member of the Fire Service Section of the Governor's Earthquake Task Force, I would agree that the hazard of fire to the city after a similar disaster today is much greater than in 1906.

This assessment of the hazard of fire to the city is reinforced by a recent engineering report funded by the insurance industry to estimate the conflagration risk to the Bay Area, and to quantify the insured fire losses that might result. The 1987 report – *Fire*

(Continued on page 137)

Jack and Charmian London were at their ranch in Glen Ellen at the time of the earthquake. They left on horseback to look at the ruins of the California Home for the Care and Training of Feeble-Minded Children, where dust still rose from the ruins.

Mr. London said to his wife – as she wrote in 1921 – "Why, Mate Woman, I shouldn't wonder if San Francisco had sunk. That was some earthquake. We don't know but the Atlantic may be washing up at the feet of the Rocky Mountains!"

Charmian London was stunned by what she saw as she and Jack walked through the streets of the doomed city: "In my eyes, there abides the face of a stricken man, perhaps a fireman, whom we saw carried into a lofty doorway in Union Square. His back had been broken, and as the stretcher bore him past, out of a handsome, ashen young face, the dreadful darkening eyes looked right into mine. All the world was crashing about him and he, a broken thing, with death awaiting him inside the granite portals, gazed upon the last woman of his race that he was ever to see. Jack, with tender hand, drew me away."

Jack London told his wife, "I'll never write about this for anybody, no, I'll never write a word about it. What use trying? One could only string big words together and curse the futility of them."

However, when Collier's offered him the then-enormous sum of 25 cents per word for his story on the Great Earthquake, Jack London, in serious debt, wrote a 2500 word article for the magazine. It was the most money per word he was ever paid for his writings.

Mr. London was not happy with the results, and said, "It's the best stagger I can make at an impossible thing." Later, he wrote poet George Sterling: "(James) Hopper's article in Everybody's (magazine) is great. Best story of the Quake I've seen. My congratulations to him."

Dear Merle —

You bet I was in the thick of it. Routed out of bed at quarter past five. Half an hour later Mrs. London and I were in the saddle. We rode miles over the surrounding country. An hour after the shock, from a high place in the mountains, we could see at the same time the smoke of burning San Francisco and of burning Santa Rosa. Caught a train to Santa Rosa — Santa Rosa got it worse than S. F. Then in the afternoon, Wednesday afternoon, we got into San Francisco and spent the whole night in the path of the flames — You bet, I saw it all.

Am glad all of you escaped O.K.

Do I understand that you are going to move to Oakland.

Affectionately
Your Uncle Jack

Jack and Charmian London.

Aerial view of thousands of wood-frame row houses in San Francisco's Sunset District.

(Continued from page 135)

Following Earthquake – Estimates of the Conflagration Risk to Insured Property in Greater Los Angeles and San Francisco – written by Dr. Charles Scawthorn, estimates that a minimum of 79 fires may start in San Francisco after a major earthquake; 39 of which will require fire department response greatly in excess of available fire equipment and personnel. The report also says a minimum of 142 fire engines will be needed to cope with those fires. This is almost four times the number of fire engines in service in San Francisco in 1989. The number of buildings destroyed by fire is estimated to be from 22,500, to as high as 48,000, depending on wind velocities, climatic conditions and the city's fire defense. Business and home property losses from this next great disaster, says the report, will run between 2 and 5 billion dollars, but it doesn't attempt to estimate life loss or injuries from the postulated earthquake. Included in the report are estimates of prop-

erty losses in surrounding communities, and it emphasizes that the post-earthquake fire risk is three to four times higher in San Francisco than in other Bay Area communities.

It is my considered opinion that the number of fires and the dollar loss estimates are relatively accurate, but in some cases are understated. The 1971 San Fernando earthquake, magnitude [M] 6.4, resulted in a total of 109 fires in the area, and the 1987 Whittier-Narrows earthquake, magnitude [M] 5.9, generated 36 structure fires. Richter scale increases are measured logarithmically by a factor of ten. In other words, a magnitude [M] 8 earthquake is not twice as strong as a magnitude [M] 4, but 10,000 times stronger, 10x10x10x10, [10]. So, using these figures, the engineering prediction of 79 fires in San Francisco following a magnitude [M] 8 earthquake appears to be conservative.

BUILDING CODE STANDARDS REDUCED –
FIRE HAZARD CONTINUED

Experience from the 1906 Earthquake and Fire uncovered severe defects in building code provisions both for earthquake and fire resistance. These building defects were repeated in the reconstruction of San Francisco's business district and the major expansion of residential areas.

Further, in the great haste to rebuild the city, building code standards were actually reduced from those in effect before the Great Fire. Wind loads, floor loads and roof loads were reduced by almost 50 percent over the subsequent years. This reduction in building code standards was described by Henry Dewell, a noted engineer, in his comments before the San Francisco Commonwealth Club in August 1925. "The office building or similar structure designed in accordance with today's San Francisco building ordinance," he said, "is very much weaker than the building designed immediately after 1906. With respect to safe design against earthquakes, we have only not progressed but we have actually seriously retrogressed." However, neither he, nor anyone else at the time, commented on one of the greatest building defects from the standpoint of fire hazard – the continuation of the practice to allow row housing to be built with wooden side walls abutting the adjacent building without barriers to arrest the spread of fire from one building to another.

For example, in the outer residential districts in the western part of the city, a block usually consists of 24 houses built with wooden side walls touching one another. As far as fire protection is concerned this is effectively a single block-sized structure. Each of these blocks represents a single fire load of combustible construction exceeding 30,000 square feet. Under major fire conditions this fire load would tax the best efforts of an entire metropolitan fire department. There are, unfortunately, thousands of such houses across the city. This building code defect was finally corrected in 1984, but by then the damage

was done. Primarily because of this one construction defect the city, in recent years, has experienced numerous multi-building fires. In 1959, 36 buildings burned in the Western Addition; a 1979 fire burned 26 buildings in the area of Seventh and Harrison Streets, and 11 buildings were destroyed on Divisadero Street in 1983. During the 1979 fire at Seventh and Harrison Streets all San Mateo fire departments were alerted by the San Francisco Fire Department to stand by for response into the city, because of the heavy commitment of city fire units to the fire. These were single location blazes, where the entire fire department was available to fight the fire.

Visualize, if you will, the impossible task placed upon the fire department when multiple fires in buildings of this type of construction erupt throughout the city after the next major earthquake.

POLYURETHANE AND POLYSTYRENE –
THE NEW COMBUSTIBLES

The term "fire load" means both the combustible materials used in building construction and the contents. The composition of building contents, such as furniture, carpets and so on, has changed dramatically in the last 30 years, unfortunately in a manner that greatly increases the fire risk. Most furnishings, in the past, were composed of cellulosic material such as wood and cotton batting in mattresses and upholstered furniture that, when set afire, usually smolders for a considerable period of time before bursting into flame.

Most furniture and furnishings in the past 30 years have been manufactured from synthetic materials. When ignited, they burn fiercely, and throw off great clouds of dense smoke that make escape from burning buildings more dangerous, and increases the difficulty in putting out the fires. Gordon Vickery, Director of the Foundation for Fire Safety, warned of the life risk created by these synthetic materials. "They burn twice as fast,

San Francisco's City Hall complex rests atop part of the old Mission Swamp. This aerial view from Market Street and United Nations Plaza [Fulton Street] shows *the site of the old City Hall to the left of the underground parking exit at Larkin Street.*

twice as hot and can give off up to 500 times as much toxic gases as more conventional materials."

Extensive fire tests at the Richmond Field Testing Station of the University of California were conducted with rooms furnished with modern synthetic materials such as polyurethane and polystyrene modular furniture. They burned rapidly and reached "flashover stage" – when the entire room explodes in flames – in five minutes or less, which is four or five times faster than similar test fires in ordinary cellulosic fiber-based materials. Our homes and offices are now full of this type of furnishings. Synthetic materials have greatly increased the fire risk in modern buildings and will magnify the fire problem in the multiple fires that will break out after a serious earthquake.

This increased fire threat was tragically demonstrated during the 1983 Cathedral Hill Hotel fire in San Francisco. Fuel for this fire was composed of about 165 chairs padded with polyurethane stacked around the perimeter of an assembly area on the mezzanine floor and constituted the only furniture in the area. The resulting fire fed by these chairs raged through the building and killed two people. Dollar loss from this fire exceeded $12 million.

TOXIC AND HAZARDOUS MATERIALS – SIGN OF THE TIMES

Proliferation of toxic and hazardous materials in the city has added another serious dimension to our fire risk. Accidental releases of hazardous materials have caused the evacuation of major portions of U. S. cities in recent years, and similar dangerous releases will certainly happen in a major earthquake. There are well over 1,000 locations in the city that contain some form of hazardous and toxic materials such as solvents, acids, and other chemicals used in manufacturing and other industrial processes. Large tanks of liquid hydrogen presently in San Francisco, for example, are used for the treatment of vegetable products and in related industrial processes. These processes are normally very safe, but a rupture caused by a major earthquake will be extremely dangerous. A leaking high-pressure hydrogen joint will usually take fire immediately and will rapidly expand as the liquid vaporizes into a gas. The hazard is more severe, and this is quite ironical, if the hydrogen does not catch fire, because the vapors will flow like water and also spread rapidly. When liquid hydrogen does vaporize, it expands at a ratio of one-to-850 cubic feet with a tremendous explosive range. If the gas permeates enclosed areas there is an immediate probability of a serious explosion.

This is only one of many hazardous material dangers. Any of them would require evacuation of major parts of the city under normal circumstances and would also hinder access of emergency personnel.

(Continued on page 142)

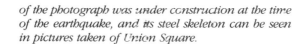

The St. Francis Hotel at Union Square. This part of San Francisco contains some of the City's most valuable commercial real estate. The tall building at the bottom of the photograph was under construction at the time of the earthquake, and its steel skeleton can be seen in pictures taken of Union Square.

Dramatic view of dense clusters of high-rise buildings at Post and Montgomery Streets.

It was impossible for emergency vehicles to move through many of San Francisco's streets after the earthquake and fire of 1906 because of the rubble.

In 1906, thousands of tons of brick rubble surround the wrecked City Hall.

Nob Hill to the bay encompasses some of the largest population densities in the United States. Chinatown alone has hundreds of unreinforced masonry structures and narrow streets and alleyways.

(Continued from page 139)

NATURAL GAS – A CONTINUING HAZARD

There were more than 30 gas line explosions during the 1906 earthquake and fire that created 15-to-30-foot craters in the streets. These explosions added to the conflagration, and ruptured nearby water mains as well as underground telephone and telegraph conduits. Most of the gas in the 1900s was distributed under low pressure from the large gas holder tanks that were visible in various parts of the city. Today, all of these large gas holders have disappeared; more efficient, higher pressure gas supply lines have made them unnecessary.

High pressure transmission, and the complexity of gas supply distribution systems add to the potential fire threat. Within the last ten years a ruptured gas line in the downtown area forced me to evacuate 30,000 people. Escaping gas was not cut off for nine hours. The serious hazard of these gas distribution lines was demonstrated in the October 1987 earthquake in the Los Angeles-Whittier area, where there were 80 gas main ruptures. This was a magnitude [M] 5.9 earthquake – creating far less devastation than would be caused by an earthquake approaching magnitude [M] 8 on the Richter scale.

HIGH-RISE BUILDINGS –
POTENTIAL FOR DISASTER

There are about 500 high-rise buildings in San Francisco, including some that survived 1906. Most engineering assessments say that well-built steel-frame buildings with good foundations will survive a major earthquake. This is small comfort to those inside in the event of a complete burnout of the combustible contents.

The TransAmerica building on the site of the Montgomery Block, and all high-rise buildings built thereafter, with one exception, are equipped with a life-safety system that includes a sprinkler system and an on-site water supply to provide continuing protection even if water mains are ruptured by an earthquake. However, there are nearly 400 high-rise structures that pre-date these modern buildings, equipped with what can only be described as basic fire protection equipment: a vertical standpipe and portable fire extinguishers.

Here is the problem: fires in this class of high-rise building require firefighters – lots of them – to physically carry portable equipment to the fire. A "smoke showing" report by first arriving fire units causes an immediate call for 60 firefighters. With the probability of several such fires after a major earthquake, the fire department incident commander will be faced with the same decisions that Captain Charles J. Cullen of Fire Engine No. 6 had to make: whether to commit personnel or to abandon a building. If the lives of occupants are, however, at risk, the commander will have no choice, as Captain Cullen had no choice, but to commit – as long as there are rescue personnel available.

If this paints a grim picture, consider that in Los Angeles City in 1988, a fire in a single high-rise building required 383 department

California Street from Market Street to the Richmond District. The buildings in the foreground are all built on "made ground."

personnel to bring it under control. This represented nearly fifty percent of their available resources. If a similar fire occurred in one of San Francisco's numerous high-rise buildings the fire department could not mount a similar effort; there is a total of only 315 firefighters available to protect the entire city – at this writing.

WATER SUPPLY – A CITY'S LIFE BLOOD

It is a little known fact that there was sufficient water in the Spring Valley Water Company reservoirs in San Francisco to combat the 1906 fire, even with the serious breaks in the main lines outside the city. Breakdown of the water supply was due to the failure of distribution mains within the city, and thousands of ruptured, patchwork household water connections. Many of these deficiencies still exist today.

In 1985, the Engineering Department of Cornell University published findings based on its investigation of the San Francisco municipal water system. This report recog- nized the importance of the Fire Depart- ment's Auxiliary Water Supply System, but predicted the possibility of serious difficul- ties associated with pipeline breaks. During a great earthquake, the majority of city water mains crossing zones of lateral earth spreads will be broken, crippling the firefighting capability of the municipal system, particu- larly in the eastern part of the city. This sec- tion, unfortunately, also includes the finan- cial district. Here, the only water would come from the fire department's Auxiliary Water Supply System – if it is, in fact, still operable.

WIND FORCES – THE UNKNOWN FACTOR

San Francisco is subject to prevailing west- erly winds, an important factor in the City's fire defense. However, there has been little study of the effects of winds generated by large fires in metropolitan areas and their escalation into firestorms. One of the few authoritative reports on this subject, "Fire and the Air War," was published in 1946. Edited by Horatio Bond, Chief Engineer of the National Fire Protection Association (N.F.P.A.), the publication is a compilation of expert observations of fires set by incendiary and atomic bombs during World War II.

The firestorm phenomenon was de- scribed as a column of burning gases and hot air rising over a fire and strong air move- ment is drawn toward the center of the fire from all sides to replace the oxygen being consumed. The destruction inside the fire- storm was usually complete.

The report contains a reliable eyewitness account of the viciousness of a firestorm in a metropolitan city. Professor Graeff of the Hamburg Military Defense Area gave this vivid description of the destructive force of the firestorm in that city.

"The heat [of the fire] increased rapidly and produced a wind which soon was the strength of a typhoon. In public squares and parks it broke trees, and burning branches shot through the air. Trees of all sizes were uprooted. The firestorm broke down doors of houses and later the flames crept into the doorways and corridors. The firestorm looked like a blizzard of red snowflakes.

"The heat turned whole city blocks into a flaming hell. As the temperatures increased in the streets from the spread of large-scale fires many of the occupants of the air raid shelters realized the precariousness of the situation, yet very few tried to escape into areas not endangered by the fire. In the course of hours the air in the shelters became increasingly worse. Matches or candles did not burn. People lay on the floors because the air was better there and they could breathe easier. Some vomited and became incontinent. Some became tired and quiet and went to sleep. Many stated that the air 'just didn't come out any more' and breathing became very difficult. Otherwise they did not feel anything, and the rest went on over those who had fallen."

The N.F.P.A. report also commented on problems faced by the fire department during the firestorms. "The tremendous hurricane of fire caused the air to be drawn toward the fire from all directions with such a terrific velocity that it tore trees apart, and prevented firemen from coming close enough to be within range of hose streams. Soon it caused building walls to collapse into streets, and further prevented the department from bringing apparatus into the area."

The Hamburg Fire Department estimated that 55,000 persons lost their lives. Thousands of victims, later found in basement shelters, showed no indication of having been burned, but apparently they died from lack of oxygen, heat inhalation, or asphyxiation from coal and other gases.

The N.F.P.A. differentiated between the firestorm phenomenon and a conflagration:

"The chief characteristic of the conflagration was the presence of a fire front, an extended wall of fire moving to leeward preceded by a turbid mass of pre-heated vapors. The progress and destructive features of the conflagration were therefore much greater than those of the firestorm, for in the conflagration the fire continued to spread until it could reach no more combustible material."

At the start of the 1906 fire, wind speeds measured by the U. S. Weather Bureau were less than ten miles per hour, but a few hours later, Lieutenant Frederick N. Freeman, a trained naval officer, reported the generation of "gale force winds" (30-35 mph). A fire official described the severe wind drafts created by the Great Fire, and Midshipman Pond reported that wind drove the fire up Rincon Hill and outran men and women in flight, sweeping the hill clean in less than an hour.

San Francisco, fortunately, has had no modern experience with firestorms. But the strong, fire-winds like those of April 1906, comparable to the firestorms that destroyed European and Japanese cities in World War II, will seriously impede standard firefighting practices after the next Great Earthquake. An awestruck Jack London, with his vivid account of the 1906 firestorm, was forty years ahead of his time in his accurate description of the destructive firestorms that were to de-

The remodeled Call Building (now Central Towers) still dominates the intersection of Third and Market Streets. At the extreme upper right of the photograph is the Meridien Hotel on the site of the Winchester House on Third Street. The rebuilt electic powerhouse on Jessie Street is in the lower right hand corner.

stroy Hamburg, Dresden and Tokyo.

WHAT CAN HAPPEN AFTER
AN EARTHQUAKE

There are several fire possibilities which cannot be accurately predicted, no matter what the severity of an earthquake. In a magnitude, [M] 8 earthquake, however, the potential fire can be gauged by what we know of the 1906 earthquake, the Coalinga earthquake, the San Fernando earthquake, the Mexico City earthquake, and from my thirty years of experience as a San Francisco firefighter.

This is the future I see for San Francisco: After the first great shock subsides and before fires grow to serious proportions, people would attempt to escape from collapsed buildings as others try to report fires and call for help to rescue trapped occupants. These people will experience a new jolt – no telephones. During recent major earthquakes telephone communications have been disrupted because of damage to phone cables or central office equipment, or simply because of an overload of calls. There is no other way to quickly seek assistance, or to provide information to the emergency services. The Municipal Street Telegraph System, with the familiar red fire alarm boxes, will be inoperable because of damage to underground conduits.

Loss of communications between the public and the emergency services – police, fire, medical – will be critical. Without information as to where fires have started, or where building collapses have trapped occupants, the fire department must begin a time-consuming survey to assess the magnitude of the disaster. Time of day will largely determine the number of injuries and deaths. During the weekday, with schools in session and businesses in full operation there will be over one million people in San Francisco. Collapsed buildings, sunken and caved in pavement, debris in the street and flooding caused by ruptured water mains will seriously hamper emergency vehicles. There are narrow, Gold-Rush width streets in Chinatown and high-occupancy masonry and wood frame buildings; in the Tenderloin there is a preponderance of unreinforced masonry buildings, and many of them will suffer partial collapse and fill the streets with debris.

After the 1983 Coalinga earthquake, Fire Chief Fred Frederickson said every fire engine in his department suffered flat tires from glass and debris. San Francisco will fare no better. Indeed, the financial district may prove to be the most difficult access area for fire fighting and rescue operations. Tall buildings will shed glass in large quantities, adding to the debris in the streets and pose a serious barrier to emergency vehicle access.

As blazes grow in various parts of the city, the fire department will be spread thinner and thinner, responding to new fires and trying to maintain control of existing ones, all without the assistance of those firefighters already committed to evacuating and rescuing people trapped in collapsed structures.

(Continued on page 150)

The Transamerica pyramid occupies the site of the Montgomery Block where members of the 22nd Infantry began their looting spree. Hundreds of post-earthquake unreinforced masonry structures occupy the former Warehouse District to the right of the photograph.

1906 wreckage of Chinatown buildings along Dupont Street (Grant Avenue) between California and Sacramento Streets.

Fire Engine Station No. 26 at 327 Second Avenue in the Richmond District. This engine company put out many small fires in wood-frame buildings immediately after the earthquake and fire of 1906.

To prevent looting, soldiers guarded the wreckage of Chinatown after the fire of 1906. Twenty members of the National Guard of California were arrested by the U. S. Army and charged with looting the ruins.

The need for housing was so great after the 1906 earthquake and fire that many surviving structures were "remodeled" or reconstructed, oftentimes without city permits. Here, a one-story saloon became the nucleus of a new three-story structure.

Beulah Street dead ends into Cole Street, between Waller and Frederick, in the Haight-Ashbury district. This type of dense row house construction dominates many of The City's residential districts.

Dolores Street (center) separates the old city from the new. Twentieth Street, the southern border of Mission Dolores Park, was where the Great Fire was stopped in the Mission District. Wood-frame houses were again built in this area that suffered such earthquake destruction in 1906. The east side of Dolores Street from Market Street to Mission High School was dynamited to create a firebreak.

Smouldering rubble of buildings at Mission and East (The Embarcadero) Streets shortly after the fire of 1906

as photographed from the Ferry Building tower. The surviving Audiffred Building is at far left.

After the 1906 earthquake and fire, battles over fire insurance kept many property owners from clearing the rubble from their property until settlements were

made with insurance companies. It was several months before rubble was removed from Clay Street between Nob Hill and the Ferry Building.

Land use in the South of Market District remains surprisingly similar to that of pre-earthquake San Francisco. The Southern Pacific Company yard at the bottom of the photograph is where thousands of refugees camped to wait out the Great Fire. Nearly all of the buildings to the south and west of the James Lick Freeway are on "made ground."

(Continued from page 145)
Media will converge on San Francisco in unbelievable numbers, and their coverage should produce a far better understanding of the disaster response than we have of 1906, for which we will one day be grateful. San Franciscans, in 1906, reported incredible delays in locating their families, particularly when no one in the family read English. Newspapers did publish lists of names of the missing and injured, but they were not in any particular order. Perhaps newspapers will publish missing and survivor lists alphabetically. Yet the media will unavoidably add to the unpredictable confusion and disorganization. You cannot fight fires, get to fires, or evacuate wounded if the path is blocked by media and other vehicles, particularly those with flat tires. In Coalinga, hovering news media and emergency services helicopters created problems for triage stations.

However, fire remains the big threat. With electric power lines down in streets, gas supply lines severed, chemical spills and hazardous materials released, there is a potential for firestorms or conflagrations throughout the city.

FIRE FIGHTING ASSISTANCE FROM OUTSIDE THE CITY

Mutual aid assistance from outside the Bay Area will be delayed in arriving in San Francisco. Both the Golden Gate and the Bay bridges will be closed by ground failure at the approaches. Predictions are that peninsula access will also be impaired because of liquifaction of filled-in land and damaged overpasses. In effect, the city will be isolated for hours, if not days. Airlifts can provide personnel and supplies, but fire vehicles of necessity, will have to be brought to the city on surface roads and streets. Help from off-duty personnel will also be limited, because more than 70 percent of the members live in suburban areas, which will suffer their own disasters.

DEMAND ON FIRE DEFENSE STRATEGY

In the hours immediately following the earthquake, with the number of fires growing and merging, the San Francisco Fire Department chief officers will have to make drastic changes in fire defense strategy. With approximately 300 personnel on duty, and many of those involved in rescue operations, the department will not be able to combat all fires on an individual basis. It will be necessary to shift to perimeter fire control measures. This type of fire control is rarely used in a metropolitan city, because when it is used it tacitly acknowledges that all properties within the established perimeter are doomed. The strategy involves placing high-powered master stream nozzles at specific locations on a fire front where it is believed that they will stop the fire or, without water as in 1906, the creation of firebreaks. It may be possible to position and maintain some of these master streams with the limited number of personnel and volunteers available. The crucial factor for success in this strategy is sufficient water to maintain effective fire flows. Since master streams are normally first located downwind, a shift in wind direction, caused by the magnitude of the fire –

San Francisco's post-earthquake population spread to the Richmond and Sunset Districts, where thousands of wood-frame row houses were built, with no fire-rated separation between structures

possibly reaching firestorm proportions, can be disastrous.

The burden that is placed upon the fire department by perimeter firefighting was demonstrated during the 1959 Western Addition fire that destroyed 36 buildings. Master streams were positioned on the perimeter to contain the fire, but burning brands carried by a surging wind started secondary fires as far as five blocks from the original fire. Requests for additional assistance at these other fires were denied – there were only two engine companies available to protect the rest of the city. This was probably the closest the city came to being without adequate fire protection since 1906.

If fire crosses the perimeter at any point there is usually very rapid spread due to the extremely high fire temperatures. (Fire temperatures in the Great Fire reached 2700 degrees Fahrenheit.) Fires will jump streets and rapidly spread, particularly in hilly areas. The western residential section of the city will be most vulnerable to this form of fire extension because of the up-slope terrain and the prevailing westerly wind.

SECTIONAL FIRE DEFENSE – THE FALLBACK POSITION

When fires jump perimeter boundaries it will be necessary to resort to sectional fire defense. This kind of fire defense attempts to confine fires to multi-block areas. In addition to the use of master streams, this strategy relies on the use of open spaces, fire barriers, and if feasible, removal or demolition of uninvolved buildings. This type of fire defense has not been used in San Francisco since the Great Fire when three battalion chiefs used it successfully to save major portions of the Mission District. This is obviously a last resort – short of abandonment – and will cause multi-million dollar fire losses and possibly numerous fatalities, if the areas beyond the perimeter have not been previously evacuated.

For sectional firefighting to achieve any success, planning must have identified open areas, wide streets, expressways, parks and similar areas that can effectively isolate the involved section from unburned areas. This calls for extensive and detailed pre-disaster fire planning. If fire extension reaches such proportions as to make sectional firefighting necessary, major parts of the city will be destroyed and the threat of a conflagration or firestorm becomes very real.

WHO IS IN CHARGE – FEDERAL, STATE OR LOCAL AUTHORITIES

The 1906 experience revealed serious conflict of authority in the disaster response. Similar conflict occurred in the 1983 Coalinga earthquake. This conflict will not change. In the event of a major disaster in San Francisco, the local authority will be the fire department as declared by the late Mayor George Moscone and endorsed by succeeding mayors. However, some other governmental agencies apparently feel they are not bound by this directive.

I am troubled to see how many state and federal agencies have highly centralized views of disaster management and control. Many of these agencies have a disaster or-

Wood-frame home with buckled floors and plaster stripped from the lath after the 1906 earthquake.

ganizational chart which place that agency in total charge of communications, as well as the direction and control of the disaster response.

STATE AGENCY PERSPECTIVE

Earthquake Planning Scenario for a Magnitude 8.3 Earthquake of the San Andreas Fault in the San Francisco Bay Area, was published in 1982 by the California Department of Conservation, Division of Mines and Geology. This report said, "The principal challenge in responding to the consequences of this event will be the transport of people and material within as well as from outside the stricken region." There is no mention of fires in this report and state officials arriving on the scene may have a big surprise in store for them.

FEDERAL PERSPECTIVE

The Federal Emergency Management Agency (FEMA) published *Preparing For Disaster* in 1983. Please consider one tasteless and suspiciously cavalier statement from this report. "Planning should be based on what is likely to happen, not on the worst conceivable scenario. One of the problems that sometimes paralyzes planning is that people construct in their own minds scenarios that are so impossible that they quit thinking about them. They will say, 'Okay, what if you have 50,000 casualties?' Now that is a staggering thing to talk about. Our response, however, would be to get 15 hospitals and 250 doctors. They might ask, 'Where would you get them?' We reply, 'The same damn place that you are getting those casualties.' Deal with a scenario that is possible or probable. Deal with the types of emergencies that you are likely to have in your community. Do not sit around worrying about the Immaculate Conception scenarios that occur about every 2,000 years."

Ironically, the estimate of 50,000 casualties ridiculed by FEMA is the estimate of another federal agency, the National Oceanic and Atmospheric Administration (NOAA). Actual number of casualties estimated by NOAA for a magnitude [M] 8.3 earthquake occurring in the Bay Area at 4:30 p.m. during the work week was 10,360 deaths and 40,360 hospitalized injuries for a total of 50,720 casualties. Divergent views by two federal agencies, with responsibilities in the same area, is an indication of the confusion and lack of coordination that will occur when several governmental agencies are involved in a major disaster.

When the next major earthquake occurs in the Bay Area, I hope a strong chain-of-command will be in place that will be recognized and accepted by all governmental agencies. This conflict about accurate assessments of the number of casualties has been a continuing problem with the many agencies involved in natural disaster prediction and mitigation activities.

DEATH AND INJURY

In her work to more accurately record the number of victims in the 1906 disaster, Gladys Hansen, Archivist for the City and County of San Francisco faced this problem. The U. S. Army estimate of the earthquake

Lincoln School at Fifth and Mission Streets was badly damaged by the 1906 earthquake, then destroyed by the fire. Public school building codes were greatly im- *proved by the passage of the Field Act following the Long Beach earthquake of 1933.*

casualties at the time totaled 498. Mrs. Hansen found that injuries and deaths resulting from psychological trauma such as suicides and severe depression, as well as long term illnesses were not included in the casualty total. To assist in her project, and to provide a more accurate description of an earthquake casualty, this definition was developed by the author and Donald Cheu, M.D., F.A.C.S., a member of the Governor's Earthquake Task Force.

EARTHQUAKE CASUALTY/ EARTHQUAKE DEATH

An earthquake death is an immediate fatality resulting from an earthquake or an earthquake-caused injury or illness that becomes fatal within a period of one year following the earthquake.

DIRECT CASUALTY

This definition includes injury or death resulting from structures or other objects falling on the victim, burns caused by hot or caustic material falling on the victim, or the victim being thrown or falling into the caustic or hot material; contact with charged electrical wires; injury or death resulting from blast or explosion; or injury or death resulting from falls caused by earth shaking.

INDIRECT CASUALTY

A. Psychological Trauma – including suicides.
B. Injuries such as laceration resulting from stepping onto glass or other sharp or jagged material.
C. Sickness and disease resulting from unsanitary conditions caused by the earthquake, including plague; release of toxic materials; escape of radioactive materials and mutagens from protective containment; released gases and airborne contaminants.
D. Injuries and deaths related to the enforcement of laws by members of the military or civilian law enforcement agencies, or death by homicide.

Gladys Hansen's casualty search project conforms to the these guidelines, and at the time of this printing her total of 1906 earthquake and fire deaths had reached 3,000.

THE FUTURE OF SAN FRANCISCO

The disaster prediction you have read here is unfortunately possible, even probable. It is predicated on a magnitude [M] 8 earthquake, combined with experience retrieved from 1906, as well as my personal experience in over 30 years of firefighting in San Francisco. I caution anyone against thinking this the "worst case." This is my conservative projection based on the proven earthquake and fire experience of San Francisco – an experience none of us wish to see repeated. But if it is repeated, I hope that the mayoral and supervisoral administrations in office after the disaster will heed the lessons that were never learned after the 1906 earthquake and fire.

I hope these observations and thoughts will guide the rebuilding of San Francisco after the next Great Earthquake and Fire as a city safe for people – safe from fire – if not from future convulsions of the earth.

Emmet D. Condon
April 1989

Fire insurance companies paid thousands of dollars for photographs of earthquake-damaged buildings. Agents for the insured, as well, bought all available photographs of damaged buildings and then destroyed the pictures. Photographs such as these were used in court cases following the 1906 disaster, and were also used as the basis for denial of claims under the fallen building clause.

Map of San Francisco commissioned for a scientific report on subsidence in parts of the City that occurred during the 1906 earthquake.

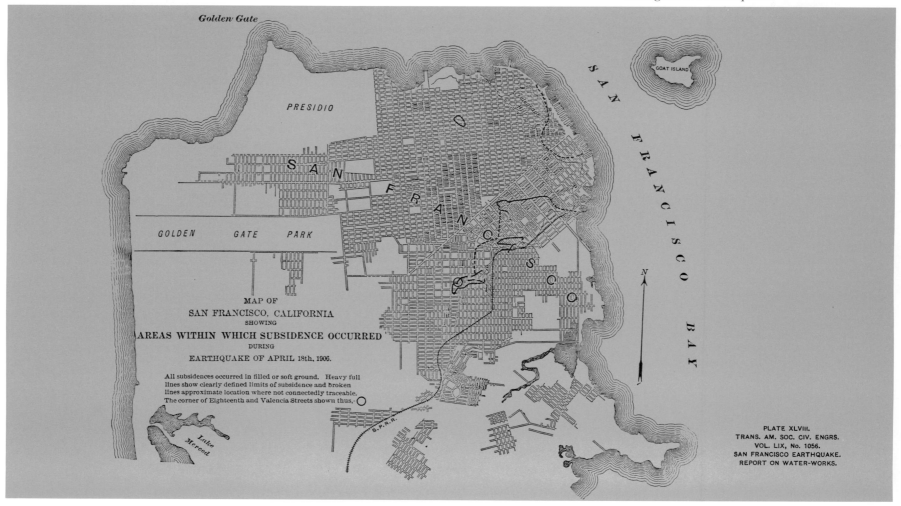

Index

Selected Bibliography

BOOKS

Adams, H. Austin. *The Man John D.
Spreckels.* San Diego: Frye & Smith,
1924.
Aitken, Frank. *A History of the Earthquake and Fire.* San Francisco: E. Hil-
ton Co., May 1906.
Alden, C. H., Jr. *Burnt Clay Construction
at San Francisco.* Brick Builder, May
1906.
Allen, Clarence R. *Earthquakes and
Mountains Around the Pacific.* Pasadena: California Institute of Technology, 1963.
Andrews, Allen. *Earthquake.* London:
Angus & Robertson Ltd., 1963.
Atherton, Gertrude. *Golden Gate Country.* New York: Duell, Sloane & Pearce,
1945.

Baccari, Alessandro. *Saints Peter & Paul
Church: the Chronicles of "The Italian
Cathedral" of the West, 1884-1984.*
San Francisco: Alessandro Baccari, Jr.,
for Saints Peter and Paul Church,
1985.
Bancroft, Hubert Howe. *Some Cities and
San Francisco, and Resurgam.* New
York: The Bancroft Co., 1907.
Banks, Charles E. *The History of the San
Francisco Disaster and Mount Vesu-
vius Horror.* San Francisco: C. E.
Thomas Co., 1906.
Barrymore, John. *Confessions of an
Actor.* London: Robert Holden & Co.
Ltd., 1926.
Bean, Walton. *Boss Ruef's San Francisco.*
London: Cambridge Univ. Press, 1952.
Beans, Rowena. *"Inasmuch . . . " The
One Hundred-year History of the San

Francisco Ladies' Protection and Relief Society, 1853-1953.* San Francisco: J. J. Gillick, 1953.
Bennett, John Edward. *Rebuilding of
San Francisco With Special Reference
to Ways and Means for Reconstruct-
ing the Private Edifice.* San Francisco:
1906.
Berry, James. *The Earthquake of 1906.*
Privately printed, 1907.
Best, Alfred M. *Best's Special Report Upon
the San Francisco Losses and Settle-
ments of the 243 Institutions In-
volved in the Conflagration of April
18-21, 1906.* New York: Alfred M. Best
Co., Inc., 1907.
Bicknell, Ernest P. *Pioneering with the
Red Cross.* New York: the Macmillan
Co., 1935.
Bilobrk, Nedelko. *San Francisco's First
Earthquakeproof and Fireproof Build-
ing.* California State Western Univ.,
1975.
Bishop, Harris. *Souvenir and Resume of
Oakland Relief Work to San Fran-
cisco Refugees.* Oakland, Ca.: Press of
Oakland Tribune, 1906.
Blanding, Gordon. *Notes on Earth-
quakes Along the California Coast
Line.* 1908.
Boardman, Mabel T. *Under the Red Cross
Flag at Home and Abroad.* Philadel-
phia: J.B. Lippincott Co., 1915.
Bogart, Sewall. *Lauriston.* Portola Valley,
Ca.: Alpine House Publications, 1976.
Bolt, Bruce A. *Earthquakes: a Primer.*
San Francisco: W.H. Freeman, 1978
Bolt, Bruce A. *Nuclear Explosions and
Earthquakes: The Parted Veil.* San
Francisco: W.H. Freeman & Co., 1976
Bonnet, Theodore F. *The Regenerators.*

San Francisco: Pacific Printing Co.,
1911.
Borel, Antoine. *San Francisco is No
More.* Menlo Park, Ca.: 1963.
Briggs, Peter. *Will California Fall Into
the Sea?* New York: D. McKay Co.,
1972.
Bronson, William. *The Earth Shook, the
Sky Burned.* New York: Doubleday,
1959.
——. *Still Flying and Nailed to the
Mast.* New York: Doubleday, 1963.
Brooks, George W. *The Spirit of 1906.*
San Francisco: The California Insur-
ance Co. of San Francisco, 1921.
Brown, Helen Hillyer. *The Great San
Francisco Fire.* San Francisco: Leo
Holub, 1956.
Bruce, John. *Gaudy Century.* New York:
Random House, 1948.
Buchanan, Dorothy A. *To Go Among
Strangers.* Ilfracombe, Devon: Arthur
H. Stockwell, Ltd., 1969.
Burnham, Daniel H. *Report on a Plan
for San Francisco.* San Francisco:
1905.
Byerly, Perry. *Earthquakes in Northern
California.* Berkeley: Univ. of Calif.
Press. 1940.
Byington, Lewis Francis, ed. *The History
of San Francisco.* Chicago, San Fran-
cisco: The S.J. Clark Co., 1931.
Byrne, James W. *Recollections of the Fire.*
San Francisco: Privately printed, 1927.

Carnahan, Melissa. *Personal Experiences
of the San Francisco Earthquake of
April, 1906.* Pittsburg, Pa.: Pittsburgh
Printing Co., 1909.
Carroll, Luke M. *Holy Cross Parish and
Lone Mountain District of San Fran-

cisco.* San Francisco: October, 1937.
Caruso, Dorothy. *Enrico Caruso: His Life
and Death.* London: J. Werner, Laurie
Ltd., 1946.
Castellini, Mary M. *A Victorian Heritage
in Old Cow Hollow.* San Francisco:
1976.
Chandler, Arthur. *Old Tales of San Fran-
cisco.* Dubuque, Iowa: Kendall/Hunt
Publishing Co., 1977.
Christopher, R. Patrick. *Historic Struc-
ture Report Western Grounds Old
Parade Ground and MacArthur Av-
enue Fort Mason Golden Gate Na-
tional Recreation Area.* Denver, Co.:
U.S. Dept. of the Interior, Sept. 1980.
*The Church in San Francisco; How it
Suffered From Fire and What can Be
Done to Rebuild It.* New York:
Domestic and Foreign Missionary So-
ciety of the Protestant Episcopal
Church, 1906.
Clary, Raymond H. *The Making of
Golden Gate Park: The Early Years
1865-1906.* San Francisco: California
Living Books, 1980.
Clay Products Institute of California.
*Earthquakes and Building Construc-
tion.* Los Angeles: 1929.
Cogan, Sara G. *The Jews of San Francisco
& The Greater Bay Area 1849-1919.
An Annotated Bibliography.* Ber-
keley, Ca.: Western Jewish History
Center, Judah L. Magnes Memorial
Museum, 1973.
Coleman, Harry J. *Give Us a Little Smile
Baby.* New York: Dutton, 1943.
*Committee of Forty on Reconstruction
of San Francisco. Transcript of joint
proceedings of sub-committees on:
Municipal departments (including*

police): Special session of the Legislature and state legislation: Charter amendments: Judiciary. May, 1906.
Crespi, Cesare. *San Francisco e la sua catastrofe.* San Francisco: Tipografia Internazionale, 1906.
Crowell, John Chambers. *Displacement Along the San Andreas Fault, California.* New York: Geological Society of America, 1962.
Crown Zellerbach Corporation. *The City of Gold; the Story of City Planning in San Francisco.* San Francisco: Crown Zellerbach Corp., 1960.

Daniels, Douglas Henry. *Pioneer Urbanites.* Philadelphia: Temple Univ. Press, 1980.
Davidson, C. *Great Earthquakes.* London: Murby, 1936.
Derleth, Charles, Jr. *Destructive Extent of the California Earthquake.* San Francisco: A.M. Robertson, 1907.
Devol, Carroll A. *The Army in the San Francisco Disaster.* Washington, D.C.: 1907.
Dickelmann, William. *San Francisco Earthquake Fire April 18, 1906.* San Francisco: 1906.
Dillon, Richard H. *San Francisco: Adventurers and Visionaries.* Tulsa, Ok.: Continental Heritage Press, 1983.
———. *The Hatchet Men.* New York: Coward-McCann, Inc., 1962.
———. *North Beach.* Novato, Ca.: Presidio Press, 1985.
Dobie, Charles Caldwell. *San Francisco A Pageant.* New York, London: D. Appleton-Century Co., 1933.
Douty, Christopher Morris. *The Economics of Localized Disasters. The 1906 San Francisco Catastrophe.* New York: Arno Press, 1977.
Dow, Gerald R. *Bay Fill in San Francisco.* San Francisco State Thesis, July 1973.
Drury, Clifford M. *San Francisco YMCA 1853-1953.* Glendale, Ca.: The Arthur H. Clark Co., 1963.
Duke, Charles M. *Bibliography of Effects of Soil Conditions on Earthquake Damage.* San Francisco: Earthquake Engineering Research Institute, 1958.

Ellery, Nathanie. *Permanency in Building Construction; The Modern Problem Confronting Every Owner and Builder.* San Francisco: H.S. Crocker Co., 1913.

First Unitarian Society of San Francisco. *One Hundred Years of the First Unitarian Church of San Francisco, 1850-1950.* San Francisco: The Grabhorn Press, 1950.
Freedman, Bernard I. *An Unimportant Place.* San Francisco: State Compensation Insurance Fund, 1980.
Freeman, J.R. *Earthquake Damage and Earthquake Insurance.* New York: McGraw-Hill, 1972.
Fried, John J. *Life Along the San Andreas Fault.* New York: Saturday Review Press, 1973.
Funston, Frederick. *Memories of Two Wars.* London: Constable and Co., 1912.

Gilbert, Grove Karl. *The San Francisco Earthquake and Fire of April 18, 1906, and Their Effects on Structures and Structural Materials.* Washington: Government Printing Office, 1907.
Gilliam, Harold. *San Francisco Bay.* Garden City, NY: 1957.
Gilliland, Adam. *Looking Back Over the Years.* Hartford, Conn.: 1937.
Givens, James David. *San Francisco in Ruins.* Denver: Smith-Brooks, 1906.
Glimpses of the San Francisco Disaster, Graphically Depicting the Great California Earthquake and Fire. Chicago: Laird & Lee, 1906.
Golden Jubilee Souvenir, 1863-1913. San Francisco: St. Brigid's Parish, 1913.
Goodrich, Mary. *The Palace Hotel.* San Francisco: 1950.
Great Earthquake, April 18,1906. Mountain View, Ca.: Pacific Press Pub. Co., 1906.
Guilfoyle, Merlin Joseph. *San Francisco "No Mean City."* Fresno, Ca.: Academy Library Guild, 1954.

Harlan, George H. *San Francisco Ferryboats.* Berkeley, Ca.: Howell-North Books, 1967.
Henry, Neil. *Complete Story of the San Francisco Earthquake.* Chicago: the Bible House, 1906.
Heppenheimer, T.A. *The Coming Quake.* Time Books, 1988.
Hewitt, R. *From Earthquake, Fire and Flood.* New York: Charles Scribner's Sons, 1957.
Hill, Keppel W. *The Cow Hollow Church.* 1967.
Himmelwright, Abraham Lincoln Artman. *The San Francisco Earthquake and Fire; A Brief History of the Disaster.* New York, N.Y., The Roebling Construction Co., 1906.
Holden, Edward S. *A Catalogue of Earthquakes on the Pacific Coast 1769-1897.* Smithsonian Institute Annual Report, 1898.
———. *Earthquakes in California in 1890 and 1891.* Washington, D.C.: U.S. Government Printing Office, 1892.
Holmes, Harold C. *Some Random Reminiscences of an Antiquarian Bookseller.* Oakland, Ca.: Holmes Book Co., 1967.
Hopper, James. *Our San Francisco.* New York: 1906.
Hunt, Rockwell D. *California and Californians.* Chicago: The Lewis Publishing Co., 1926.

Iacopi, Robert. *Earthquake Country.* Menlo Park, Ca.: Lane Book Co., 1964.
Insley, Russell B. *The Story of Roos Bros.* San Francisco: Privately Printed, 1945.
Irving, Robert. *Volcanoes and Earthquakes.* New York: Alfred A. Knopf, 1962.
Irwin, William H. *The City That Was.* New York: B.W. Huebsch, 1908.
Issel, William. *San Francisco, 1865-1932.* Berkeley: Univ. of Calif. Press, 1986.

Jackson, Joseph Henry. ed. *The Western Gate.* New York: Farrar, Straus and Young, 1952.
Jacobson, Pauline. *A Fire-Defying Landmark.* San Francisco: 1912.
James, Paul. *California Superquake.* Hicksville, NY: Exposition Press, 1974.
Johnson, Paul C. *San Francisco: As It Is, As It Was.* Garden City, N.Y.: Doubleday, 1979.
Jones, Clarence Miller. *Earthquakes.* Columbus, Oh.: 1907.
Jones, Idwal. *Ark of Empire.* Garden City, NY: Doubleday & Co., 1951.
Jordan, David S. *The California Earthquake of 1906.* San Francisco: A.M. Robertson, 1907.
Joseph Dixon Crucible Co. *Through Frisco's Furnace.* 1906. (pamphlet)

Kahn, Edgar M. *Cable Car Days in San Francisco.* Stanford, Ca.: Stanford Univ. Press, 1940.
Kahn, Judd. *Imperial San Francisco.* Lincoln, Neb.: Univ. of Nebraska Press, 1979.
Kavanagh, D.J. *The Holy Family Sisters of San Francisco.* San Francisco, Ca.: Gilmartin Co., 1922.
Keeler, C. *San Francisco Through Earthquake and Fire.* San Francisco: P. Elder & Co., 1906.
Kemble, John Haskell. *San Francisco Bay.* Cambridge, Md.: Cornell Maritime Press, 1957.
Kennedy, John Castillo. *The Great Earthquake and Fire, San Francisco, 1906.* New York: Morrow, 1963.
Key, Pierre V.R. *Enrico Caruso: A Biography.* Boston: Little, Brown & Co., 1922.
Kinnard, Lawrence. *History of the Greater San Francisco Bay Region. Vol. 2.* New York and West Palm Beach: Lewis Historical Publishing Co., 1966.
Klauber, Laurence. *Two Days in San Francisco, 1906.* San Diego: Laurence Klauber, 1906.
Krueger, Catherine M. *How Oft Shall Phoenix Rise?* New York: Vantage Press, 1981.

Lafler, Henry A. *How the Army Worked to Save San Francisco.* San Francisco: Calkins Newspaper Syndicate, 1906.
Levinsohn, John L. *Cow Hollow.* San Francisco: San Francisco Yesterday, 1976.
Lewis, Oscar. *San Francisco; Mission to Metropolis.* Berkeley, Ca.: Howell-North Books, 1966.
———. *San Francisco Since 1872.* San Francisco: Ray Oil Burner Co., 1946.
Linthicum, R. and T. White. *The Complete Story of the San Francisco Horror.* Chicago: Hubert Russell, 1906.
Livingstone, Alexander P. *Complete Story of San Francisco's Terrible Calamity.* San Francisco: Continental Publishing House, 1907.
Livingston, Edward. *A Personal History of the San Francisco Earthquake and Fire in 1906.* San Francisco: Windsor Press, 1941.
London, Charmian. *The Book of Jack London.* New York: The Century Co., 1921.
Longstreet, Stephen. *The Wilder Shore.* Garden City, N.Y.: Doubleday, 1968.
Los Angeles Chamber of Commerce. *Report of the Citizens' Relief Committee of Receipts and Disbursements of Funds and Work for the Relief of Sufferers from the Earthquake and Fire Which Occurred at San Francisco, Apr. 18, 1906.* 1908.

Mack, Gerstle. *1906: Surviving the Great Earthquake and Fire.* San Francisco: Chronicle Books, 1981.
Macondray & Co.,Inc. *One Hundredth Anniversary, 1848-1948.* San Francisco.
MacPhail, Archibald. *Of Men and Fire; a Story of Fire Insurance in the Far West.* San Francisco: Fire Underwriters Association of the Pacific, 1948.
Manson, Marsden. *Report of Marsden Manson to the Mayor & Committee on Reconstruction on those Portions of the Burnham Plans Which Meet Our Commercial Necessities.* San Francisco: 1906.
Marsh, Clifford W. *Facts Concerning the Great Fire of San Francisco.* Bridgeport, Conn.: The Marigold-Foster, 1907. (pamphlet)
Mason, Jack. *Earthquake Bay.* Inverness, Ca.: North Shore Books, 1980.
Merchants' Association of New York. *Committee for the Relief of the San Francisco Sufferers.* Report. 1906. (pamphlet)
Meyer, Larry L. *California Quake.* Nashville: Sherbourne Press, 1978.
Michaelis Publishing Co. *Ruins of San Francisco.* Kansas City, Mo.: 1906.
Mighels, Ella Sterling. *San Francisco Redi-vivus!* Oakland, Ca.: 1907.
Millard, Bailey. *History of the San Francisco Bay Region.* San Francisco, New York: The American Historical Society, 1924.
Mississippi Wire Glass Co. *Earthquake and Fire, 1906.* San Francisco. New York: 1907.
Moran, D. F. *Earthquake and Fire.* San Francisco: Earthquake Engineering Research Institute, Committee on Fire Protection, 1958.
Morgan, Roland. *San Francisco Then and Now.* San Francisco: Bodima Books, 1978.
Morris, Charles. *The San Francisco Calamity by Earthquake and Fire.* Philadelphia, Chicago: Winston, 1906.
Morrow, William W. *The Earthquake of April 18,1906 and the Great Fire in San Francisco.* San Francisco: 1906.
Motely, James Marvin. *San Francisco Relief Survey, the Organization and Methods of Relief Used After the Earthquake and Fire of April 18,1906.* New York: Survey Associates Inc., 1913.
Moulin, Tom, ed. *San Francisco Creation of a City.* Millbrae, Ca.: Celestial Arts, 1978.
Muscatine, Doris. *Old San Francisco.* New York: G.P. Putnam's Sons, 1975.
Myrick, David F. *San Francisco's Telegraph Hill.* Berkeley, Ca.: Howell-North Books, 1972.
McGloin, John Bernard. *Jesuits by the Golden Gate.* San Francisco, Ca.: Univ. of San Francisco, 1972.
———. *San Francisco, the Story of a City.* San Raphael, Ca.: Presidio Press, 1978.
McLaren, Norman L. *Business and Club Life in San Francisco.* Berkeley, Ca.: Regional Oral History Office, Bancroft Library, Univ. of Calif.

Narell, Irene. *Our City, The Jews of San Francisco.* San Diego, Ca.: Howell-North Books, 1981.
National Assoc. of Credit Men. *Report of Special Committee on Settlements Made by Fire Insurance Companies in Connection With the San Francisco Disaster.* New York: 1907.
National Fire-proofing Company. *Trial by Fire at San Francisco.* New York: 1906. (pamphlet)
Neil, Henry. *Complete Story of the San Francisco Earthquake.* Chicago: The Bible House, 1906.
Newman, W.A. *What the Earthquake Actually Did to California Federal Buildings.* 1906. (pamphlet)
Nichols, William F. *A Father's Story of the Earthquake in San Francisco April 18, 19, 20, 1906.* San Francisco: 1906.

Older, Cora Miranda. *San Francisco; Magic City.* New York: Longmans, Green, 1961.
Older, Fremont. *My Own Story.* New York: the Macmillan Co., 1926.
Olmsted, Nancy. *Vanished Waters; A History of San Francisco's Mission Bay.* San Francisco, Ca.: Mission Creek Conservancy, 1986.
Olmsted, Roger R. & Nancy L. Olmsted. *Rincon De Las Salinas Y Potrero Viejo – The Vanished Corner.* San Francisco Clean Water Management Program, November, 1981.
———. *San Francisco Waterfront.* San Francisco Wastewater Management Program, Dec. 1977.
Omori, Fusakichi. *Note on the San Francisco Earthquake of April 18, 1906.* 1906. (Earthquake Investigation Committee. Publications 21, appendix 2.)
100th Anniversary, St. Boniface Parish, San Francisco, Ca., 1860-1960.

Panoramic Views of San Francisco, Showing the "Golden Gate City" Destroyed by Earthquake and Fire, April 18, 1906. San Francisco and Oakland, Ca.: S. Bieber, 1906.
Park, Andrew G. *The City Beautiful; San Francisco Past, Present and Future.* Los Angeles, Ca.: Houston & Harding, 1906.
Petersen, Carl E. *The Champion Globetrotter, Twice Round the World Without Money.* Berkeley, Ca.: 1928.
The Picture Story of the San Francisco Earthquake, Wednesday, April 18, 1906. Los Angeles: Pierce, 1906.
Plan of Proposed Street Changes in the Burned District and Other Sections of San Francisco. May, 1906.
Pough, Frederick H. *All About Volcanoes and Earthquakes.* New York: Random House, 1953.
Preliminary Report of the State Earthquake Investigation Commission. Berkeley: 1906.
Proceedings on the Occasion of the Presentation of the Gold Medal to the City of San Francisco by the Republic of France at the Hands of her Ambassador His Excellency Jean Jules Jusserand. San Francisco: Stanley-Taylor, 1909.
Purdy, Helen Throop. *San Francisco As It Was, As It Is, And How To See It.* San Francisco: Paul Elder, 1912.

Reconstruction Committee, Sub-Committee on Statistics. Report. April 24, 1907. Pamphlet.
Record of the Fireman's Fund Insurance Company in the San Francisco Disaster of April 18-21st, 1906. San Francisco: Britton & Rey, 1907.
Redwood Association. *Redwood in the San Francisco Fire.* San Francisco: 1906.
Reed, S.A. *San Francisco Conflagration of April, 1906.* Special Report to the National Board of Fire Underwriters. Committee of Twenty. New York: 1906.
Reid, Whitelaw. *The Story of San Francisco for English Ears.* London: Harrison & Sons, 1908.
Report of the General Masonic Relief Fund Incident to Earthquake and Fire of April 18, 1906, Received and Disbursed by Motley Hewes Flint, Grand Master Free and Accepted Masons of the Jurisdiction of California, October 1, 1906. San Francisco: 1906.
Report of the Committee of Five to the "Thirty-five Companies" on the San Francisco Conflagration, April 18-21, 1906. New York: Mail & Express, 1907.
Report of the Sub-committee on Statistics to the Chairman and Committee on Reconstruction. San Francisco, Ca.: April 24th, 1907.

Report of the Sub-Committee on Water Supply and Fire Protection to the Committee on the Reconstruction of San Francisco. San Francisco: 1906.

Rieder-Cardinell Co. *San Francisco Before and After the Fire.* Los Angeles and Oakland: 1906.

Rieder, Michael. *San Francisco, the Doomed City. Earthquake and Fire, April 18, 1906.* Los Angeles: 1906.

Riesenberg, Felix Jr. *Golden Gate.* New York: Tudor Publishing Co., 1940.

Ritchie, David. *Superquake! Why Earthquakes Occur and When the Big One Will Hit Southern California.* New York: Crown, 1988.

Rodriguez, Marie. *The Earthquake of 1906.* San Francisco: Barry, 1951.

Rolle, Andrew F. *An American in California.* San Marino, Ca.: Henry E. Huntington Library. 1956.

Root, Henry. *Henry Root, Surveyor, Engineer and Inventor.* San Francisco, Ca.: Privately Printed, 1921.

Russell Sage Foundation. *San Francisco Relief Survey.* New York: Survey Associates, Inc.

San Francisco; A City of Ruins. Alameda, Ca.: T. P. S. Publishing Co., 1906.

San Francisco and Vicinity Before and after its Destruction. Portland, Me.: L. H. Nelson, 1906.

San Francisco and Vicinity Before and After the Big Fire, April 18, 19th and 20th, 1906. Los Angeles: Rieder-Cardinell Co., 1906.

San Francisco. Chamber of Commerce. *Special committee on insurance settlements. Report of the Special committee of the board of trustees of the Chamber of Commerce of San Francisco on insurance settlements incident to the San Francisco fire. Approved at a meeting of the Board of trustees, November 13, 1906.*

San Francisco Council of Churches. *Heritage and Hope. A History of the Protestant, Anglican & Orthodox Church Movement in Francisco.* San Francisco: 1979.

San Francisco Municipal Reports. Various years.

San Francisco of Yesterday and Today. San Francisco: C. Weidner.

San Francisco Relief and Red Cross Funds . . . Department Reports as Submitted to the Board of Directors at the Regular Monthly Meeting, March 19th, 1907. San Francisco: Starkweather, Latham & Emanuel, 1907.

San Francisco Relief and Red Cross Funds, Finance Committee. Rules of Procedure to Define the Accounting System Covering the Business of the Finance Committee. April 30, 1906. (Pamphlet).

San Francisco Relief and Red Cross Funds. Preliminary Report. November, 1906.

San Francisco Relief Survey. New York: Survey Associates, 1913.

San Francisco, the City of Destruction. Portland, Me.: L. H. Nelson, 1906.

San Francisco Then and Now. San Francisco: Pillsbury Picture Co., 1909.

San Francisco, the Imperishable. San Francisco: Southern Pacific Co.

Saul, Eric. *The Great San Francisco Earthquake and Fire, 1906.* Millbrae, Ca.: Celestial Arts, 1981.

Scenes of the San Francisco Fire and Earthquake, April 18, 1906. Series no. 3: Before and After. San Francisco: Phoenix Photo Co., 1906.

Scharlach, Bernice. *House of Harmony: Concordia-Argonaut's First 130 years.* Berkeley, Ca.: Western Jewish History Center, Judah L. Magnes Memorial Museum, 1983.

Schler, W. D. *Report to the Massachusetts Association for the Relief of California.* San Francisco, Ca.: Sept. 27, 1906.

Schoenstein, Louis J. *Memories of a San Francisco organ builder.* San Francisco: Cue Publications, 1977.

Schussler, H. *Water Supply of San Francisco, California, Before, During and After the Earthquake of April 18, 1906, and the subsequent Conflagration, 1906.*

Searight, Frank T. *The Doomed City.* Chicago: Laird & Lee, 1906.

Seeing San Francisco by Kodak. Los Angeles: Chamber of Commerce Relief Fund, 1906.

Shanks, Ralph C., Jr. *Lighthouses of San Francisco Bay.* San Anselmo, Ca.: Costano Books, 1976.

Shreve & Co., San Francisco. *San Francisco, a photographic review.* 1906.

Siefkin, David. *The City at the End of the Rainbow.* New York: Putman, 1976.

———. *Meet me at the St. Francis.* San Francisco: St. Francis Hotel Corp., 1979.

Silverman, Ruth. ed. *San Francisco Observed.* San Francisco: Chronicle Books, 1986.

Sixteen Views of the San Francisco Fire and Earthquake, April 18, 1906. San Francisco: Green Pub. Co., 1906.

Smallwood, Charles. *The Cable Car Book.* Millbrae, Ca.: Celestial Arts, 1980.

Smith, Temple. *Views of Santa Rosa & Vicinity, Before & After the Disaster, April 18, 1906.* Los Angeles: Rieder, Cardinell & Co., 1906.

Southern Pacific Company. *San Francisco Imperishable.* San Francisco: 1906.

Steele, Rufus. *The City That Is. The Story of the Rebuilding of San Francisco in Three Years.* San Francisco: A. M. Robertson, 1909.

Steinbrugge, Karl V. *Earthquake Hazard in the San Francisco Bay Area: A Continuing Problem in Public Policy.* Univ. of Calif., Berkeley: Institute of Govermental Studies, 1968.

———. *"Seismic Risk to Buildings and Structures on Filled Lands in San Francisco Bay."* San Francisco Bay Conservation and Development Commission, 1967.

Stellman, Louis John. *The Vanished Ruin Era.* San Francisco: P. Elder and Company 1910.

Stetson, James Burgess. *Narrative of my Experiences in the Earthquake and Fire at San Francisco.* Palo Alto: Lewis Osborne, 1969.

———. *San Francisco During the Eventful Days of April 1906.* San Francisco: The Murdock Press, 1906.

Strack, Marilyn JoAnne. *The San Francisco Earthquake and Fire of 1906; an Annotated Bibliography.* San Jose: 1976.

Strother, French. *The Rebound of San Francisco.* New York: 1906.

Sutherland, Monica. *The Damndest Finest Ruins.* New York: Coward-McCann 1959.

———. *The San Francisco Disaster.* London: Barrie & Rock-liffe, 1959.

Swanberg, W. A. *Citizen Hearst.* New York: Charles Scribner's Sons, 1961.

"Thirty-Five" Companies. *Committee of Five-Report of Committee of Five to the "Thirty-Five" Companies on the San Francisco Conflagration.* 1906.

Thomas, C.E. *Complete History of the San Francisco Disaster and Mount Vesuvius Horror.* 1906.

Thomas, Gordon. *The San Francisco Earthquake.* New York: Stein and Day 1971.

Thomas, Lately. *A Debonair Scoundrel.* New York: Holt, Rinehart & Winston, 1962.

Thompson, Erwin N. *The Rock: A History of Alcatraz Island.* 1847-1972. Denver, Co.: National Park Service. 1971.

Todd, Frank Morton. *A Romance of Insurance.* San Francisco: H.S. Crocker Co., 1929.

Townley, Sidney D. and Maxwell Allen. *Descriptive Catalog of Earthquakes of the Pacific Coast of the United States 1769 to 1928.* Berkeley, Ca.: Univ. of Calif. Press, 1939.

Turner, Patricia, ed. *1906. Remembered.* San Francisco: Friends of The San Francisco Public Library, 1981.

Tyler, Sydney. *San Francisco's Great Disaster.* Philadelphia: P.W. Ziegler Co., 1906.

Van Der Zee, John. *The Gate.* New York: Simon and Schuster, 1986.

Views of San Francisco before and after earthquake. San Francisco: E. P. Charlton & Co., 1906.

Wagner, Jack R. *The Last Whistle.* Berkeley, Ca.: Howell-North Books, 1974.

Walker, Bryce S. *Earthquake.* Alexandria, Va.: Time-Life Books, 1982.

Walsh, James P. *The San Francisco Irish 1850-1976.* San Francisco: Smith McKay Printing Co., 1978.

Weatherred, Edith Tozier. *San Francisco on the Night of April 18, 1906.* San Francisco: Bachrach & Co., 1906.

Webb, Edith Buckland. *Indian Life at the Old Missions.* Los Angeles: Warren F. Lewis, Publisher, 1952.

Wenkam, Robert. *The Edge of Fire. San Francisco:* Sierra Club Books, 1987.

Willard, Ruth Hendricks. *Sacred Places of San Francisco.* Novato, Ca.: Presidio Press, 1985.

Wilson, Carol Green. *Gump's Treasure Trade.* New York: Thomas Y. Crowell Co., 1949.

———. *Chinatown Quest; the Life Adventures of Donaldina Cameron.* Stanford, Ca.: Stanford Univ. Press, 1931.

Wilson, James Russel. *San Francisco's Horror of Earthquake and Fire.* Philadelphia: Percival Supply Co., 1906.

Wilson, Neill C. *Southern Pacific.* New York, London, Toronto: McGraw-Hill Book Company, Inc., 1952.

Wollenberg, Charles. *Golden Gate Metropolis.* Berkeley, Ca.: Institute of Governmental Studies, Univ. of Calif., 1985.

Wood, Harry Oscar. *Destructive and Near destructive Earthquakes in California and Western Nevada, 1769-1933.* Washington: Government Printing Office, 1934.

Wood, Robert Muir. *Earthquakes and Volcanoes.* New York: Weidenfeld and Nicolson, 1987.

Woodruff Co. *Our Story: Reinforced Concrete and Methods of Using It.* 1906 (Pamphlet).

Yanev, P. *Peace of Mind in Earthquake Country.* San Francisco: Chronicle Books, 1974.

Yip, Christopher Lee. *San Francisco Chinatown: An Architectural and Urban History.* University Microfilms International, 1985.

Youd, T.L. *Historic Ground Failures in Northern California Triggered by Earthquakes.* Washington: U.S. Government Printing Office, 1978.

Young, John P. *San Francisco: A History.* Chicago: J. J. Clarke Publishing Co., 1928.

Zarchin, Michael M. *Glimpses of Jewish Life in San Francisco.* Berkeley, Ca.: The Judah L. Magnes Memorial Museum, 1964.

Zeigler, Wilbur G. *Story of the Earthquake and Fire.* San Francisco, Ca.: L. C. Osteyee, 1906.

GOVERNMENT RECORDS AND RELATED PUBLICATIONS

Byerly, Perry. *Pacific Coast Earthquakes.* Eugene, Oregon, Eugene, Oregon State System of Higher Education, 1952.

California. State Earthquake Investigation Commission. *The California Earthquake of April 18, 1906.* Report of the State Earthquake Investigation Commission . . . Washington, D. C., Carnegie Institution of Washington, 1908-10.

Gilbert, G. K., R. L. Humphrey, J. S. Sewell and Frank Soule. "San Francisco Earthquake and Fire of April 18, 1906, and Their Effects on Structures and Structural Materials." BULLETIN 324, U. S. GEOLOGICAL SURVEY. September, 1907.

Calif. Dept. of Natural Resources. Div. of Mines. *San Francisco Earthquakes of March 1957.* (Special Report 57) ed. Gordon B. Oakeshott. Ferry Building, San Francisco, 1959.

Calif. State Earthquake Investigation Commission. *The California Earthquake of April 18, 1906.* Report of the State Earthquake Investigation Commission, Washington, D.C., Carnegie Institution of Washington, 1908-1910.

Coffman, Jerry L. and Carl A. Von Hake, eds. *Earthquake History of the United States.* U. S. Dept. of Commerce Publication 41-1. Washington, U. S. Government Printing Office, 1973.

Deacon, J. Byron. *Disasters and the American Red Cross in Disaster Relief.* New York, Russell Sage Foundation, 1918.

Earthquake in California April 18, 1906. Special Report of Maj. Gen. Adolphus W. Greely, U. S. A., Commanding the Pacific Division, on the Relief Operations Conducted by the Military Authorities of the United States at San Francisco and Other Points, With Accompanying Documents. Washington, Government Printing Office, 1906.

Greely, Maj. Gen. Adolphus, U.S.A. *Special Report on the Relief Operations Conducted by the Military Authorities of the United States at San Francisco and Other Points with Accompanying Documents. 1906.*

Kahn, Julius. *The San Francisco Disaster, Honest and Dishonest Insurance.* Speech in the house of Representatives, Thursday, June 28, 1906. Washington, 1906.

Lawson, Andrew C. *The California Earthquake of April 18, 1906.* Washington, D. C., Carnegie Institution of Washington, 1908.

McAdie, Alexander G. *Catalogue of Earthquakes on the Pacific Coast, 1897 to 1906.* Smithsonian Institution Annual Report, 1907.

Mills, W. H. *Influences that Insure the Rebuilding of San Francisco.* State Board of Trade, Bulletin No. 15. 1906.

State Earthquake Investigation Commission. *The California Earthquake of April 18, 1906.* Carnegie Institution of Washington, D.C. 1908-1910. (Preliminary report, 1906).

U.S. Geological Survey. *The San Francisco Earthquake and Fire of April 18, 1906 and Their Effects on Structures and Structural Materials.* Washington, Government Printing Office, 1907.

U.S. War Department. *Army Supplies at San Francisco.* Message from the President . . . transmitting a letter from the Secretary of War. . . . Washington, D. C., Government Printing Office, 1906.

U.S. War Dept. *Employment of Labor at Mare Island Navy Yard, etc.* Message from the President . . . , transmitting communications from the Navy Department . . . 1906. (59th Congress, 1st Session, Senate Document 405.)

U.S. War Dept. *Relief of San Francisco.* Message from the President . . . , submitting a letter of the Secretary of War, with accompanying documents. . . . Washington, D.C. Government Printing Office, 1906.

Waters, R. J., & Co. *Reproduction from Official Map of San Francisco, Showing the District Swept by the Fire of April 18, 19, 20, 1906. Area, approximately 7 square miles.* San Francisco, 1906.

Wood, Harry. *Earthquake History of the United States; Part II, Stronger Earthquakes of California and Western Nevada.* Washington, D. C.: U. S. Government Printing Office, 1951.

NEWSPAPERS, CALIFORNIA

Berkeley Reporter
Los Angeles Express
Los Angeles Herald
Los Angeles Times
Oakland Herald
Oakland Enquirer
Oakland Tribune
Press Democrat
Retail Grocers Advocate
San Francisco Bulletin
San Francisco Call
San Francisco Chronicle
San Francisco Examiner
San Francisco News
San Jose Herald
San Jose Mercury

NEWSPAPERS, OTHER

Chicago Record Herald
New York Globe
New York Journal of Commerce
New York Morning Telegraph
New York Press
New York Sun
New York Times
Omaha Herald
Portland Oregonian
Portland Telegram
Pueblo Chieftan
Seattle Post Intelligencer
St. Louis Star Chronicle
Utica Herald Dispatch
Vancouver Daily Province

Earthquake Update: October 17, 1989, 5:04 P.M.

7.0 QUAKE STUNS BAY AREA
MARINA DEVASTATED BY FIRE
TERROR ON THE BRIDGE
AT LEAST 250 KILLED

These headlines filled California newspapers with graphic descriptions of the major disaster that devastated seven counties in California. Detailed media reports gave a vivid description of the wide spread damage from Santa Cruz north to the Bay Area, including the tragic loss of lives on the I-880 Freeway. The number of deaths on the freeway are still uncounted as this is written, two days after the disaster.

In San Francisco alone, property loss exceeded two billion dollars and it was estimated that over 30 structures in the Marina District would have to be demolished. Damage to other buildings numbered in the hundreds. This did not include the buildings destroyed in the major fire in the Marina, that as reported, "Pressed the San Francisco Fire Department to the limit." The rupture of water mains in the area compounded the firefighters' problems and required hose lines to be stretched from the city's single fireboat several blocks away. However, the most horrifying tragedy that stunned the public was the disaster that occurred on the I-880 Freeway when the top tier of the freeway came crashing down on the lower level smashing a mile-long line of rush hour traffic and killing the majority of the occupants. As a result of this tragedy, protions of the Embarcadero and southern freeways in San Francisco will remain closed for months due to the similarity of construction to the I-880 Freeway.

A large section of the Bay Bridge collapsed, killing one person and severing a major transit link between San Francisco and the East Bay. It illustrates how quickly the city of San Francisco can be isolated from immediate help from the rest of the Bay Area.

How does this disaster compare with the predictions made in the preceding chapter? Are they valid and can they be used to target necessary corrections which are vitally needed to lessen the impact of a magnitude [M] 8 earthquake in the Bay Area?

Unfortunately, I believe the predictions remain valid and are understated. The comparison between a magnitude [M] 7.0 and a magnitude [M] 8.0 on the Richter Scale has been described in the statements of several scientists, that a magnitude [M] 8.0 earthquake on the Richter Scale is 30 times more powerful and destructive than the magnitude [M] 7.0 earthquake that has ravaged one hundred miles of California's cities and towns.

It is difficult to comprehend the scope of such a damaging disaster, but it does provide great emphasis to those same scientists' statement that, "This is not the Big One they know is certain some day."

But there are many corrective measures that can, and should be initiated to lessen the impact of the predicted "Great Earthquake."

San Francisco is ringed with many areas of filled land, much of it unstable. Large sections are covered with residential and industrial buildings. These are the same areas where building collapse was prevalent in 1906. Previous chapters in this book illustrate the folly of building on infirm ground. It should not be allowed to happen again. Any new construction in these infirm areas should be strictly controlled and require detailed foundation requirements designed and supervised by highly qualified engineers.

Over 2,000 unreinforced masonry buildings have been identified and listed in San Francisco alone and many of them will surely collapse and cause large numbers of deaths when the "killer" earthquake strikes. The technical knowledge exists to properly brace and strengthen these dangerous buildings, but the city has been reluctant to face the anticipated opposition of property owners. Surely this tragic earthquake should give city officials the impetus to initiate the necessary corrective legislation.

A bond issue is on the November 1989 ballot that will provide for strengthening and bracing city owned buildings, many of which house emergency service vehicles and personnel. I am sure that the citizens of San Francisco will support and approve this positive measure.

A 1986 bond issue is already providing for underground cisterns and extension of the Fire Deparment's high pressure system into heavily populated residential areas, which will hopefully lessen the possibility of a repetition of the Marina District fire. The single fireboat Phoenix cannot be relied upon to provide emergency water supplies into all the sections of land fill in the city.

There still exists the danger of rupture of the many gas and water mains that serve the infirm, land fill areas of the city. They will remain a constant threat to the city until modern technology and public insistence require the installation of excess flow valves or similar preventive devices that will automatically shut down or control these utilities when major ground movement occurs in the infirm areas.

But even when these and other corrective measures are achieved the saving of many lives will rely on people; the eager citizen volunteers who crawled through rubble and debris, risking their lives, to free trapped victims as they will do in the next disaster; the trained and properly equipped emergency service personnel of the city, supplemented by disciplined military personnel, willing to help in any way.

The San Francisco Fire Department is below the daily manning level that any experienced chief officer knows is necessary to provide adequate service to the city. Three departments, the Municipal Railway and the Fire and Police Departments account for more than fifty percent of the personnel budget for the entire city, so it continues to be a losing battle to receive sufficient funds to maintain needed staffing.

To help offset this shortage, Admiral Toney, then stationed on Treasure Island, was contacted by the San Francisco Fire Department in 1986 and asked if he could provide assistance. The Admiral readily agreed to supply personnel and equipment to the Fire Department during serious emergencies, as long as he was in command at Treasure Island.

A training exercise was held in early 1987 to test the system. The Navy sent personnel to the city by boat, assuming that the Bay Bridge would be closed after a major disaster (as it was in the earthquake). Municipal Railway coaches, waiting at the piers, transported the sailors and marines to fire stations throughout the city and effectively doubled the strength of the Fire Department in approximately two hours.

Admiral Toney has been reassigned, but the present admiral, John Bitoff has the same dedication and commitment to helping the city. His frustration could be sensed when he was quoted in the newspaper that he had 1,650 sailors and marines awaiting a call to duty. "They are leaning forward in the trenches. They are a cocked pistol ready to go. But like a good neighbor, I don't want to rush into someone's house before I am invited." Sadly, the invitation never came during the height of the disaster in San Francisco.

These trained and well disciplined military personnel are one of the greatest assets the city has, and agreements should be remade and nurtured to supply the help that the Navy is so eager to give, as they did give during the 1906 Earthquake and Fire.

With their help and the help of our citizen volunteers as well as the city's emergency personnel the Phoenix will continue to rise above any natural disaster visited upon San Francisco.

— *Emmet D. Condon*
October 19, 1989

Sunday Mercury and Herald

SAN JOSE, CALIFORNIA, SUNDAY MORNING, APRIL 22, 1906—SIXTEEN PAGES. NO. 112.

PLAGUE IS NOW THREATENING THE HOMELESS

The horrors of a plague threaten San Francisco. Typhoid fever, as a result of unsanitary conditions, has made its appearance. Four cases are now receiving medical attention. Smallpox and scarlet fever, too, are reported. General Funston has caused to be posted throughout the city notices of sanitary regulation. Water for drinking purposes must be boiled. All refuse and swill must be buried. These methods, with proper medical supplies and tents to live in, it is hoped, will check the threatened epidemic.

AUTHORITATIVE STATEMENT OF THE FINANCIAL OUTLOOK

SAN FRANCISCO, April 21.—The first authoritative statement of the financial outlook can now be made. The Bank Commissioners find financial conditions much better than they expected, consider them excellent in fact, and such as to warrant public confidence in a speedy and satisfactory adjustment of the banking machinery throughout the State.

The Commissioners are in continuous session and are consulting with bankers all over California, and making a thorough investigation of the monetary situation so as to be fully informed before deciding upon a definite plan of action. They have the situation well in hand, and have no fears of the result. Measures are being taken to have cash released from the United States Mint on telegraphic order, as soon as the banks reopen for business.

The Commissioners recognize that the monetary situation affects the entire State, and are therefore opposed to the reopening of any bank in California till a plan has been matured that will meet the interests of all concerned, it being their opinion that the interests of the general public are a paramount consideration in this exigency. No precipitate action will be permitted that is likely to create complications or hinder an adjustment which will restore confidence and protect all interests.

At half past ten o'clock Monday morning the San Francisco Clearing House Association will meet and discuss the local condition, and be prepared to submit as comprehensive a report when the State Clearing House Association meets in Oakland on Tuesday, at 2 o'clock p. m., as can be made in advance of opening the vaults, which have all been found to be uninjured, which insures the safety of their contents.

When the State Clearing House Association meets on Tuesday the general situation will be discussed and steps taken to formulate a line of future action subject to contingencies and developments. It can be stated that the Commission finds the banks throughout the State in excellent shape.

It is realized that the most pressing need is to provide a supply of ready money for immediate necessities, and steps will be taken at the earliest practicable moment to relieve the temporary stringency caused by the closing of the banks pending a general adjustment to meet all conditions. It can be stated, however, that a way will be devised to relieve the most pressing monetary needs.

Money is flowing in from every direction in the meantime, and as soon as plans and rules applicable to the banking situation of the entire State can be formulated, there promises to be an abundance of cash for all commercial needs. But it will take some time and thought to perfect a policy adjusted to all interests and localities. A channel will be provided for placing a certain amount of money in circulation to supply immediate necessities.

Physical obstacles will necessarily delay the opening of the vaults of the San Francisco banks, and it is recognized that no plan of action can be decided on till the vaults are opened.

The Commissioners are keeping the Governor fully advised at every stage of development, and whatever steps they decide to take will be with his full knowledge and concurrence.

And as the State banks are under the jurisdiction of the Bank Commissioners they will all be compelled to abide by any rule formulated by the Board. The National banks are in thorough accord with the State bankers, and can be relied on to co-operate in all measures prescribed by the State Commission.

INSURANCE MEN HEDGING.

An important meeting of the San Francisco Board of Fire Underwriters was held this morning at its permanent headquarters at Reed's Hall at Twelfth and Harrison streets. The sense of the meeting was that the impression should not be given out that the insurance companies had money to throw away or that any losses would be paid until they had been properly adjusted and only such losses as the companies are responsible for will be paid.

This matter was brought to the attention of the board by Rolla V. Watt, manager of the Royal and Queen insurance companies, who said: "I met ex-Mayor Phelan on the street yesterday and he asked me to get some sort of a notice given out to the public that their losses would be paid. I do not believe that this is the proper thing and I told him so. The companies I represent will pay what they are liable for and no more and it is better for those whose spirits are drooping to allow them to droop rather than to buoy them up with false hopes."

DISTINCTION AS TO LOSSES.

The sentiment was generally concurred in. From the remark made there is no doubt that the companies will draw a fine distinction between the general loss and that by fire and will only pay for what was actually burned. The question of property devastated by dynamite was not touched upon and will probably be the cause of endless litigation.

CONGRESS ADDS MILLION AND HALF

WASHINGTON, April 21.—Secretary Taft presented the need for additional appropriation for the San Francisco sufferers to the House Committee on Appropriations this morning, suggesting that $1,500,000 more should be appropriated. To this the committee readily assented, and the appropriation will be made today. The Secretary explained that a special message from the President together with a letter of detail from himself, was on its way to Congress.

COUNTY CLERK HAS QUARTERS GIVEN HIM

The Misses Welsh, at First and St. James streets, have kindly offered room to County Clerk Pfister for the transaction of the business of his office. Mr. Pfister has accepted the offer and on Monday morning will resume business.

AUTHENTIC PHOTOS OF SAN FRANCISCO.

IN SAN FRANCISCO
All that remains of the City Hall. —Photo Wales.

IN SAN FRANCISCO.
Newspaper row, showing the gutted Phelan and Call Buildings. —Photo J. V. Haley.

IN SAN FRANCISCO.
A corner of the Palace Hotel. —Photo J. V. Haley.

ONE HUNDRED AND FIFTY MORE PEOPLE ARE BURNED TO DEATH

SAN FRANCISCO, April 21.—It is estimated that more than 150 people were burned to death last night in the vicinity of Telegraph and Russian Hills and on Union street. While the fire was raging the people were cut off from retreat. In twenty buildings bodies have been recovered. Two babes were found where they had been dropped in mad flight.

DON'T HEED FOREBODERS BUT USE COMMON SENSE

Father Ricard, of Santa Clara College, writes the Mercury as follows:

The earthquake period is gone. Once the pent up forces of nature have had a vent, nothing of a serious nature need be apprehended. At the most a succession of minor shocks, may be felt and that's all. It is not reasonable, therefore for people to continue in dread of a new destructive tembler. People should fearlessly go to work and repair mischief done and sleep quietly at night anywhere at all, especially in wooden frame.

Never mind foreboders of evil: they do not know what they are talking about. Seismonetry is in its infancy and those therefore who venture out with predictions of future earthquakes when the main shock has taken place, ought to be arrested as disturbers of the peace.

Hotel St. James.

The residents of the Hotel St. James have regained their composure. No further damage is expected to ensue from the earthquake. The building was damaged, but not seriously. The hotel resumed regular business last evening.

SMALLPOX AND FEVER THE LATEST HORRORS

SAN FRANCISCO, April 21.—The fire has been extinguished at all points. After having devoured nearly four-fifths of the buildings of the city, the progress of the flames, at twelve o'clock today, was stayed. Square miles of ruins bear testimony to their fierce appetite.

The city is already, Phoenix-like, preparing to rise from her ashes. While the embers of the greatest fire of modern times are still smouldering, corps of architects, retained by the large property owners, are mapping out plans for rebuilding.

After four days of horror, the people are awakening to a full realization of the calamity. They are undaunted and determined to replace the ruined metropolis with a city of even greater beauty and grandeur.

Famine, which threatened the hundreds of thousands of homeless, has been warded off. Relief trains, loaded down with foodstuffs, have reached the city by dozens. The scarcity of water has been relieved. Efficient organization is gradually providing shelter for the homeless.

Disease, smallpox, scarlet and typhoid fever, have appeared to add to the horror of the situation. Prompt and efficient medical assistance and a complete sanitary organization, only can ward off the threatened epidemics.

The entire water front has been swept away by flames. While the Ferry Building still remains intact, the fire authorities have warned the people that it is anything but safe. It may topple over at any moment if a stray wind came up.

All along the front the grain sheds are piled on the docks and the wharves and piers are cracked, smashed and twisted out of shape for practical use.

SWEPT BY FLAMES.

During the night the all devouring flames swept from the top of Telegraph Hill down to the level, where the lumber yards stood. Thence they whirled out toward the military reservation, where over twenty thousand men, women and children are encampd.

For a time there was fear that the blaze would get the few remaining houses along Bay street and at the foot of Van Ness avenue, but they finally quenched themselves apparently from exhaustion.

MENACED BY OIL.

Some feared the heat from the hills above the beach might ignite the great oil and gas tanks near Meiggs' wharf. Had this occurred thousands would certainly have been killed by resulting explosions. But, thank God, the flames failed to affect these oil and gas vats.

Today many people have come down town to view the spectre of the business portion of San Francisco. Where the great sky-scrapers and massive warehouses stood hills of ashes and bent and twisted pillars of iron alone remain. Here and there the portion of a wall remains in sufficiency to indicate the character of the structure of which it was once a part; but that is all.

BANKS TO REOPEN.

The banks are doing everything in their power to reopen. The Union Trust Company's vaults are in splendid condition. The safe deposit annex is also reported safe.

In fact, the clearing house people say that a considerable portion of the money on deposit in commercial and saving institutions will be available in a few days.

Many of the big business concerns are wiring to their Eastern representatives for ready money, in order to begin again with least possible delay.

The heads of a number of the agencies for large Middle West, Eastern and European concerns have received assurances that everything possible will be done to rehabilitate the San Francisco end of their ventures.

TAKING HEART.

So it is at least comforting to know that the outside world has not had its great confidence in the future of this once great city shaken.

The people of San Francisco are taking heart.

With the dawn came plenty of provisions for the vast multitudes who have been deprived of food and shelter by the fire.

PLENTY TO EAT.

In all of the parks and squares where the homeless are camped members of the Relief Committee and the military went about distributing bread, coffee and canned goods.

There was a sufficiency for all.

The night was a bit rough owing to a brisk breeze, but the people never for a moment lost heart. And what was lacking in physical comfort was made up in good cheer.

PANIC STARTED.

A panic was started this morning by the rumor that another blaze had started in the Western Addition. Fortunately this was without foundation, and when this became known quiet was restored.

Mayor Schmitz and General Funston with their corps of aids are getting things in splendid shape. They have their schemes for relief and reconstruction down to a practical and working basis, and hold out every hope for success.

CONFIDENCE IN MAYOR.

And the great feature of it all is that the grief-stricken people have every confidence in the ability of the Mayor and the representative of the Federal and State governments to cope with the situation.

SPLENDID WORK.

The military is doing splendid work. While their methods

(Concluded on Page Two).

Weather Forecast: FAIR.

An Industrious Incubator!
3,968 WORLD WANTS
1,311 DAILY ONLY.
More Than Same Day Last Year.
WATCH WORLD WONDERS WHICH
Golden Gate Adv. Co'y 2402-2406 16th St.

The World.

"Circulation Books Open to All."   "Circulation Books Open to All."

Weather Forecast: FAIR.

"His Fortune."
A Story in a Picture.
FREE
With Next Sunday's World.
ANOTHER CHARLES DANA GIBSON DRAWING.

VOL. XLVI. NO. 16,313.   Copyright, 1906, by the Press Publishing Company, New York World.   NEW YORK, FRIDAY, APRIL 20, 1906.   PRICE ONE CENT in Greater New York and Jersey City. TWO CENTS outside of Greater New York and Jersey City and on trains.

GENERAL VIEW OF THE RANGE OF THE EARTHQUAKE AND VIEWS AND BULDINGS IN THE PRINCIPAL TOWNS.

GOLDEN GATE PARK WHERE TENTS WILL BE PITCHED FOR THE HOMELESS.

HALL OF RECORDS, OAKLAND.

HOTEL DEL MONTE, MONTEREY.

VIEW FROM CITY HALL at SAN JOSE.

COURT HOUSE at STOCKTON.

SAN LUIS OBISPO.

SANTA MARIA.

HOTEL POTTER, Santa Barbara.

SANTA BARBARA CHANNEL

50 MILES

CAPITOL BUILDING AT SACRAMENTO

FIRES YET RAGING LAY ALMOST ALL THE CITY OF SAN FRANCISCO IN ASHES.

Flames Sweep Into the Wealthy Residence District, Destroying the Magnificent Mansions on Nob Hill and Adding Millions to the Loss, Now Estimated at Perhaps $300,000,000.

MILE OF HOUSES DYNAMITED IN A VAIN ATTEMPT TO CHECK THE FIRE.

300,000 People Made Homeless—Hosts Camp in the Parks and on the Unoccupied Sand Hills—A Frantic Rush to Flee the City—Provisions Scarce and Famine Threatens—Loss of Life May Exceed One Thousand.

The situation at 2 A. M. to-day is as follows:

1. San Francisco is a heap of ashes.
2. The property loss is placed at from $250,000,000 to $300,000,000.
3. A conservative estimate places the loss of life at 1,000, but this number may be increased. In fact, the present estimate is mere guesswork.
4. More than twenty cities and towns other than San Francisco have been destroyed in part or in whole.
5. The property loss in outside places is estimated at $30,000,000.
6. The loss of life in outside places is estimated at 800.
7. The people made homeless exceed 300,000.
8. The only public or semi-public building standing in San Francisco is the United States Mint.
9. A slight tremor shook the Pacific coast yesterday from San Francisco to Los Angeles without doing great damage.
10. Measures for relief were undertaken by the nation, States and cities. More than $3,000,000 was raised.

(Special to The World.)

SAN FRANCISCO, April 19.—The city is destroyed. Three hundred thousand people are homeless to-night.

The fire spread everywhere to-day, borne by an everchanging wind. The section of the city west of Van Ness avenue, which contains the homes of the wealthy, was fired at 6 o'clock to-night. The district was soon surrounded by fire and could not be saved.

From noon until 6 o'clock soldiers, police and firemen demolished the splendid homes on the easterly side of the broad avenue by dynamite and black powder.

They carried the devastation for a distance of one mile, under orders from Mayor Schmitz and the Council and Gen. Funston.

Buildings were still toppling under the dynamite, when the fames leaped across the area of destruction, and the district that a million dollars' worth of property had been destroyed to save was doomed.

300,000 Are Now Homeless.

The Deputy Chief of the San Francisco Fire Department got out the following bulletin:

"At 7.30 to-night the fire was still under headway, gathering force and spreading. Two-thirds of the business section of the city has been devastated. The fire is heading for the residential district. Efforts to fight the flames have proved futile. Three hundred thousand are homeless to-night. By Saturday San Francisco will be an ash heap."

There was much confusion at night concerning the loss of life. This forenoon there were twenty-seven corpses lying in Portsmouth Square, gathered from various sections. It was said that elsewhere bodies were lying in the streets, there being no means available to remove them. In Market a reporter saw three bodies lying in the debris, some rude covering having been thrown over them.

Already Planning the Restoration.

As far as the eye could reach from Nob Hill to the South, to the East and far out to the West lay in fantastic heaps, charred and smoking, all that remained of the prosperous city.

It was another day of an uneven struggle of man against an unconquerable element. Acre on acre has been ground into dust and ashes, despite the heroic perseverance of the firemen to limit the conflagration.

To-night there was a hope that the worst had been nearly reached, and that when to-morrow dawned the end may have come; but the hope was faint. If the flames can be barred from the western addition then the end will be written to the great disaster.

San Francisco was not discouraged to-night. Its best and highest class began at once to plan for restoration and to care for the stricken ones and the relief was immediate and effective. Total subscriptions of $180,000 were announced to-night. Arrangements were made for the immediate relief of the needy.

The baking of 50,000 loaves of bread daily will begin to-morrow. Free transportation will be provided by the Southern Pacific Railroad to destitute persons desiring to go to interior points.

Few Sections Escape the Flames.

At 5 o'clock this afternoon it was reported by officers of the army who have been through the city that practically all of San Francisco was burned or burning. There were a few scattered spots where the fire had not yet touched. But their area was small.

Sergt. Binkley, U. S. A., reported at that time:

"Everything out Market street to about Twenty-third street is burning fiercely. Everything is gone except the Mint. The Sub-Treasury is in ruins. The Post-Office was injured only by the earthquake. Only

PANIC IN LOS ANGELES FOLLOWS TWO SLIGHT EARTHQUAKE SHOCKS.

Men, Women and Children Ran to the Parks Fearing the Buildings Would Fall—Business Abandoned and the City in Anxiety Fearing Fate That Befell San Francisco.

(Special to The World.)

LOS ANGELES, Cal., April 19.—Two slight shocks of earthquake were felt here soon after noon to-day. Tall buildings swayed a little, windows rattled and chandeliers moved. No damage was done. At any other time little attention would have been paid to such a disturbance, but owing to the San Francisco disaster people became terror-stricken and for one hour the city was in a panic.

The shocks came about six minutes apart and lasted only a few seconds. They were followed by occasional very faint tremors that died away after an hour.

So great was the fright that business was suspended generally for the remainder of the day. In every home to-night there is fear and trembling. Many people are remaining out of doors, apprehending a reewal of the shocks during the night.

Fled In a Wild Panic.

When the quaking began at noon hour large crowds were gathered around bulletin-boards eagerly reading the news from San Francisco. As the ground trembled beneath their feet they were paralyzed with terror for a moment. Then panic seized the throngs. Men, women and children ran aimlessly about, fearing that tall buildings would fall on them. From stores, office buildings, factories and homes thousands more fled toward open spaces and parks.

When it was found that the earth had quieted and no damage had been done there was a cautious return. Every nerve of the city is on edge, and the slightest disturbance would be the signal for another panic.

G. E. Franklin, head of the United States Weather Bureau in this city, in his report of the earthquake, ten minutes after it occurred, said:

"There was nothing at all unusual in the shock. It was of hardly suffi-

(Continued on Second Page.)

More Than $3,000,000 Raised Yesterday for Relief Fund.

More than $3,000,000 cash was raised throughout the nation yesterday for the San Francisco sufferers. The principal contributors in this city and elsewhere were:

John D. Rockefeller	$100,000
New York Stock Exchange	100,000
Clarence H. Mackay	50,000
Ladenburg, Thalmann & Co., the United Railways Investment Company, Patrick Calhoun, Sidney Shepard, and Ford.	
Bacon & Davis	25,000
H. Guggenheim's Sons	25,000
J. P. Morgan & Co.	25,000
Carnegie Hero Fund	25,000
Adolph K. Jessup	25,000
August Belmont	25,000

Disaster Cost 1,845 Lives and $283,180,000 in Property.

In the following list of California cities, towns and villages blighted by earthquake and fire the casualties and damages reported are in each are estimated from the most conservative reports:

City, Town or Village	Population	Damage	Casualties
San Francisco	345,000	$250,000,000	1,000 +
Oakland	70,000	500,600	5 +
Alameda	17,000	400,000	2
San Jose	35,000	3,000,000	50 +
Agnew (State Hospital for Insane)	800	400,000	275 +
Palo Alto (Stanford University)	5,000	5,000,000	3
Salinas	3,000	2,000,000	None
Napa	5,500	250,000	?
Hollister	1,900	200,000	?
Vallejo	8,000	40,000	?
Sacramento	30,000	25,000	?
Redwood City	1,800	30,000	?
Port Richmond (Terminal of Santa Fe RR.)	400	?	?
Suisun	1,000	50,000	?
Santa Rosa	7,000	800,000	500 +
Watsonville	3,000	70,000	?
Monterey	2,500	25,000	8
Loma Prieta	500		4 +
Stockton	18,000	40,000	?
Brawley	500	100,000	?
Santa Cruz	7,000	150,000	Conflict'g
Gilroy	2,500	100,000	?
*Healdsburg	1,900	Reports conflicting.	
*Cloverdale	1,000	Reports conflicting.	
*Geyserville	500	Reports conflicting.	
*Hopland	600	Reports conflicting.	
Ukiah (State Hospital for Insane here)	2,000	Reports conflicting.	
Totals		$283,180,000	1,845

*Indicates probable greater loss of life.
Note—The last five towns are reported wiped out; $20,000,000 would not cover property loss.

SOUTHERN PACIFIC TRAINS RUNNING.

Tracks Repaired to 'Frisco and Refugees Are Being Handled.

The Southern Pacific Railroad Company received information at its New York offices yesterday afternoon that trains were running from San Francisco south down the peninsula toward San Jose. Refugees were being handled as speedily as possible.

The company's station at Third and Townsend streets, San Francisco, while damaged, was not destroyed, and was being used as a terminal.

A despatch from Sacramento said the Southern Pacific had repaired its tracks and telegraph lines south of San Francisco yesterday and resumed traffic in the afternoon between Sacramento and Oakland.